# THE AGE OF
# ATHELSTAN

# THE AGE OF
# ATHELSTAN
## BRITAIN'S FORGOTTEN HISTORY

PAUL HILL

*To my Father, Richard*

*Cover picture:* Athelstan panel on Maggie Humphry's
mural in Eden Street, Kingston upon Thames.
*Photograph courtesy of Kingston Museum and Heritage Service*

First published in 2004 by Tempus Publishing

Reprinted in 2008 by
The History Press
The Mill, Brimscombe Port,
Stroud, Gloucestershire, GL5 2QG
www.thehistorypress.co.uk

Reprinted 2011

British Library Cataloguing in Publication Data.
A catalogue record for this book is available from the British Library.

ISBN 978 0 7524 2566 5

Typesetting and origination by
Tempus Publishing Limited
Printed and bound in Great Britain by
Marston Book Services Limited, Didcot

# CONTENTS

Map of lowland Britain during the Age of Athelstan. To the south of the treaty line under Alfred and Edward was the kingdom of the Anglo-Saxons. Later, a kingdom of the English would stretch at least as far as the Humber.

# ACKNOWLEDGEMENTS

There are many people who have given me a great deal of help in various aspects of this work, some of them consistently over a number of years. My wife Lucy, who has gone out of her way to provide me with enough time and space to indulge myself, is deservedly my first acknowledgement.

To Simon Davies, I must extend my thanks. He has shared with me a passion for this period of British history for a long time and has had to endure at my request the hunt for the battle of Brunanburh both in the field and on the tabletop. The countless experiments we have conducted to assess the military capabilities of armies of the Viking period have proved extremely useful in the formation of this book.

To Professor Simon Keynes of Cambridge University I owe a special note of gratitude for guiding me to meaningful research material and sharing with me some of his thoughts on Athelstan and his era. Similarly, I thank Professor Elaine Treharne of Leicester University, who has given me a welcome insight from the point of view of medieval English litera-ture into the lasting reputation of King Athelstan.

Julie Wileman and Judie English, colleagues who have given their support and advice regarding many of the theories presented here, including the supply of illustrative material and an examination of the first draft manuscript, have been a continued source of support and encouragement.

Any quest for Athelstan must always include a visit to Malmesbury. Had I not been treated with such respect and enthusiasm by Cllr John Bowen, I would not have felt able to tackle some very important issues.

I am profoundly grateful to have been introduced to people and places in one of England's most remarkable and beautiful towns.

The town of Tamworth shares with Malmesbury a fondness for Athelstan and also for his remarkable aunt who had one of her bases there. I am grateful for the help I have received from John Harper of the *Tamworth Herald* and for the remarkable photographic skills of Paul Barber.

For his advice on the background to the earliest aspects of Freemasonry, I am thankful to Michael Lear. His efforts in exploring the legend of Athelstan's connection to the institution were most welcome. To Dave Potts for his endless supply of useful research material, and to Robert Silburn for his recollections, I am also grateful. Also, my thanks to Tim and Shaan Everson and to Paul Boardman for their help.

Many public institutions have assisted in the production of this work and some have been particularly helpful. To Jill Ivy of Durham Cathedral Library I owe a great deal of thanks for arranging for a photograph of a manuscript in the collection there to be made available, and to the staff of countless reference libraries in Ireland and across the north of England I extend my gratitude, chief amongst which are those at Dublin and Doncaster. I am also grateful to the staff of my local library for their co-operation.

My parents' support and kindness has extended itself to a level of technical back-up which would bring peace of mind to any author in the modern age of electronic wizardry and for this I am eternally grateful.

But there is one place left. It is the place where the book was born. The town where King Athelstan was crowned gave me an opportunity to explore aspects of Anglo-Saxon history which I had not yet discovered. The museum staff at Kingston continue to be a source of great help. To Anne McCormack, Jill Lamb, Emma Rummins, Cheryl Smith and Johanna Norton, I extend my profound gratitude for their role in the provision of visual and research material for the volume. It is hard to imagine how *The Age of Athelstan* could ever have been written without them.

*Paul Hill*
*Motspur Park, 2003*

# FOREWORD

This book tells the story of the emergence of a nation born amid the drama of Viking attacks and devastation. It was an age which saw the last great Anglo-Saxon kingdom of the pre-Viking era almost destroyed by Scandinavian aggression, only for its heirs to establish their claim to total power in Britain some fifty-nine years after their darkest days, somewhere on a windswept heath in the north of England. The man who led his countrymen to victory that day in 937 owed his success to the achievements of his father and grandfather and in no small way to the extraordinary characteristics which he himself embodied. He was Athelstan, the first king of England. His piety, strength of leadership and international reputation quickly made him a legend to people at home and abroad.

Few of us, however, can help but view our history through the filter provided by the times in which we live. Our hunt for the truth is clouded by our modern perceptions of what we think is the most reliable way to find it. Modern thinking assures us that the truth lies in substantiated fact in the form of written or archaeological evidence. This is certainly true. But in Britain's colourful early medieval history, the recording of events has often included the words of the storyteller. Rhyme and verse is easy to remember and can be passed from generation to generation. It was also the vehicle for a high form of praise, accepted as such in society. And amongst it, the more open-minded scholar may find useful notions. Such things are treacherous to those who seek the plain truth, however, and we must tread carefully, allowing ourselves not to be seduced by those who have their own reasons to say what they say. The art of understanding lies in finding common ground between the proven and the lyrical.

This volume uses the testimony of many historians, old and new. Some texts are reliable, while others wax and wane between the plausible and the legendary. One of the twelfth-century historians whose material is often quoted in relation to the reign of Athelstan is William of Malmesbury. He had discovered some authentic material in old books on the king and told us that much of his material was reliable. He also admitted to his reader that some of what he said had come from old popular songs and poems about Athelstan and that he could not vouch for its authenticity. It is this material which some historians have found attractive. Where it is used in this volume its dangers are outlined, but use it we must. Indeed, now and then such material can be tested against other more reliable sources.

Nowhere in Anglo-Saxon history is this problem of reconciling multiple and conflicting sources more profound than in the great hunt for the battle of Brunanburh, fought by Athelstan against a northern coalition in 937. The history of the hunt, which includes some amusing red herrings, forms the core of the book. One suspects that the hunt will continue for centuries to come.

The historical texts upon which we rely give the names of people involved in the events portrayed here. For the sake of clarity, I have adopted the most popular and accepted forms of the names. Olaf, for example, appears as Anlaf in Old English, Óláfr in Old Norse and Amlaíb in the Irish texts. The name even appears as another variant in seventeenth-century copy texts of earlier material as Awley. I choose Olaf here. The Old English dipthong Æ, is retained where it makes sense to do so. The more common Æthelflæd is used in preference to the modern Ethelfleda, when describing the extraordinary life of the Lady of the Mercians. There are one or two obvious exceptions to this approach. Athelstan, the main subject of the book, is written the modern way for the sake of convenience, as indeed are the names Edward and Alfred, which are still in use today.

The main purpose of this book is to bring to light the achievements and context of one of Britain's most extraordinary kings, a man who was seen by fellow countrymen and outsiders alike as of singular importance in his time. I have chosen to begin the work with the first appearance in the British Isles of the Scandinavian warrior whom we call the *Viking*. Understanding the Viking phenomenon as a whole is essential to understanding the different ways in which people reacted to it and why in the age of Athelstan the political stakes had become so high.

There is much that still needs to be discovered about how Athelstan ruled his great kingdom and some of the ideas put forward here are an appeal to scholars to take up the challenge. Military organisation, continental relationships, ecclesiastical reform and the ever-present fight for independence in the north of England are all themes covered here.

But somewhere down the centuries the English people lost Athelstan. If we were fortunate, we might have been told at school about Alfred the Great, but rarely will we have sat down at a lesson dedicated to the work of his most illustrious grandson. And so the book concludes with an analysis of why the legend of the great king may have gone missing many centuries after it grew into a popular conception of medieval kingship.

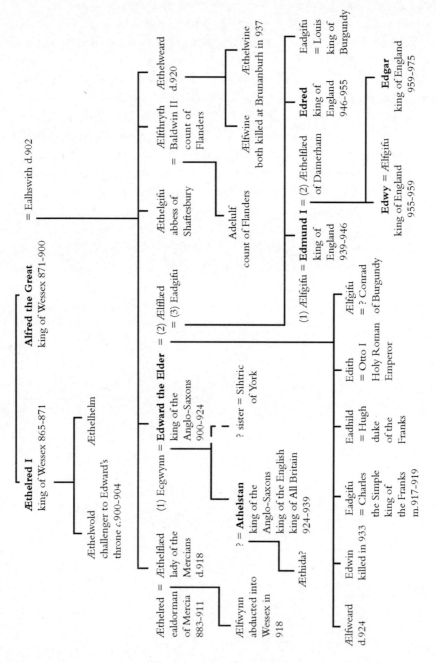

Rulers of Wessex and England from Alfred the Great to Edgar.
Names in bold indicate kings.

# INTRODUCTION

Some places in England evoke an overwhelming feeling of history. I was lucky enough to grow up within yards of the battlefield of Hastings, where English history was profoundly changed on one long day in October 1066. As a young man I was struck by the difficulty that I encountered in finding out more about what had happened in England during the long era that had preceded Hastings. At school, they simply did not tell us. One might encounter a story or two about an English king on the run from the Vikings and his seeming inability to prevent a handful of cakes from burning. Or perhaps a romantic tale about Viking warriors bearing evocative names such as Eric Bloodaxe or Ivar the Boneless. These tales trickled through the giant barrier to learning which was erected around the famous date of 1066 by those who thought that our understanding of the story of England should begin at the very point where so much of it ended.

Slowly, it seems, things are changing. Anglo-Saxon history is firmly back on the map, even if it is being taught today in England at a very introductory level. But it is not all good news. How many people in Britain can honestly say that they have heard of a man who was arguably one of the greatest rulers in the island of Britain since the departure of the Romans?

The name *Athelstan*, whose literal translation from the Old English means 'Noble Stone', has preyed upon my mind for some time. It is written on the plinth of the coronation stone at Kingston upon Thames. Kingston, unlike Battle, has no abbey or battlefield, but it does have this extraordinary monument to the kings of the tenth century and it seeks to educate its visitors in a different and perhaps more subtle way. The Royal Borough of Kingston upon Thames has a council dump situated just off Athelstan Road, a quiet and predictably unappealing place. The children of King Athelstan Primary School are regularly reminded of the reason why their school is named the way it is and their school badge carries the image of a king. And when one looks through the old copies of newspapers held in the Kingston Local History Room, the town's fascination with pageantry is openly revealed. In 1902 and 1924 there were huge celebrations organised by proud civic officials to commemorate the millennial dates of the coronations of Edward the Elder and Athelstan respectively. The town has always been proud to wear the title of Royal Borough.

In any quest to discover Athelstan, one is inevitably drawn to Malmesbury in Wiltshire. Here Athelstan's empty tomb lies in the remarkable church, once a great abbey which housed some of the finest scholars of Europe. People talk about him there every day. There is a feeling in Malmesbury that I only came across in Battle, but this feeling is for Athelstan, not for Harold Godwinson. The legend of Athelstan is palpable in Malmesbury and the passion is strong. Here there is another Athelstan Road, an Athelstan Garage, an Athelstan Museum, a flourishing second-hand shop known humorously as Athelstan's Attic and some time ago there was a Mr Mott's Athelstan Cinema, a place remembered with affection by the townsfolk. But there is so much more. The Old Corporation traces itself back to the time of the great king who granted them local land at the end of his reign 'on account of their help in my struggle with the Danes'. And if one drives down the ancient Kingsway, which links sites of royal and ecclesiastical importance, one travels across a landscape created by generations of Anglo–Saxon monarchs. These things alone are enough to justify the position which Malmesbury takes in this book.

But to be fair, other towns and places can tell a similar story. Axminster Town Council in Devon has a coat of arms which playfully includes two axes and the posthumously issued arms of Athelstan, for it was he, who after the famous battle of Brunanburh in 937, endowed the church there with lands so that prayers could be offered for the souls of his leaders who fell at the famous confrontation with the Danes and Scots.

There are in fact twenty-three Athelstan Roads in England and one in Tywyn in Wales. There are a further eight Athelstan Closes, one Athelstan

Lane and one Athelstan Park in England. There is even a settlement called Athelstan in Iowa in the USA, with a population of just thirty-one people. Sadly, it is only in these few places where a street name here, a place name or monument there, reminds us of one of Britain's most successful and admired rulers. Admired, that is, until the time was right to forget.

The subsequent history of England cannot have been foreseen by those who fought at Senlac Ridge in 1066, not even by the most admiring of the Duke of Normandy's followers and chroniclers. That the Norman *milites* and barons would replace almost every indigenous thegn and nobleman, that the laws of the land would change, its language forever altered, that the focus of English political aspirations would shift dramatically to the continental and Frankish world and no longer to that of the Scandinavian diaspora, none of this could have been predicted.

One of the last Englishmen in William the Conqueror's service was killed in action whilst attempting to protect his king. His name was Toki. That this man had a Danish name should be of no surprise to anybody. The last English king, Harold Godwinson, was half-Danish himself and his brothers famously held land and political or military appointments across the country. Gathered around Harold beneath the Golden Dragon of Wessex on that fateful evening at Hastings were his housecarles, a semi-professional bodyguard of heavy infantrymen descended from the men who had landed themselves a special military position in the English army during and after the great wars between Canute and Æthelred II Unræd in 1016. The truth of the matter is that the last man to fall around the English standard at Hastings probably spoke Danish as well as he spoke English. The pre-conquest history of England is inextricably linked to that of the Scandinavian world.

The story of England's gradual formation in the two centuries preceding 1066 is a fascinating one. The achievements of monarchs and other leaders of a great variety of cultures are seldom commented upon, such was the impact of conquest in 1066. This conquest has come to represent a seductively simple turning point in the fortunes and destiny of an emerging nation. The shock of overwhelming defeat has had a profound effect on the English mind. It seems that the barrier erected around 1066 was designed to prevent us from getting hurt. If we really knew of the glory of the tenth-century Anglo-Saxon Empire, the next

200 years might seem to us to be a painful journey of cultural re-discovery. They were just that.

The age of Athelstan was a time when more than one great and powerful invader was overcome, when multiple military and political successes and calamities changed the face of culture, language and settlement in many parts of Britain; a time when a string of leaders fought for supremacy within the British Isles. One man in the line of monarchs from Alfred the Great to Æthelred II stands out among the rest for the achievements he made during his short reign. He was to build upon the extraordinary successes of his father and grandfather who had met the Danish in the field of battle and struck deals with them, winning time here and territory there. But no one had ever held such a fearsome reputation at home and abroad as Athelstan. A military master and benevolent ruler, Athelstan encapsulated all that is necessary in an early medieval political leader for success in dangerous times. The rulers who followed him built upon his successes and they knew full well that they owed their position to him.

And yet we must always be cautious when we read of the great deeds of kings who it seemed could do no wrong. Athelstan did not share the same values as we do today. Early medieval power politics was brutal. It is probable that Athelstan had his own brother drowned at sea in an act that once and for all prevented an attempt on his throne from that quarter. Furthermore, the men who had caused Athelstan such a headache during his reign out-lived him and swept back into the north of England to continue their challenge to the kingdom south of the Humber. Nevertheless, this curious figure was one of the few English kings, with the exception of the Mercian king, Offa and Athelstan's own grandfather Alfred, whose reputation survived the centuries which followed the Norman Conquest. But when history was re-written again in the Tudor period, Athelstan was all but lost. Now we must rejoin the tale at a time when there were no powerful Dukes of Normandy with designs on the English throne, a time when threats to political stability lurked around every corner both from within and without the island of Britain. There are surprises within these pages and there are names which have long since been forgotten, lost in a romantic mist. But what is here is something which needs to be told, for it is necessary to exorcise the ghost of Hastings.

I

# RECOVERING ATHELSTAN

## THE PEN AND THE TROWEL

The search for information regarding a relatively short fifteen-year reign of an admittedly remarkable king is always going to be fraught with difficulty. We must look either side of the reign of Athelstan (924-939) to assess what went before it and what followed it. To do this we must use a variety of means.

When historians try to piece together a narrative, things are not as simple as they might appear. The histories, chronicles, lives of saints and annals which are available to us are themselves a palimpsest of sources, some carrying over mistakes or misunderstandings from the sources upon which they draw. Fortunately, we are not short of material for the period, although its accurate interpretation will always remain controversial. In the last sixty years some great advances have been made in the understanding of aspects of the period, particularly in the reconciliation of seemingly contradictory chronologies in roughly contemporary documents.

Provided that its weaknesses and bias are properly acknowledged, the *Anglo-Saxon Chronicle* forms an admirable basic narrative for events in this period, notwithstanding a curious reluctance to expand upon some significant events in the early part of the tenth century. We should bear in mind that by and large we get a rather Anglo-centric view of

British history from the *Anglo-Saxon Chronicle*, despite the fact that its scribes clearly drew upon a number of sources. That the chronicles began on the order of Alfred the Great should also not be forgotten. History shows that his dynasty would rise from the ashes of Viking devastation to a position of ultimate power in England. However, this was the earliest attempt in any society in Western Europe to construct a narrative of events in the vernacular tongue. Without it we would be struggling for scraps of information from dubious sources for a huge period of the history of Britain.

One of the problems with this and many other chronicles, annals and histories of the period is the notion of when one year succeeds another. The feast of the circumcision, 1 January, was taken by the eleventh-century homilist[1] Ælfric as being the beginning of the year. He based his argument – if that is what we can call it – on this being in accordance with ancient Roman custom.[2] Some of the eleventh-century entries in the *Chronicle* start, however, with the year beginning 25 March, whilst other entries for earlier years take September as the year's end, following the traditional Roman system of annual taxation. In fact, this was done for the years 868, 870 and 872-5 in some manuscripts of the *Chronicle* and in Manuscript A, the Winchester, or Parker, Chronicle, for the period 890-970.[3]

We must bear in mind too that the chroniclers were using other material to compile their accounts. There are some sequences of entries which look like they were compiled at the time of the events taking place, but most are the interpretation of other sources. This is particularly true for the scribe who shows an almost paranoid interest in the progress of the huge Danish army which left England to campaign in France in the 880s. Clearly he is following a continental source for this material. For the period with which we are concerned, there is some confusion over dates and many simple entries were placed in the *Chronicle* where we might have expected something more detailed. Manuscript A, the Parker Chronicle, is the oldest of the manuscripts, and in the tenth century a number of scribes pick up the entries to 924, with another writing simple entries from the reign of Athelstan to Æthelred II Unræd. Despite the paucity of information for the period, the Parker Chronicle does at least have the famous poems celebrating the English victory at the battle of Brunanburh (937) and Edmund's recapture of the five Danish boroughs (942), along with fine poetry in praise of Edgar (975).

The two Abingdon manuscripts (B and C) seem largely to use West Saxon sources. Manuscript C has an insertion between the years 915-934, known as the Mercian Register, which deals with the exploits of the famous Æthelflæd, Lady of the Mercians. These brief annals cover the period 902 to 924 and sometimes repeat things mentioned in the main body of the text. Manuscript D (Worcester) is interesting for the characteristics it shares with northern sources. Worcester and York were closely associated in the late tenth and early eleventh centuries, being held by the same man between 972-1016. Some of the poems are there in the Worcester manuscript, except for the one dedicated to Edgar which is relegated to prose. The long-running Peterborough manuscript (E), which goes up to the twelfth century, has basic material for our period and may be an early twelfth-century copy based on a Canterbury original, replacing one which was lost in the fire at Peterborough in 1116. There is no Mercian Register or poem for the battle of Brunanburh in this version. Manuscript H is merely a fragment with a twelfth-century entry, but the bilingual epitome of Canterbury (Manuscript F) is interesting for the Latin text which accompanies the Old English. Here there are possibilities for the historian who wishes to look at the meaning of specific terms, like 'mounted army' or 'Viking', since we can see how the scribe chose to explain these things in Latin.

The excerpts from various versions of the *Anglo-Saxon Chronicle* used in this book are taken from the translation by Michael Swanton.[4] This most recent and useful edition has been carefully translated. Where it has been necessary to add a footnote explaining a particular term, this has been done for the sake of clarity, and in some cases to show that there are still some problems of interpretation for words which had specific meanings at the time of their writing.

The *Anglo-Saxon Chronicles* formed the basis for the work of the next generation of historians who added material of their own. We owe a huge debt to William of Malmesbury, Simeon of Durham and Florence of Worcester for their work on the histories of the kings and events of the age of Athelstan. For example, there is the priceless fact that the Scottish and Scandinavian-Irish allies who invaded Athelstan's empire and fought him at Brunanburh in 937 are said by Simeon and Florence to have sailed up the Humber (and not, perhaps as one would expect, up the Ribble, Mersey or Dee). Then there are William's accounts which draw from earlier work praising Athelstan. He even gives us a physical description of the man himself, and shows that he is in touch with common opinion on the memory of Athelstan. Similarly, the chronicler and nobleman Æthelweard, writing just a generation or two after the great events of the late 930s in a work dedicated to a relative in Germany, was able to say that ordinary people still regarded that struggle as 'the great war'.

We must also rely upon material which was written in a certain style, such as sagas or poems. Their difficult styles might appear to hold reliability as their main hostage, but with careful interpretation they can be useful. Poetry was the language of justification in the tenth century and if you had a poem created in your honour, it was a sign of a real achievement. So, despite the obvious bias in works of great praise and despite the struggle of some poets to find the right words to fit the meter of their art form, these works do at least mention people and places, battles and military formations which help to colour the picture.

The material is not just English. Old Norse sagas such as *Egil's Saga* are invaluable, despite being written centuries later. If they do nothing else, they capture the spirit of the time. Likewise, Irish writings are extremely useful in helping us reconcile the dates and activities of Vikings in Ireland who were also active in Britain at around the same time. Here, we look to the *Annals of Ulster*, of Clonmacnoise and perhaps to the disputed Three Fragments, which give us an idea of what might have been happening in north-west Mercia in the early tenth century (see pages 93-94). Welsh material is also available and some of it famously speaks of a British future without the over-proud rule of the West Saxon English. But to all of this material we must add the evidence that we get from archaeology, which can sometimes directly challenge the notions expressed by the writers we have mentioned here. In some cases, like that at Repton in Derbyshire, the archaeological work has been a powerful tool in discovering Viking activity in their camp which we know from historical sources was only occupied in the winter of 873-4. Here we are able to see the physical evidence for the Danish Great Army just moments before its dramatic split into two separate factions. What we know from the record of the pen can sometimes be tested by the trowel.

Archaeology has seen something of a revolution in Britain over the last twenty years. An increase in development in urban centres has led to a corresponding increase in archaeological excavations carried out by professional excavation units. The result of this activity, taking into account the great work of university research departments and the continuing contributions of amateur societies, is that we have more material information at our fingertips with which to help us interpret cultural and social aspects of Anglo-Saxon England in the age of Athelstan.

The archaeology of the great fortifications of Alfred is covered elsewhere in this book. So too, under a general discussion of the extent and impact of Scandinavian settlement in the north, is the related subject of place name studies (see pages 74-76). Here, in the first instance, we look at what archaeology has contributed to our understanding of material culture in the period generally, and to our understanding of those towns in the Midlands of England which became called the Five Boroughs of the Danelaw. They are slowly revealing their secrets. These towns are Nottingham, Stamford, Leicester, Lincoln and Derby. The nature of their fortification, layout and of the types of trade and other urban activity which went on there are beginning to be understood. This area quickly became a hybrid culture in Athelstan's era. It shows through its material remains a remarkably vibrant society, neither truly Viking nor Anglo-Saxon in nature, but a mixture of the two with other influences besides. The archaeology of the Danelaw supports the argument that this was a period of renewed trade and urban development in the Midlands of England, matched only by the royal building programme of fortifications and refuges in Alfredian and Edwardian Wessex, within which similar economic activities took place.

As far as the Scandinavian urban areas of England are concerned, to the Five Boroughs should be added the hugely important sites of York, for so long at the heart of Viking imperial designs, and Torksey, Doncaster, Cambridge, Repton, Northampton, Bedford and Huntingdon, which all saw occupation on some scale by the Danish invader and many of which were fortified and re-fortified by both sides in the great tenth-century struggle for control of central and northern England.

## THE ARCHAEOLOGY OF THE FIVE DANISH BOROUGHS

Derby is perhaps the least understood of the towns in the Five Boroughs. It is generally thought that settlement continued in the tenth century based around the early ninth-century church of St Alkmund, known as 'the north church'. In fact, before it was called Derby, the English name for the settlement was 'Northworthy', and it was to Northworthy that the body of a Mercian ealdorman, Æthelwulf, was brought after his death in battle fighting for the English against the Vikings near Reading in 871, a distance of around 100 miles. And although there was clearly settlement shift away from the nearby Roman fort of Little Chester (Derventio), some evidence exists to suggest that this site itself may have been defensible in the period of the wars of the Mercian leader Lady Æthelflæd against the Danes. Future archaeological excavations on the post-Roman levels at Little Chester are likely to reveal more detail about the fate of that fort in Viking times and the subsequent develop-ment of the settlement at Northworthy. The position of medieval Derby, on the eastern side of the river Derwent, makes less strategic sense than the position of Little Chester's fortification on the other side of the river. Derby was the most westerly of the Five Boroughs and vulnerable to attack from English Mercian forces from the east. Derby's isolation in this respect is further underlined by the fact that when English armies travelled north on their great campaigns during the mid-tenth century, they did so via Leicester and Nottingham, which had far more impor-tant central locations on the Roman road network. But there is much to be answered by investigations at Derby, not least of which is why, before the monetary reforms of Edgar in 973, the mint at Derby was by far the most prolific of the region.

The settlement at Nottingham does not share the same Roman ancestry as that of Derby, although its proximity to the Fosse Way (the road to Lincoln from the south-west) proved to be of singular importance during the campaigns of Athelstan and his brothers. Its name derives from an early Anglo-Saxon hybrid meaning 'the settle-ment of the followers of Snot', being first mentioned as *Snotengaham* when recorded as being taken over by the Danes in 868. Some evidence exists of a mid-Saxon enclosure in the town and there are ditches to the north of Fishergate, some up to 50m long, which have been dated by their pottery contents to the mid-Saxon period. The evidence as it now stands would suggest mid-Saxon occupation at the east end of the medieval town. Curiously, St Mary's, the church of the burh, lies outside this eastern zone and the assumption must be that settlement in the tenth century had by now spread westwards.

The evidence for the extraordinary events which took place in Nottingham after 868, when the Vikings first fortified the town, is reluctant to reveal itself to the trowel. There is just the one discovery of two Viking graves found on the south side of Bath Street in 1851.[5] The historical evidence points to the fact that the Danes successfully fortified the place and were able to rebuff Mercian and West Saxon forces who were unable to prosecute a siege. Later, when the settlement was taken by King Edward the Elder in 918, we are told that he repaired the fortifications and then came back two years later to build a sister fortification on the south side of the river (nothing of which has been discovered), joined to its sibling by a bridge. Later still, as with all the Five Boroughs, Nottingham was under the apparently unhappy government of Olaf Guthfrithson, the Scandinavian leader of York who was at the heart of a great struggle with the kings of the English in the 930s and 940s. Nothing has been reliably dated to this period from the archaeological record. The problem in Nottingham, it seems, is the nature of the geology. The medieval merchants' houses were built with huge cellars cut into the sandstone. Later, the Victorians made a habit of it, with their large town houses. The ground simply recommended itself to such buildings. There is even a curious reference from Alfred's biographer, Asser, who describes Nottingham as being a 'house of caves'. Since then, many features have been removed by subsequent development.

Stamford is another borough which straddles a river and is very close to a nodal point on the Roman road network. Ermine Street crosses the Welland just one mile upstream from the town. On the knoll north of Castle Row where the Anglo-Norman castle was later built, some fairly substantial ditches and a feature interpreted as a palisade trench have been found. There are a series of concentric ditches here and many of them contain material dating to around 850-900, precisely the period one would expect for the defences of Stamford to have been built up. However, it is generally thought that this area was distinctive and may represent a pre-Viking period royal estate centre. The picture is not as clear as it might be. These ditches enclose an area which lies to the west of another enclosed area, also on the north bank of the river, which is believed, with good reason, to be the original burh. To the south of the river, with St Martin's church as its central focus, runs a squarish network of roads which would appear to delineate the southern burh built by

Edward the Elder in 918. Clearly, Stamford has some fascinating secrets to reveal. It was a conspicuously fortified place and has yielded a great deal of evidence for iron-working and pottery manufacture in this period, having both a rich source of local clay and iron. Stamford pottery was very widely known in tenth-century England and included distinctively glazed wares, ranging from tableware to storage jars, and it seems that this industry was an Anglo-Scandinavian phenomenon of some note.

One of two of the Five Boroughs with a regional significance in Roman times was Leicester. The Roman town which became known as 'Ratae', a native term which indicates the presence of defences, was the capital of the Corieltauvi. It was originally a fort in the days when this area along the Fosse Way represented the Roman military frontier in Britain. Later, it was re-shaped and a civilian population moved in. Some evidence exists in the form of a variety of artefacts from the early medieval period and two early Pagan Saxon cemeteries suggest significant post-Roman activity at Leicester, some of which is supposed to have taken place in the deteriorating remains of the Forum and Basilica complex. Regrettably, there is virtually nothing surviving from the ninth and tenth century, an era which clearly saw some intense political activity in the town. Olaf Guthfrithson and Wulfstan, the independently minded archbishop of York, actually escaped from the burh in 940 whilst they were under siege from the West Saxon army. What little does survive from this era suggests a similar role in the local economy for Leicester to that of the other boroughs of the Danelaw – the stoke pit of a pottery kiln at Southgate Street would appear to contain pottery sherd forms consistent with the latter part of the tenth century, which, if true, would indicate that Leicester was also a manufacturing centre of commercial goods at this time.

Perhaps the most militarily significant Roman town of all of those which later became the Five Danish Boroughs was Lincoln. Notwithstanding its regional importance to the Roman military machine in the first and second centuries, Lincoln became a provincial capital by the early fourth century. It is easy to see why Lincoln retained its strategic significance for so long, being on the junction of Ermine Street and the Fosse Way. But there does seem to have been something of a hiatus at Lincoln: the early Saxon evidence is sparse and the archaeology suggests that some of the Roman roads through the town were blocked by debris and the construction of later buildings in the centuries which followed the departure of the Romans. But it was to this town that St Paulinus, the famous missionary, paid a visit in 628 and built a church. Lincoln was taken over by the Vikings during their settlement of 877 and it is thought that the town's defences at this time must have been founded on the strength of the existing Roman system. Although there is no evidence for their modification in the age of Athelstan, it is true to say that the medieval defences were almost exclusively based upon the line of the Roman ones. In fact, there is evidence that quite a few Roman structures survived into the Anglo-Saxon period in one form or another, but that the chief casualty was the road system.

Rubbish pits, chance finds of finger rings, beads, silver pieces and sunken-floored buildings, are among the discoveries which are helping to elucidate Lincoln's Viking past, and excavations at St Mark's church, Wigford, have revealed the existence of a tenth-century timber church. Also, there is evidence along the banks of the Witham that land had begun to be reclaimed for industrial purposes along the waterfront in the tenth century. Fish traps were laid in the Witham during the tenth century in stretches that had been cleared and which had apparently been virtually stagnant in the late Roman period. The presence of sherds from a ninth-century Syrian vessel and a fragment of a ninth-century Chinese stoneware bowl shed light on the extent of the foreign contact of the inhabitants of Lincoln in the Viking period. Further to this, as a die-cutting centre and important mint, Lincoln's coinage output was vast, being topped only by that of London and York.

But how is archaeology helping in other areas of ninth- and tenth-century study? The answer to this is that more and more aspects of material culture which were once used to define neat cultural groups, are now being recognised as indicative of a society engaged in a wide-ranging production and exchange network. Scandinavian settlement brought with it an influx of materials from all over Europe and elsewhere. The Scottish isles provided steatite bowls, Scotland and Ireland fine jewellery and accessories, from Germany came pottery and jewellery, and special lava quern-stones from the Mayen region. Byzantine silk and Islamic coins and pottery also came to England at this time. Additional to this cosmopolitan material culture are the fascinating culturally hybrid artefacts and monuments which fuse Anglo-Saxon and Viking styles to form something new. Jewellery, coinage and stone sculpture all display such aspects, particularly in the case of coinage where St Peter often shares his place quite comfortably with Thor's hammer. Indeed, Viking coinage of the north of England was being minted to commemorate the English East Anglian king, St Edmund, the very man who had been murdered by the Danish Great Army just a generation before these coins were struck.

Further evidence of the extraordinary diversity of culture in the Danelaw comes in the nature of the burial practices there. Sometimes there is inhumation without grave goods and sometimes with swords and spears and other accompaniments. Burials were not just restricted to church graveyards in this brave new world, either. New barrows were sometimes erected and in places such as Heath Wood at Ingelby, arguably a truly 'pagan' Viking site, whole cemeteries were built in this way. But it is the appearance of English-style goods such as the easily identifiable Anglo-Saxon swords in individual graves traditionally labelled as Scandinavian which has aroused the passion of archaeologists in recent times. Are these warriors purely pagan men who refused to give up their burial practices? Or is the case more complex than was once thought? It could be that these burials simply represent the appearance of a new era of competition between warriors as there is nothing particularly unusual about burial with goods in a Christian context.[6]

The use of commemorative stone sculptures has received much attention as it is by means of these that lords were expressing themselves through a mixture of proudly displayed Scandinavian mythological motifs and prudent observations of Christian custom. Some have argued that the increasing power of Wessex in the eastern Danelaw, particularly in Lincolnshire, led to the gradual reduction in Scandinavian motifs on stone carvings and that such artistic trends reflected the politics of the time.[7] In any case, these great stone sculptures of the north seem to act as signposts along our road to understanding the wealth and intentions of those who had them made. They stand for a form of cultural identity, however hybrid, which separates them from the styles of Wessex at a time when the men of Lindsey (Lincolnshire) and Northumbria would have feared an erosion of their independence from the south.

## A FAMOUS PLACE IN SURREY

Every man burns to show the king how keenly he supports him; one fears, another hopes, and hope's fullness drives out fear. The palace seethes, it overflows with the rich living that befits a king. Everywhere foaming wine, and in the great hall a busy tumult; lackeys run to and fro, and servants hurry to their tasks. Food fills their stomachs, music fills their minds; one man plucks the strings, another rivals him as he beats time, all sing one burden: 'Thine O Christ, be the praise, Thine the Glory'. The king with welcome in his eye accepts this show of loyalty, and deigns to grant them all a share in his affections.

William of Malmesbury
*Gesta Regum Anglorum*

Athelstan was not the only king to be crowned at Kingston upon Thames in Surrey. This great royal occasion had happened once before and would happen again here several more times. The traditional claim of Kingston is for Edward the Elder, Athelstan, Edmund, Edred, Edwy, Edward the Martyr and Æthelred II. The historians of that town guard Kingston's claim to be the seat of ancient coronations just as jealously as Lancashire and Yorkshire historians guard their candidates for the site of the lost battle of Brunanburh. There is every reason for this pride, although the coronation stone upon which seven tenth-century Anglo-Saxon kings were crowned has a somewhat chequered history. The name of the town does not, as was widely believed, derive from the presence there of the coronation stone. The notion that the word *Kingston* comes from the phrase 'King's stone' is an invention of the Victorian period, or perhaps later. It has been a line of argument for people who have sought to emphasise Kingston's royal connections. But the town does not need much help in that regard, since the evidence for Kingston's relationship with royalty has always been emphatic.

The coronation stone today stands proudly outside the Guildhall in the centre of Kingston, still mounted within its Victorian design, enclosed by railings with a 'Saxon'-style spearhead at the apex of each of the seven corners. Set within the plinth on seven sides is a coin of the realm of each of the kings who are thought to have been crowned here. Since at least the seventeenth century, when the town was described as 'the chair of majesty', a connection between the stone and the kings has been postulated. But it was not until the early Victorian era that the unusual-looking sarsen block that had been in the market place for as long as anyone could remember, was finally recognised for what it was. This squarish block of silicious sandstone must have come from the area around Salisbury Plain where similar local stones were quarried to build parts of the monument at Stonehenge. What was it doing in Kingston? The answer to that question before 1850 was that it was being used as a mounting block for horsemen. The townsfolk decided to erect a monument for the stone and gave it an unforgettable inauguration ceremony in the grandest of styles. In 1850 a public festival was held to celebrate the ancestry of the stone, an event which conspicuously linked the West Saxon monarchy with the presiding Queen Victoria, and the civic authority has scarcely looked back since. Royal associations with the town would continue after the Norman Conquest, with the granting of certain rights to the townsfolk by King John in an early charter of 1200, a copy of which survives in a 1208 version. These rights and more besides were reaffirmed throughout the centuries by various monarchs and Kingston's history during the English Civil War was largely, though not exclusively, a royalist one. But the town will forever be associated with the coronations of the Saxon kings. Street names, school names and even the occasional public house celebrate the memory of the Anglo-Saxon era.

The name Kingston was, in fact, surprisingly common in Anglo-Saxon England. It simply means 'The King's Tun' or estate. Early records spell the word in a form that makes this point clearer: *cyninges-tun*. A *cyninge* is the chief kinsman – a king. The Old English word should be pronounced 'kewninge'. It is true that the word 'tun' is an ancestor of our modern word 'town', but if we imagine Kingston upon Thames as a tenth-century city then we are misleading ourselves. The first mention of the settlement during the period is a revealing one. In 838 a council was held here over which Egbert, king of Wessex, presided. Also present were Æthelwulf, underking of Kent, Archbishop Ceolnoth of Canterbury and leading members of the clergy of the day. The writer who records this council refers to 'That famous place which is called Kingston in the region of Surrey'. The council itself decided on some important measures for the cementing of relationships between Canterbury and the West Saxon monarch. Canterbury would have to get used to West Saxon dominance now that the expansion of that kingdom had swallowed Kent and Sussex with it. Egbert restored land to Christchurch at Canterbury and allowed free elections of abbots and abbesses in Kentish monastic communities. The intriguing thing about this early reference is that it suggests very firmly that Kingston, or at least the place which became Kingston, had roots deeper in history than the reign of Egbert. What was a royal estate in the ninth and tenth centuries clearly was a place well known enough in the early Dark Ages to acquire the fame which our 838 writer observes. Quite what this early activity had been is anyone's guess. The river Thames at Kingston has revealed artefacts from the Palaeolithic period to the modern age in more or less equal weight. The Roman period is represented by a multitude of coins and jewellery which appear to have been thrown into a tributary of the river, perhaps slow running, over a long time. Archaeologists have postulated that there may have been a shrine there in the Roman period and that the religious significance of Kingston as a crossing place on the Thames (a function for which it was to be widely recognised when its medieval bridge was built in the twelfth century) may have continued into the Dark Ages and Anglo-Saxon period, when it became one of the king's many royal estates. There had never been a Roman settlement in the urban sense at Kingston – the nearest being *Pontes* at Staines, but there was clearly Roman activity.

What exactly went on in an Anglo-Saxon tun is an interesting question. At the heart of the tun was the royal official, the reeve, whose job it was to administer the tun in the absence of his lord. These used to be the places where the taxation for a surrounding district was collected and stored. In the earlier Anglo-Saxon period, much of this produce would have arrived on the hoof or in carts, with financial payments increasingly replacing the old food-rents. This meant that the form of the settlement in the tenth century would probably have consisted of scattered wooden houses to the north of the parish church and, further south, some large timber buildings and a central timber hall of some reasonable size. However, when the king visited Kingston, several new buildings would have been built to accommodate the royal household and its retainers. These were the days of itinerant governments and the preparations for hosting the king at one of his tuns would have been immense. For a brief period, as happened in Athelstan's reign and again in 972 and c.1020, the population of the settlement would have swollen out of all proportion to its capacity for housing people. More than seven times in one century a crowd of important people visited Kingston either to witness the coronation of the most powerful ruler in Britain, or to accompany him on his itinerary.

As well as having this key secular role, Kingston also appears to have had a Minster church.[8] Minster churches were frequently based at royal vills and it is suggested that the large size of Kingston's medieval parish is due to the fact that in the Anglo-Saxon period it had been the ecclesiastic centre for a large area.[9] John Leland, the sixteenth-century writer, recorded on his visit to Kingston 'that wher their toun chirche is now was sumytyme an abbay'. In the grounds of the church today can be seen the remains of the foundations of the walls of the chapel of St Mary, whose ancestry is supposed to go back to the Anglo-Saxon period. The chapel, which may have been the church in which Athelstan was crowned, is no more than 60ft long and it was excavated by Dr Finny, a hugely enthusiastic local antiquarian, in the late 1920s. This may only be part of the Minster church, which would have been a larger building in the tenth century, perhaps much of it wooden. Carolingian parallels with the postulated Kingston church have been drawn and it is suggested that there may well have been a continental-style balcony chapel from which the kings could be displayed to the masses.[10]

Why had the coronation of the West Saxon monarch shifted its focus to Kingston in the tenth century? Historians have struggled to find the answer to this question. Our only hope is in the analysis of the prevailing politics of the time, coupled with the practical needs of organisation and geography. Being on the Thames, at the head of the tide, or close to it, will have helped attendants reach their destination. Kingston is situated at the extreme edge of Wessex and is close to London, which had become English once again after 886. It is easily reachable from other parts of Surrey, Sussex and Kent inside a day and, importantly at this time, reachable from Mercia, the English kingdom to the north of the Thames, which before the ninth and tenth centuries had held so much sway in the region of Surrey. It had a Minster church and it also belonged to the West Saxon king. Everyone who should need to get here could do so, at least for the time being. It was not a great urban settlement, which made it the ideal place for a grand open-air gathering of the type which sometimes went on for days after events such as coronations and royal christenings. In short, the royal administration needed plenty of space to stage the event.

But what of the authenticity of the claims for the crowning of kings at Kingston? One should say that there are really only two contemporary or near-contemporary reliable references to the event and that both of these are in the *Anglo-Saxon Chronicle*. The others, for various reasons, could be discounted, or so it is argued. This is probably a little unfair, but the two coronations recorded in the *Anglo-Saxon Chronicle* which are generally taken at face value are those of Athelstan and of Æthelred Unræd:

> Here King Edward died at Farndon in Mercia and very soon, sixteen days after, his son died at Oxford; and their bodies lie at Winchester. And Athelstan was chosen king by the Mercians and consecrated at Kingston; and he gave his sister across the sea to the son of the king of the Old Saxons.
>
> *Anglo-Saxon Chronicle* entry for 924,
> Worcester Manuscript (D)

> In this year, Æthelred was consecrated as king on the Sunday, fourteen days after Easter, at Kingston; and there were at his consecration two archbishops and ten diocesan bishops. The same year a bloody cloud was seen, many times in the likeness of fire; and it appeared most of all at midnight; and it was formed thus of various beams; then when it became day it glided away.
>
> *Anglo-Saxon Chronicle* entry for 979,
> Abingdon Manuscript (C)

The other sources which can be added to the *Anglo-Saxon Chronicle* entries are the twelfth-century accounts of William of Malmesbury, Florence of Worcester, Henry of Huntingdon, Roger of Hovedon, Ralph de Diceto and the early fifteenth-century account by Johannes Brompton and Holinshed's chronicles of 1578.[11] Malmesbury, Huntingdon and Hovedon were probably using versions of the *Anglo-Saxon Chronicle* amongst other documents to compile their histories. This does not necessarily discount what they have to say, of course. Ralph de Diceto was a dean of St Paul's who died in *c.*1202, and much of his chronicle is based on, among others, Henry of Huntingdon, who gives the names of just two kings as being crowned at Kingston. Ralph, it is suggested, simply filled in the gaps. The monk Florence of Worcester, whose work is based on a version of the *Anglo-Saxon Chronicle*, suggests that Edred and Edwy were also crowned at Kingston. A charter of 946 which seems to have survived at Worcester, records the granting of land in Warkton in Northamptonshire by Edred. This was a grant that had been made whilst the king was at 'Kingston'. We do not know which Kingston this was, nor do we have the charter to examine since it has been destroyed. Florence would have seen it though and presumably used this as his evidence. And so, perhaps, one more candidate for Kingston can be put forward. But quite where Florence got Edwy from, we do not know.

The Kingston tradition is certainly safe in the respect of the two kings mentioned above. It may well be that there are other lost sources which some of our historians used to justify the inclusion of the others, but we may never find them. Clearly, Kingston was an important strategic place in the tenth century and its long history of royal association did not happen by accident.

### A REWARD FOR MALMESBURY

Athelstan's association with the abbey and settlement in the burh at Malmesbury seems to have been very strong. Even today there is a deep sense of identity in the town focused on the personality and memory of the king. Instead of being buried at Winchester or Glastonbury as other monarchs of the age were, Athelstan was buried here. He shares the same level of fame in the town as St Aldhelm and the twelfth-century historian William of Malmesbury, from whom we learn so much colourful detail about Athelstan. For much of its history, this quiet country town was part of both a physical and ideological frontier.

Today, Malmesbury abbey is the parish church of the town. It has a history which goes back to the seventh century, when a monastery was founded there by an Irish monk called Maeldulph. One of Maeldulph's students was Aldhelm, a kinsman of Ine, the great law-making king of Wessex. Aldhelm, whom Athelstan justifiably claimed as an ancestor, later came back to Malmesbury after a period at Canterbury, and in the year 676 he reconstituted the monastery under the Benedictine Rule. Malmesbury soon fell under the sway of the increasingly powerful and expansionist kingdom of Mercia in the late seventh century. It seems to have done little harm to the abbey, which, along with Abingdon, received new lands during the period of Mercian rule. The reigns of the West Saxon monarchs of Caedwalla and Ine saw Wessex regain ownership of Malmesbury at the end of the seventh century, and the bishopric of Dorchester, whose dioceses represented the whole of Wessex, was moved to Winchester as a legacy of the West Saxon and Mercian struggle.

The Winchester diocese in 705 was split into two, with the eastern part retaining the name and the city, having much the same shape as it does today, and the western part becoming the diocese of Sherborne, its first bishop being Aldhelm. Sherborne's *cathedra* would later move first to Old Sarum and then to Salisbury. Aldhelm had been the first in line of the bishops of Salisbury whilst retaining his post as abbot of Malmesbury, this privileged position owing much to his own competence and much to his associations with the royal house of Wessex. When he died in 709, Aldhelm was brought to Malmesbury and buried there as he had left instructions to this effect.

So, West Saxon royalty and the abbey of Malmesbury had a long history of relations. In Athelstan's time this was still the case. The manor of Foxley, just a mile away, was owned by the king and he had property at nearby Norton. It is of interest that after the battle of Brunanburh Athelstan arranged for two of his cousins, Ælfwine and Æthelwine, who had fallen in that tumultuous struggle against the Danes, to be brought back to Malmesbury and buried there. The splendid gifts brought by the Count of Flanders in 926 with the embassy of Hugh, Duke of the Franks, had been presented at Abingdon but were given to the abbey at Malmesbury where they helped draw many pilgrims.

But this was not all that Athelstan did for Malmesbury. Clearly, the townspeople had helped the king in no small way. Just a mile or two outside the town is a place known as the King's Heath. It is situated alongside the Common Road leading south-west out of the town. It covers an area of about 600 acres, or five hides – enough land to qualify a single owner as a thegn. This is said to have been given to the men of Malmesbury for services rendered to the king at the time of the battle of Brunanburh in 937.[12] The charter is thought to have been granted in about 939 and its original no longer exists. The oldest medieval copy has the text in a confirmation charter granted by Richard II in 1381. A copy of the charter exists in a patent roll of Henry IV, parts of which are quoted below:

> I, Athelstan, King of the English, grant for myself and my successors, to my burgesses and all their successors of the borough of Meldulf, that they may have and hold forever, all the powers and free customs as they held them in the time of King Edward, my father, undiminished and honourably... And I give and grant to them that royal heath of five hydes of land, near my village [vill] of Norton, on account of their help in my conflict with the Danes...

What had the people of Malmesbury done to deserve this reward? The answer to this question is not known for sure, but the fact that the place was an important royal and ecclesiastical centre, with an influence over a broad landscape, must be important. Furthermore, the town is very close to the Fosse Way, which in the age of Athelstan would have been the main military high road into the Danelaw. Perhaps Malmesbury's thegns and their retainers excelled themselves at Brunanburh, or perhaps the quality of the townspeople's estate management led to the provision of horses and supplies for the army, we may never know, but Athelstan was a notable gift-giver, although he only ever seems to have given things for a good reason.

The land given to the citizens of Malmesbury remained the property of the freemen of the borough. Before 1866 it was the responsibility of an alderman and twelve burgesses elected by the freemen. When the town became a municipal borough, the Old Corporation was allowed to remain in being mainly in order that this land could be continually managed. The King's Heath had been a common upon which freemen had the right to graze their cattle, but after 1821 it was enclosed and broken up into allotments for the freemen, any one of which could obtain a life-hold share provided that they live in the borough. A local historian quotes one peculiar custom from the eighteenth century:

> On a certain day of the year, the inhabitants would be awakened in the early morning by the cry in the streets of 'Drive Heath',

announcing to the owners of cattle grazing on Malmesbury Common that all the cattle were being rounded up into the great Penn or Pound of the Common, whence they must be claimed by their owners; this to ensure that none but lineally descended Commoners were making use of the five hydes of Common given to their ancestors by K. Athelstan.[13]

The seriousness with which the Old Corporation took their connections to the ancient monarch is best exemplified by the peculiarity of the initiation ceremony of a commoner. Along with a steward, the new commoner goes to the holding which will become his. They cut a turf together and place a twig from a hedge in the sod. The steward then presents this after he has placed 2s in the hole in the ground having chanted the following refrain:

> *This turf and twig I give to thee*
> *As free as Athelstan gave to me*
> *And I hope a loving brother thou wilt be.*

The money did not remain in the hole, but was used to contribute to the King Athelstan Feast, a ceremony held in the week following the initiation. Today, the landscape still carries the marks of the original land apportionment and, despite enclosure, it ranks as one of the few cases where we are able to see with modern eyes more or less what five Anglo-Saxon hides should look like on the ground. The land covered by the common is surprisingly large.

Athelstan himself was brought after his death to Malmesbury and buried under the altar of the church of St Peter. The two princes Ælfwine and Æthelwine, who lost their lives at Brunanburh, had been brought to Malmesbury too, giving the place the feeling of a royal mausoleum. The church of St Peter is unknown, but under the reign of Edgar (959-975), during a period of great monastic and cultural revival, the abbey church was rebuilt and dedicated to St Mary. Perhaps Athelstan's tomb and that of St Aldhelm (commissioned by Athelstan) were moved into the new church. Perhaps they were moved yet again into the grand building belonging to the twelfth century (the surviving portions of which can be seen today) in order to attract pilgrims. Tradition has it that Athelstan and Aldhelm were located in the chapel at the eastern end of the tenth-century church, the chapel – which became known as St Michael's chapel and which outlasted the main body of the church itself – becoming attached to the southern transept of the present church. John Leland visited the town and wrote of this chapel in his *Itinerary*:

> Ther was a litle chirch joining to the south side of the transeotum of thabby chirch, wher sum say Joannes Scottus the great clerk was slayne about the tyme of Alfred king of West Saxons…Weavers hath now looms in this litle chirch, but it stondith and is a very old pece of work.

If that chapel, now gone, did date from the time of Alfred, then it may be a candidate for the pre-Edgar building and the resting place for Athelstan. It is difficult to see how this position could be 'under the altar', though. Furthermore, our hunt is hampered by subsequent events. At the end of the fifteenth century a huge tower and spire which had been added to the church in the fourteenth century collapsed and the whole church, from the crossing eastwards, was destroyed. This event alone may have accounted for the disappearance or destruction of the tombs. Moreover, as with so many stories of missing saints and cult figures, the wholesale destruction during the dissolution of the monasteries in the mid-sixteenth century may have something to do with it. Local opinion suggests that the remains of Athelstan may have been spirited away to a safe place during this time, the secret of their location dying with those who took them.

The tomb of Athelstan which exists today at Malmesbury may indeed date from the thirteenth or fourteenth centuries. It has certainly been in the abbey since the eighteenth century, and presumably longer. There is some doubt as to whether it started its life as Athelstan's monument, however. Firstly, the tomb is not particularly grand. One would expect something more of a showpiece to attract the pilgrims of the fourteenth century. Secondly, the figure on the tomb has clearly undergone dramatic change: the head and the lion at the figure's feet have been replaced at least once, probably in response to some desecration of the tomb at some stage.

Today Malmesbury is a beautiful country town rising on an imposing hill. The attractiveness of its gardens and the pleasing remains of its abbey church make it hard to imagine that in the late ninth and tenth centuries it was a frontier settlement greatly involved with the struggle for control of the country which would become the kingdom of the English. There remains one last evocative link between the town and its most famous benefactor and it is in a name which conjures up images of the heroic age of Brunanburh. There is a bridge just outside the town which crosses the Avon and which has variously been known as Turtle or Truckle bridge. The road leads to the King's Heath and then on to Bristol. The old abbey register has this bridge as Turketyl Bridge. Turketyl, as we shall see, was one of the leading Scandinavian mercenaries who was given a command at Brunanburh and who fought loyally for the English monarch. The Ingulf tradition as written down in the chronicles of the abbey of Croyland stated that Turketyl became a monk and abbot of Croyland. It is tempting to think that Athelstan ordered that this important bridge in his favourite town be named after one of his most steadfast soldiers.

## WARFARE AND LORDSHIP BEFORE ATHELSTAN

Going to war in the age of Athelstan was a duty. Much has been written on this subject, but it is only relatively recently that historians have begun to get to the bottom of the search for the personal bonds between men which made warfare work. And yet, even now, the new and plausible theories are not without their challengers.[14]

Personal lordship ties, honour, bravery and tradition seem to characterise the English response to the challenge of warfare. This is not to say that English armies were not well organised – they could even work in conjunction with naval operations – but it does mean to say that the English came to battle in much the same way as their Germanic ancestors had done in centuries gone by.

Although it was the right of every freeman to bear arms, the men who did most of the fighting ought to be seen as a semi-professional elite body who owed service to their lord and who themselves would have been notable local landowners. The contemporary name given to the Anglo-Saxon army was 'fyrd'. This peculiar word is pronounced as if the medial 'y' was a 'u' as in the French *tu*. It is traditionally taken to mean 'expedition' and some have used this translation to give it

the modern meaning of 'Expeditionary Force'. However, this interpretation was very much a product of its time and there are other
more useful ways of viewing the Anglo-Saxon fyrd. For many years
military historians sought to define the late Saxon fyrd in terms of two
distinct groups – a 'Select' group (the nobles and immediate retainers)
comprising heavily armed and armoured warriors, and a 'General' or
'Great' Fyrd of unarmoured, free peasantry. The Select Fyrd would ride
on campaigns with their lord and the Great Fyrd would in effect be
a local militia. This convenient compartmentalisation attracted many
followers due to its simplicity. In fact, the nature of military obligation
was rather more complex.[15]

The key to understanding military service in this period is in the
concept of personal lordship ties. In the early Saxon period the king,
when he summoned the fyrd, would expect his personal retainers
(*Gesithas*, or companions) to arm themselves and would also expect
the duties of his *Duguð*[16] (senior landed retainers) to be fulfilled.
They would turn up for campaign with their own retinues. Early English
fyrds were an aristocratic institution based on the lordship bond. The
lesser-armed men who appear in the ranks of the English armies in the
whole period from Ine of Wessex to Harold II of England were not the
'Great Fyrd' or the local levy, but were the men of the men who owed
military service to their lord. Despite multiple reforms in the way in
which armies were recruited and organised, this personal lordship bond
seems to have remained intact until at least the Norman Conquest, if
not later. Punishment for neglecting the duty of military service could
be exacted and would be applicable across the classes. The law codes of
the early West Saxon king Ine spell it out clearly:

> If a gesiðcund man who holds land neglects military service, he shall
> pay 120 shillings and forfeit his land; [a nobleman] who holds no land
> shall pay 60 shillings; a cierlisc [free peasant] shall pay 30 shillings as
> penalty for neglecting the fyrd.

Clearly, it was not a good idea to neglect military service in early Wessex.
It soon became apparent, however, during the age of Bede in the
eighth century, that, across the whole of the seven Saxon kingdoms of
England, there was a giant loophole in the arrangements for military
service where land tenure had been granted to the holder as 'Bookland'.

The problem with Bookland was that it was granted in permanent isolation from the king's financial and administrative system. It was usually granted to monasteries, who would not be expected to give any of the usual services in return for it, except, it seems, for the important work of securing the king's soul in heaven. The explosion of monastic institutions in the seventh and eighth centuries had compounded the problem as these had held their Bookland free from obligation to the king. This meant that there was less land to reward warriors with and the risk of losing otherwise loyal military men to other courts or to foreign shores was greatly heightened. It was one of the biggest governmental headaches of the eighth century, and it came just as the first Viking assaults on England were taking place.

The answer to the problem was provided in Mercia. This, the great middle Saxon kingdom of King Offa, was the most powerful kingdom in the immediate pre-Viking era. Some attempts had been made to insist on military service in exchange for Bookland, but it was the Mercian practice of introducing the 'Common Burdens' which rescued the situation. Military service, the duty of building fortifications against the pagans and the repair of bridges, were demanded of anyone who held land by hereditary right. Soon, all the other Anglo-Saxon kingdoms followed suit. Bookland was no longer a problem as far as military service was concerned.

The Common Burdens remained with the English as a tool of government for some time. The shift in power away from Mercia to Wessex in the ninth century meant that West Saxon monarchs had to employ all their administrative skill to make the system work in the face of the unprecedented threat from the Danes. The Danish armies had succeeded in eliminating all but one of the early English dynasties and it would fall to Alfred the Great to once again reorganise the English military system to cope with a new and potentially fatal threat.

Alfredian changes were profound. Alfred's story is set out below (pages 59-80), but the main issue which concerns us here is the way in which he reorganised fyrd duty. We can see the chief characteristics of the pre-reform West Saxon army by examining one of the most revealing entries in the *Anglo-Saxon Chronicle* of the ninth century:

> ... And that year there were nine national fights[17] fought against the
> raiding army in the kingdom to the south of the Thames, besides

those forays which Alfred, the king's brother, and ealdormen and king's thegns, often rode on, which were never counted...

*Anglo-Saxon Chronicle* entry for the year 870 [871]

Peterborough Manuscript (E)

There seems to have been a kingdom-wide host which fought large-scale pitched battles in that year. Also, there were the mounted forces of the king's brother, king's thegns and of the regional ealdormen. The difference between these two types of force was in the time they took to muster. The retainers of the individual ealdormen and powerful thegns would have acted like a rapid-reaction force, but their numbers would have been relatively small. The national host would have taken at least two weeks to assemble but would have had numbers to bring to bear. But all of these forces available to an Anglo-Saxon king depended on the bond of lordship and upon the loyalty the king could expect from his men. The achievement of Alfred in this respect was nothing short of miraculous. Early in 878, he was almost out of the equation, a refugee in his own country. Danish forces were marching into his kingdom and demanding subjection from each Wessex village they passed through. Alfred was losing men's loyalty as, everywhere he looked in his dwindling kingdom, they switched allegiance under duress to a new Danish overlord. Somehow, his personal strength of character brought fresh allegiance from the thegns of the West Country and Alfred won a famous victory over his adversary at Edington in that year. It marked the beginning of one of the most remarkable and sustained military and political comebacks in Western European history, and it is probably due to the strength of the ancient lordship bond of Old England, together with the competence of a string of rulers, that the kingdom was reborn.

The fyrd was split between those who were to be on active military service, those who would continue to till the land until their turn for campaigning came, and those who were on garrison duty in the newly-built forts of Alfred's kingdom. This arrangement was a wise use of human resources. The emphasis on mounted men had become important by Alfred's time. Alfred had demanded the provision of horses as compulsory for fyrd duty and this was further emphasised in Athelstan's reign (924-939). Athelstan demanded that 'every man shall provide two well mounted men for every plough', a demand which will have produced a great deal of mounted warriors. The preponderance of mounted fyrdsmen in English armies of the period has lead to a misunderstanding of their method of employment. They were not true cavalry as such, but moved through the landscape at great speed, often overtaking their enemies. The fyrdsman's preference for dismounting and fighting on foot does not suggest that the armies of this period used their horses inefficiently or ineffectively. The same goes for the Scandinavians. From their arrival in England in the 860s, the Danes showed themselves to be proficient in acquiring mounts and are often described as a mounted force. They did not restrict the practice to their activities in England either. In 891 a Danish army was campaigning on horseback in Brabant in Belgium when they were caught and defeated by the mounted forces of the East Frankish and Saxon armies at the battle of Leuvan on the river Dijle. Their enemies had managed to defeat them before the Danish ships could provide support. The very same force is described as bringing everything it had to England the next year, horses and all. The young Prince Edward's army, which overtook part of this invasion force, is described as riding in front of it. Again, in 937 when the Scandinavians invaded far into England on a mission to regain the Viking kingdom of York, they were described by William of Malmesbury's Latin source as doing so in mounted companies.

In short, the fyrdsman who faced the Danish and Norse threat was a professional warrior. At first, the organisation of the fyrd was found wanting, although clearly there were professional aspects to the service. Later, through the work of Alfred, Edward and Athelstan, a great re-structuring made the fyrdsman a powerful presence everywhere in the kingdom and beyond. What bound them all to each other was the ancient bond of lordship. Athelstan, through the awarding of land to middle-ranking officials, created a wider base from which to draw on lordship ties, thereby increasing manpower resources.

The military history of the age of Athelstan cannot be divorced from the political. Leaders took to the field with their retainers and followers. Military campaigns were a regular feature of tenth-century political life and must not go ignored. But for now we must look at the evidence for the impact of the Scandinavians in the early years of their descent upon Britain and trace the response to the threat, for the nature of the response has profound implications for the reign of Athelstan.

Western Europe was poorly prepared for the explosion of pirates and larger seaborne armies which came from the north. Trade, economy, religion, military organisation and urban settlement, such as it was, were all transformed by the Viking phenomenon and it is true to say that responses differed from place to place. But whatever the arguments for the far-reaching extent of the impact of the Scandinavians on Britain, there is one thing that all are agreed upon: it all started in the late eighth century with the appearance on the high seas of large numbers of pirates whose freedom to behave the way they did was the consequence of both political and economic problems which prevailed in the Scandinavian homelands. We must now examine why darkness fell upon the shores of Britain on the eve of the age of Athelstan.

# 2

# IN THE SHADOW OF
# THE VIKING

Here Beorhtric took King Offa's daughter Eadburh. And in his days
came first three ships of northmen from Hordaland and then the
reeve [named Beaduheard] rode there and wanted to compel them
to go to the king's town because he did not know what they were;
and they killed him. These were the first ships of the Danish men
which sought out the land of the English race.

*Anglo-Saxon Chronicle* entry for 787 [789],
Peterborough Manuscript (E)

With these words the *Anglo-Saxon Chronicle* announced the descent of
the heathen upon England. There is some confusion in the accounts
as to the origin of the northern men in these three ships, with
the Winchester version of the Chronicle (A) not mentioning their
origin at all, whilst manuscripts B and C (Abingdon) and D (Worcester)
describe them as 'northmen' and E (Peterborough) and F (Canterbury)
state their origin in Hordaland, the district around Hardanger
Fjord in West Norway. E and F both state that they were Danes,
despite also mentioning the Norwegian connection. The Dane and
the Northman were to become common terms in the contemporary
literature, with the Norwegian more readily identifying himself to
scribes as time wore on, but this first reference is still a little puz-
zling. Dane or Norwegian, these three shiploads of men demonstrated

the characteristics which were to typify their kind for centuries. The shadow had arrived.

Much ink has been spilled upon the question of trying to define exactly what a 'Viking' was. Theories have varied over the years regarding this controversial issue and they have ranged from the plausible to the ridiculous. There are a number of ways to approach the subject and one of the most popular has been through etymology, or the study of the origins of words. It was mooted that 'Viking' might mean 'oarsman' and that it was derived from a word that was used to describe the distance covered in each shift by an oarsman.[1] But this explanation provides relatively little meaning for a word which has haunted chroniclers for centuries. Another view, also etymological, suggests that the term arose on the shores of Anglian and Frisian Europe and that it subsequently found its way into Old English (a very similar language to Old Frisian). The word is suggestive of the temporary encampments which the coastal raiders threw up on foreign shores to protect themselves, it is said. But we know that a *wic* was a trading settlement, not an encampment of pirates. And if they were named after their penchant for attacking such vulnerable settlements, then we have to ask why they were not given the name of 'monastery-looters' as well.

A reasonable explanation might appear to be inherent in the Scandinavian word *Vikingr*, which is thought to mean 'Vik dweller' or 'inhabitant of the Viken area', the land flanking the Oslo Fjord. If we can provide the dynamic for why the term came so quickly to mean 'pirate', then we may have our answer. First, we must see what the different cultures of northern Europe called the men of the northern seas.

The Frankish chroniclers used the term Northmen, or Danes, much like the English. The Irish were quick to describe them as pagans, then later, 'foreigners', distinguishing the dark one (the *Dubgall*, or Dane) from the fair one (the *Finngall*, or Norseman), but it is with the English chroniclers that we find the widespread, but by no means universal, use of the term 'Viking'. Later, he could be Dane, Norwegian or Swede, but whoever he was, his activities meant trouble for all. The *Anglo-Saxon Chronicle*, using the Latin term *Pirates* (F), so described the raiding army which entered the Thames and sailed up to Fulham in 878-79, and we must assume that the word was chosen carefully. Sometimes, as in the entries for 921 (probably 917) and 897 (896), the Vikings are termed as those who man their *Aesc*, their distinctive shallow-draft keel-built long ships. The significance of the

Viking ships and their ability to cause great harm up and down the British coastline as well as to travel deep inland up the river systems was not lost on contemporary writers.

By the time of the so-called second Viking age in England, which began again during the reign of Æthelred II (979-1016), the English author of the famous *Battle of Maldon* poem refers to the Danish army variously as Vikings, Seamen, Ashmen, Danes and Heathen Warriors.[2] With such a bewildering variety of terms, it is easy to see why the confusion has arisen over the centuries. And yet it remains a matter of considerable irritation that the term 'Viking' has come to symbolise almost everything remotely Scandinavian in terms of material culture, politics and history for the era spanning the eighth to eleventh centuries. The truth about the men from the north is far more complex than the modern euphemism would suggest.

SCANDINAVIA AND THE VIKING EXPLOSION

The Scandinavian homelands had shown some degree of prosperity in the pre-Viking period. During the period known as the Vendel Culture, the presence of rich graves in the sixth and seventh centuries implies a significant contact with Frankish traders and the Mediterranean.[3] It is this trading activity which provides the main clue in our quest to understand the Viking.

Lacking the same governmental apparatus as Frankish and Anglo-Saxon Christian polities, the Scandinavian powerbase came from their extended kin group, such as it had in pagan times in early Saxon England. Naturally, this led to the rise in importance of dynastic politics in the homelands. Dynasties had begun to form, some of whose names echo through the halls of history having survived in great Anglo-Saxon works of literature such as the poem *Beowulf*. The Geatas of Southern Sweden, the Jelling in Jutland, the Ynglings in the areas around the Oslo Fjord and the Leire near Roskilde in Zealand all had their part to play in the formation of Scandinavian culture before, and to some extent, during the Viking age.

But what was it that caused the great Viking adventure? Most scholars would agree that the traditional explanation that there was land-hunger in Scandinavian homelands can only really be attributed to the western coastal areas of Norway and that there was nothing particularly new about such a phenomenon. The answer must lie elsewhere. Europe in the post-Roman period was rediscovering the value of trade. This commercial expansionist tendency manifested itself in the town-like trading ports which were established both within and without the areas of the former Western Roman Empire. Trade had not died out as such, but by the eighth century it had become controlled by increasingly powerful leaders whose role in checking piracy (as well as sometimes causing it) cannot go unacknowledged. The Frisians, a great maritime and mercantile presence in northern waters, had managed to introduce great quantities of silver into the northern economy, resulting in the widespread adoption of silver coinage. Ports such as Hamwih (Southampton), Dorestad, Quentovic (Boulogne), Fordwich (Canterbury), Ribe (on the west coast of Jutland) and Hedeby shared common characteristics: they were a hive of mercantile activity with a great degree of planning in the design and layout of the place. In many cases, most of the trading was carried out within yards of the ships which brought the goods, giving these ports another, more significant, characteristic – they were vulnerable to attack.

Ironically, it was the Scandinavians themselves who had as much to lose from the activities of the pirates of the Baltic and North Sea as anyone else. It was from Scandinavia that the finest skins, furs and pelts came to be sold at the market centres of Europe. Most crews sailing out of the northern seas were preoccupied with peaceful mercantile matters and were not marauding Vikings. The furs were accompanied by a wide range of other Baltic produce and included quality whetstones, amber and eiderdown. But although these materials had been brought to the trading ports with peaceful intent, the manner of their acquisition was quite different. Finns, Saami and Balts are all recorded in contemporary accounts as being under the subjection or coercion of the Scandinavians, particularly the Norwegians, and they paid for their subjection with huge tributes of goods such as ship ropes, walrus hides, skins, animal hides and furs. So, behind the 'peaceful' trader was a diplomatic structure which had at its head a warlord who used the sword as his chief bargaining tool. And yet, all this economic activity, the vulnerability of the new trading ports of coastal Europe and the well-documented aggression of the Scandinavian, still does not explain the phenomenon fully. For this, we must look at the politics. The ingredients for the chaos in Scandinavia in the Viking period had always been there, yet what was needed to trigger the new era was political instability. The Danes had become powerful enough by the eighth century to give their neighbours in southern Norway a difficult choice. Submit to Danish overlordship, or choose exile. Those who chose exile, particularly those who did so from the area around Viken, became Vikings, seeking wealth and adventure elsewhere, or so it is argued. But such men were not the only Scandinavians to choose to go a-Viking. After the breakdown of a strong central Danish power, it became something of a fashion.

The Frankish Empire, whilst strong under Charlemagne and his successor Louis the Pious, was able through pure politics to keep any Danish trouble at bay for a few years, despite the lack of comprehensive coastal protection. Louis is known to have granted land inside the empire to exiled Danish royals. The breakdown of the Carolingian Empire under Louis's sons (one of whom welcomed the services of a Viking fleet) seems to have marked a significant turning point in fortunes. Both French and English sources point to the start of raiding in around 834-5. Among the first victims of the raiders were the trading ports of Quentovic, and that at Hamwih, in England. Raids on monastic communities, particularly coastal ones in Francia, Britain and Ireland were also a conspicuous feature of Viking activity in this early era.

The Scandinavian homelands. The first recorded Viking attacks on England were launched from Hjordaland on the West Coast of Norway, but the Vikings may have taken their name from the region of the Vikin, further south.

In Denmark, King Godfred had been a powerful and centralising ruler between 800-810, but his murder at the hands of a retainer in 810 and the brief reign of his successor Hemming led to a war involving Godfred's sons. One of them, Horik, rose to prominence and is the leader whom St Anskar, the principal Frankish source for this period, identifies as the most powerful and most receptive ruler in Denmark. His rise was complete by 825 and he continued until 854. Despite one expedition of his own into Frankish territory, Horik was generally ill at ease with the activities of Danish pirates along the coastline and strove to check it where possible. Danish politics, however, were violent and unpredictable. His nephew, a young pirate known as Guthrum, who would later make a dramatic reappearance on the political stage in England, led an attack which succeeded in killing all but one of the whole royal court in 854, plunging the fragile kingdom into chaos once again. The breakdown of rule led to a shift in the activities of ambitious men, some of them quite important, who saw no reason not to take to the sea in search of political reward.

### THE SHADOW LENGTHENS ACROSS THE CELTIC LANDS

The Scandinavian threat to the political and religious life of northern Europe is clear. The ways in which each Western European culture responded to the threat differs from place to place and culture to culture. In fact, it is fair to say that no two groups responded in exactly the same way. The geography of Wales, for example, played an important part in keeping the incursions of the pirates and their successors to a reasonable minimum. In other places it was the strength or weakness of native ruling dynasties which influenced the intent of those larger raiding forces who were clearly bent on establishing some sort of political domination. One fact, however, remains. Each of the cultures that felt the force of the Scandinavian raids and settlement came out of it as an altered, but in many ways stronger, society. Though they did not always constitute a common enemy in this world of transient power politics, the effect of the Scandinavian descent on Britain and Ireland was that it acted as a catalyst in the development of those countries which were slowly coming into being. Native rulers had to learn the hard lessons of how to make their kingdoms stronger against the threat, and some found themselves better disposed to it than others.

The Irish suffered at the hands of the Norwegians and Danes just as much as their English counterparts across the sea, perhaps more so. The attacks fell upon Ireland in the early ninth century at around the same time as they fell upon the coasts of England and Northern France. But the story of how the Irish power groups coped with the Scandinavian threat differs in some detail from the English one, and in its telling we can discern some important differences in the nature of the politics of two similar societies.

The monastic island community of Iona was attacked in 795 during a decade which saw similar raids on communities in the north of England. Iona was not left alone. Again, in 802 the Vikings came and once more in 806 they returned and killed sixty-eight members of the community. For much the same reasons as the monks of Lindisfarne would leave their own holy island to settle their community elsewhere, so did the monks of Iona, establishing themselves at Kells where they built a new monastery between 807-14. Iona, however, did continue as a centre.[4]

Rathlin Island off the northern Irish coast was raided in 795. Then came a raid upon St Patrick's Island further south on the east coast. But it was not just the east littoral which suffered. In 807 the western island of Inishmurray was also attacked. These early attacks shared similarities with those on England and elsewhere. They do not seem to have been co-ordinated, being designed to retrieve as much portable wealth as possible from rich and vulnerable sources. Since people are portable just like chalices, books and altar pieces, it is probable that the slave trading for which later-period Scandinavian adventurers became famous, was being practised even at this early stage.

The ruling tribal leaders of Ireland were no less impotent than the English in their response. It has to be kept in mind that on both sides of the Irish sea, the Scandinavian threat was a problem which the military organisations of the day were not designed to deal with. However, in Ireland, as in England, some early successes are recorded. In 811 and 812 local leaders defeated the raiders, perhaps by virtue of being in the right place at the right time. In 828, after a period which had seen Scandinavians in Cork, Skellig and Lusk, near Dublin, the king of the Uí Chennselaig combined with a force from the monastery of Taghmon and drove the enemy away. This union of secular and religious forces in the field is not an altogether unusual feature in Irish history at this time.

In 831 the monks of Armagh took to the field to protect their property, but were soundly beaten.

The 830s saw repeated attacks in the Armagh area (three in one month in 832). Leading religious figures were ransomed and countless religious houses sacked. Still, it seems, there was no real rhyme or reason in the attacks – just an accrual of riches. It is a testimony to the extraordinary wealth of Ireland's monastic communities that so many of them were targeted by the raiders. The famous English story of Alfred, the ealdorman of Surrey, who bought back valuable books from the pirates, must have been a familiar tale to the Irish, too. The pattern of raids in these early decades of the ninth century seems to follow the logical routes along navigable rivers. Things were to change in the late 830s in Ireland, as they would elsewhere. Bigger fleets arrived and leading them were men intent on political gain, their war bands capable of far-reaching campaigns into the hinterland of the country. One such figure, a Viking called Turgeis (Thorgils), described by the twelfth-century writer of the *Cogadh Gaedhel re Gallaibh* (The War of the Irish with the Foreigners), is said to have come to Ireland with a great fleet with the idea of assuming total authority over all other Vikings in Ireland. He is said to have attacked Armagh, driven out its abbot and, taking the abbacy for himself, became leader of the whole of the north of Ireland, just as the prophecy had dictated:

> *Gentiles shall come over the soft sea*
> *They shall confound the men of Erinn*
> *Of them there shall be an abbot over every church*
> *Of them there shall be a king over Erinn.*

The *Cogadh* goes on to say that after sacking Clonmacnoise, Turgeis was captured and drowned in 845. Other, perhaps more reliable, sources record the death of a Turgesius from drowning in that year. So, however legendary the preliminary section of the *Cogadh* from which this story is taken might appear, there is a kernel of truth at its root.

The sixty or so shiploads of foreigners who arrived in 837 troubled the Irish in the region of the Boyne and the Liffey. Here, several campaigns were fought between the invaders and the men of the Uí Néill, with mixed results. The shadow was lengthening into the hinterland. This same year saw Scandinavians along the Shannon and into Lough

Derg where they sacked the holy island on this giant lake. Lough Neagh in the north suffered its own predatory fleet throughout 839, a force which stayed for some time.[5] The consequence of the permanency of the invaders was their building of protective fortifications, which encompassed fleet and army alike. Similar forts were built in England, those at Repton in Derbyshire and at Reading in Berkshire being good examples. In Ireland these are called 'longphort'. The advantage of a longphort was obvious – the Viking could easily plunder deep into the landscape and return to his stronghold with his goods. From there he could set sail to ply his trade with whatever ill-gotten gains he had accrued. The early 840s saw a proliferation of these fortifications, with Dublin being one of the earliest alongside that at Linn Dúachaill in Co. Louth. Others soon followed, including one at Lough Ree on the Shannon (845) and one at Cork (848). The Scandinavian fortification at Dunrally on the Barrow (862) was stormed under unusual circum-stances[6] although many more such fortifications continued to be built during the 860s.

Map of early
Viking-period Ireland
showing sites mentioned
in the text

As well as being a permanent and menacing presence in the Irish hinterland, the Scandinavians offered an opportunity for native dynasties to get even with each other. The first recorded example of Irish co-operation with the invaders was in 842 when Commán, the abbot of Linn Dúachaill, is described as being killed by a combined force of Scandinavians and Irish. But alliances were not always the norm. In fact, there is plenty of evidence that the native dynastic leaders were capable of defeating both the Scandinavians and their competing neighbours by themselves on a fairly regular basis. The later 840s, for example, saw the kings of Tara and Osraige defeat and destroy numerous invading forces. But still the fortifications remained, acting as strongholds and as the bases for small power blocks which became added to the patchwork of existing kingdoms and petty kingdoms. Here, the Irish experience differs from the English. The native dynasties in the north, East Anglia and Midlands of England were utterly destroyed by the invader, with puppet kings being put in their stead. The resurrection of English power in these places had to come through the coercive power of Wessex and the English rump of Mercia. In Ireland, the political map simply became more complex. This is not to say that there were no aspirations among Irish dynastic leaders for wide-ranging dominance of the island. Far from it, in fact. The Uí Néill, even at this stage of frequent foreign troubles, were often at the heart of the struggle for supremacy. But there came another twist to the Viking story in 849. This time the invaders, with many more ships than before, had scores to settle with their own kinsmen. There followed a few years where annals recorded the expulsion from Ireland of Danes by the Norse who were already resident in Ireland. The new Scandinavian enemy came not from their original homeland it seems, but probably from Scotland and the Western Isles. One such visitor from foreign shores who exacted tribute from both the Irish and the Norse in Ireland was Olaf, son of the king of Laithlind.

In Dublin, over the next two decades, the Scandinavian lead-ers Ímar (Ivar, who, as we shall see, was active in England) and Auisle dominated. Their activities were not restricted to Ireland in this brave new world. In 866 they sailed to Scotland and with a force of Vikings drawn from Scottish as well as Irish shores they attacked and overran all of the land of the Picts to the east, placing them under tribute. Their absence from Ireland allowed the northern Uí Néill to destroy many of their longphort in a sustained campaign which alarmed the enemy enough for it to return quickly from abroad. In 870-71, the year that Wessex was struggling to contain the threat in the south of Britain, Dumbarton, the capital of the Strathclyde Welsh, was sacked by Ivar, and this alarming attack was something of a wake-up call for the polities of Northern Britain. Treasure, slaves and portable wealth of all descriptions were carried away from the city. The need to contain the threat of the invader was becoming increasingly apparent to the leaders of both Strathclyde and the Scots.

The Irish leaders were learning quickly, however. The late ninth century is marked by a string of successes which led to an irrevocable split in Dublin in 893. Moreover, the Scandinavians were now squabbling among themselves. Within three years, the two main Scandinavian political camps which had risen from the ashes of an internecine and murderous struggle, had lost their leaders to murder and intrigue. The Dublin stranglehold was weakening. In 902 events demonstrated that the game was up for the Scandinavians of that city. The rulers of Brega and Leinster combined their forces in an assault on their enemy and succeeded in driving the pagans clean out of Ireland. The result was two-fold. It began in Ireland an era of self-confidence, although the pagans would return sooner rather than later. More important than this was the subsequent effect during the next twenty years or so that the expulsion had on the settlement and politics of north-west England, western Scotland and Northumbria. The fugitives, after meeting with some resistance in the north of Wales, sought settlement in Æthelflæd's Mercian kingdom (see page 93) where one leader, Ingimund, besieged Chester. Others sought out the west of Scotland, where various Scandinavian communities already existed, and from here they began campaigns which changed the whole complexion of the region. The memory of Dublin did not fade for the Scandinavians, however. Soon they would be back again with the idea of ruling an Empire which would have two centres, one on either side of the sea at Dublin and at York and the pursuit of this dream would outlast even the Vikings' greatest natural enemy, the mighty Athelstan.

The exiles campaigned widely in Scotland, particularly against the Picts, whose king they murdered in 904. Ímar ua hÍmair, king of Dublin until the expulsion in 902, was himself murdered by the Picts at Strathearn. Ten years later, another grandson of Ímar, Ragnall (the

Rægnald of the English sources) was campaigning at Corbridge and would establish for himself the kingdom of York. The dream of the Scandinavian power block was becoming a reality. Ragnall's successful northern campaigns saw him recognised by 919 as king of the Danes, a title which meant, in effect, king of the new Scandinavian patrimony of Northumbria. His kinsman, Sitric Caech, had come to Cenn Fuait on the border of Leinster, whose men were persuaded by Niall Glúndub, the king of Tara, to attack Sitric in his camp. They were soundly beaten and soon Sitric was in Dublin and, after various Irish campaigns, Ragnall was back at York. Niall attempted to oust Sitric again, but was catastrophically defeated at Islandbridge in 919. He fell there along with a number of leading Uí Néill warriors and the Irish threat to Dublin lost its impetus. Sitric succeeded Ragnall in York and ruled there until 927 (see pages 124-125). Dublin had been left in the hands of Godfrid (Guthfrith of the English sources), a Viking slaver and warrior. Godfrid attempted campaigns in the hinterland, but the strength of the Uí Néill precluded any great successes.

Dublin was never wholly safe during the absence of its Scandinavian leaders. Independent Vikings from Limerick briefly assaulted the city during one period of absence and this event is what sparked Guthfrith's famous son Olaf Guthfrithson to launch a punitive campaign on Lough Ree in August 937. The leader of the Limerick Vikings was brought back to Dublin in chains along with many captured men who would be press-ganged into service during the great Brunanburh campaign in Northumbria. Shortly after this, Olaf was involved in the largest military campaign in early medieval history in northern Britain, conjoining his forces with those of the kings of the Scots and Strathclyde in order to defeat Athelstan, the English king who had made York his own.

After the disaster at Brunanburh against Athelstan, there were some successes in England, but back in Ireland in 944 another combination of Brega and Leinstermen successfully overwhelmed Dublin and its rule passed to the kings of Tara, who now expected that role to come with their office. Perhaps the Irish had learned of the success of combined English forces at Brunanburh in 937 and tried to imitate it, or perhaps they were just combining in the same ways that they had before. The complex history of events in the later part of the tenth century, which saw Olaf Sihtricson's extraordinarily long career wax and wane in its fortunes between York and Dublin and which also saw the gradual rise to prominence of the southern Uí Néill and, later, the Dál Cais under Brian Bórama, are well documented elsewhere and not necessarily relevant to the tale told here. It is important to note, however, that the policy of absorbing the Scandinavian polities into a wider power block, by using subjection instead of attempting an outright expulsion of the foreigner, was perhaps the most significant change in Irish-Scandinavian relations in the later period. Money from Scandinavian trading was redirected and their fleets and warriors were used as a way of achieving the status of high king in Ireland, but in the age of Athelstan, the whip hand in Ireland was clearly held by the Viking.

Wales, on the other hand, has a Scandinavian history quite unlike that of any of its neighbours. It is another example of a peculiar indigenous response to an external threat. This is probably an accident of geography, with the Welsh owing much of their successful resistance to their difficult coastline, treacherous currents and mountainous terrain. But even in the lower lands and on open western beaches the Scandinavian raiding presence was not as strong as it might have been. Resistance is noted from the Welsh, particularly in the early periods of the raids. In 855, Rhodri Mawr, Prince of Gwynedd, checked Danish ambitions under the leadership of Gorm. The Scandinavian settlement of Anglesey was subsequently abandoned. During the 870s, however, even Rhodri felt the pressure enough to seek exile in Ireland. Angelsey was again attacked, unsuccessfully, by the Norse who had been expelled from Dublin in 902. But it was the south of Wales, with its lower lying and more vulnerable landscape, that felt the full force of Scandinavian contact. In 914, a host sailing from Brittany was able to raid with impunity up the southern Welsh coast and enter the Wye Valley as far as Archenfield, were they captured the Welsh bishop of Llandaff, Cyfeiliog. The bishop was considered important enough to have his ransom of £40 paid for him by the English king.

Welsh relations with the Mercians had always been strained. One of Europe's largest archaeological monuments, Offa's Dyke, bears testimony to the antagonism between Mercia and the powerful Welsh kingdom of Powys. In fact, the dyke is now being seen as Offa's defensive line against Powys and no longer as the boundary marker between two mutually respecting kingdoms.[7]

An entry for 916 in the *Anglo-Saxon Chronicle*[8] describes a campaign where Æthelflæd, the Lady of the Mercians, sent an army into Wales and broke down Brecenan Mere, a probable fortification at Llangorse Lake, where there was a dyke across the ridge which controlled traffic from England. It is against this background of constant antagonism and campaigning between the English and Welsh kingdoms that we should view the vital years of the 930s, which saw the Welsh opinion of the West Saxon (or *Iwys* as they knew them) split into two camps. It was not all open antipathy towards the English. Some were more subtle than that. One leader in particular, Hywel Dda (the Good) of Dyfed, inspired by the Imperial-style court of Athelstan, produced a coinage of his own based on the English model and issued laws which echoed those of the English king whose court machinery he was very well acquainted with. Hywel Dda in the 920s was a menacing enough campaigning presence in the south of the country to discourage serious Scandinavian attempts at settlement there. Hywel had visited Rome and, like Alfred the Great, will have seen and learned much whilst he was there. Symbolically at least, he was the ruler of a wider area of Wales than his official title would suggest and, along with Idwal the Bald of Gwynedd, he dominated Welsh politics during the age of Athelstan. The idea that Hywel was something of an anglophile, however, has been challenged over the years.[9] His grandfather had been killed by the English in 878 and Hywel had himself been effected by a humiliating submission to Athelstan at Hereford in 927. Hywel named one of his sons Edwin, perhaps not as a sycophantic acknowledgement to England, but as a way of irritating Athelstan, who had suffered a painful experience with his own younger brother Edwin. Hywel's presence at the English court, along with Idwal, was part of an arrangement necessary to be undertaken by a *sub-regulus* and was not done through choice. He was with the English court at Exeter in 928, Worthy in 931 and Middletun in 932, and it may well be that he accompanied the English king with his own military entourage on Athelstan's great expedition into Scotland in 934. Athelstan clearly kept his enemies close.

But the Scottish king Constantine's break with England in 934 may have inspired some Welsh sentiments of independence, as feelings were clearly running high. Year after year of huge tributes had to be paid to the English monarch at Cirencester, the ancient Roman seat of local government. The harsh tributes seemed too much for some Welsh writers at the time who foretold of a great Celtic uprising against the English which, although prophetic, was ironic since it is unlikely that enemies of Athelstan at the field of Brunanburh in 937 included the Welsh:

*There will be reconciliation between Cymry and the men of Dublin,*
*The Irish of Ireland and Angelsea and Scotland,*
*The men of Cornwall and of Strathclyde will be welcome among us…*
*The men of the north in the place of honour…*
*The stewards of Cirencester will shed bitter tears…as an end to their*
*Taxes they will know death.*

*Armes Prydein*

Such was the feeling about the power of the English and the subjection of the Welsh, that the author of the *Armes Prydein* spoke openly of the possibility of alliance with the Norse of the north of England, viewing them not as natural enemies but as proud warriors who shared with the Welsh a common enemy. In fact, Scandinavian settlement in Wales by the 930s was littoral and not serious, but if the Welsh poet had his way, the small settlements would be enlarged.

In Scotland however, the Scandinavian story is sometimes less clear than we would like it to be. The settlements of Orkney, Shetland and the Western Isles give perhaps the clearest picture. Despite their seeming remoteness, many of these islands have a conspicuously rich archaeological heritage which stretches back to at least the Neolithic period and much of the archaeology is still standing above ground today. The evidence, however, such that it is, shows that there was Scandinavian settlement in the northern islands from around 800 and that these settlements had a Norwegian and not a Danish connection. In particular, it seems that the settlers were coming from the western areas of Norway, around the area of Rogaland. The excavations at Jarlshof, in southern Shetland, have revealed an impressive stone farmstead built on the good fertile land of the slopes of Sumburgh Head with good access to springs and building materials with the earliest levels dating to the ninth century. The settlement had ancillary buildings with a smithy and even a feature interpreted as a sauna.[10]

The ninth and tenth centuries saw an expansion of Scandinavian settlement onto the Scottish mainland to the south and also to the Western Isles, where communities were set up that would play an important role in the politics of northern Britain throughout the tenth century. Under the leader Sigurd, Scottish Scandinavian settlements achieved something approaching political unity. It is likely that the Pictish inhabitants of north-east Scotland were under considerable duress even at this time, being described in later medieval sources as little more than pygmies who build during the morning and evening and hide terrified in subterranean dwellings during the day, when they lose their strength.

But in lowland Scotland and Strathclyde, we have a geography that was to play a profound role in the power struggles of the north during the age of Athelstan. The leaders of Strathclyde and Scotland knew very well of the Viking tendency to take a shortcut across their lands in order to get from one coast of Britain to another. The way in which they did so has particular significance in our hunt for the truth about the battle of Brunanburh.

# 3

# THE CALLING OF ALFRED

It would seem that in the beginning, England was not prepared for anything like the raiding and destruction which it suffered at the hands of seaborne pirates in the late eighth and ninth centuries. English settlements were poorly protected, armies slow to muster and move around the countryside, and the coastal trading ports of the south and east of England had ideal beaching areas both for traders and, more alarmingly, pirates. It is no coincidence that trading ports at Hamwih (Southampton) and Quentovic (a port near Boulogne, whose sacking is recorded in English as well as continental sources) were attacked in the 830s, as they offered another source of riches in the form of trading items and materials to supplement the pirates' lust for the obvious attractions of the portable wealth of monastic communities. The eventual effect of Scandinavian assault on English settlements in this early period was a fundamental change in their nature, particularly in Wessex, where fortifications were built around certain towns and other new fortified refuges erected in the gaps in the landscape in between them. Eventually, West Saxon kings would issue laws demanding that trading and minting activity took place here in these urban centres, and it is in post-Alfredian England that we see the re-emergence of the town as a focal point, a function which had been largely ignored since the fall of Roman Britannia.

After a period of relative quiet since the early raids of the late eighth century, the *Anglo-Saxon Chronicle* records for 835 the laying waste of Sheppey. The following year Egbert of Wessex is said to have fought against '35 ship loads' at Carhampton, a royal estate in Somerset, where the Danish won a victory by keeping possession of the place of slaughter. In 838, a year in which Egbert was trying to pull together his expanding West Saxon kingdom and make his peace with Canterbury, further more menacing Danish landings occurred. A great raiding army came to Cornwall in that year and Egbert took his army to meet them. In the ensuing battle, Egbert took the victory, but his enemies are described as both Danish and British, implying a western Celtic antipathy towards the West Saxon monarch.

In 840 an ealdorman, Wulfheard, had to take the field against the aggressor near Hamwih and won a victory for his pains. At Portland in Dorset, ealdorman Æthelhelm did just that in the same year, but lost his life along with many of his retainers. These two incidents do at least show that ealdormen could lead their own small armies into the field in direct response to raids without the presence of the king and his large army. But the results of such defensive arrangements could never be guaranteed. Further raids are recorded in the 840s along the Kent coast, in Lincolnshire and significantly at the port of London and in Rochester.

Danish forces were beginning to over-winter in England. They did so at Sheppey and Thanet, ideal places for mooring their ships, but it soon became a permanent arrangement on the mainland. Another English victory was won at the mouth of the Parret in the West Country in 845, but it was clearly going to take the king himself to administer what could be described as a decisive victory over the enemy.

The concern on both sides of the English Channel about the size and extent of these Danish forces was palpable. The huge force which is described as sacking Canterbury and London in 851, and which put Berhtwulf and his Mercians to the sword, was 350 shiploads strong. West Saxon forces drawn from the whole kingdom by the king tracked it and managed to bring it to battle in Surrey at a place called Aclea (possibly Oakley). Here they secured a much-needed victory. Continental sources followed the progress of this Danish force with much the same paranoia as the *Anglo-Saxon Chronicle* followed the progress of the Great Army of the 880s across northern France. In a significant statement, the Danes, they said, were 'beaten by the English with the aid of our Lord Jesus Christ'.

This victory, compounded by Egbert's recent conquests of Mercia and annexation of Kent, Sussex and Surrey, confirmed Wessex in a position of great power in England. It seemed to be the only kingdom with just about enough resources to catch and defeat an invading Danish army, but it was clearly under great threat. The vulnerability of Wessex cannot have been helped by the prolonged absence of Æthelwulf, Egbert's son, whose devout disposition led him on a pilgrimage to Rome, leaving power in the hands of his eldest son Æthelbald. On his return, Æthelwulf was only allowed to receive back the eastern parts of his kingdom that his father had won, leaving historic Wessex still in the hands of his son. At his death in 858, Æthelwulf's second son, Æthelbert, succeeded to these territories of Sussex, Surrey and Kent and, two years later, Æthelbald died. So, in 860 the culmination of a dangerous period of potential civil war and weakness in the face of foreign danger seemed to have passed with the reuniting of Egbert's Greater Wessex under Æthelbert. Six years later, however, Æthelbert died without issue and the whole of Wessex passed to another brother of the West Saxon house, Æthelred. Æthelred I and his younger brother Alfred would have to face a sterner test of their ability to protect their corner of Christendom than any of their predecessors. The Danish assault on England from now on would have serious political motives and greater organisation than before.

## THE GREAT ARMY

In the autumn of 865 a large Danish army landed in East Anglia. Its full size is unknown, but more important than its size was its intent. There would be no going home. The *Anglo-Saxon Chronicle* gives the name of the force as *Ðas Micel Here*, which means 'the Great Army'. Its leaders were determined to stay in England. They gathered thousands of horses from the kingdom of East Anglia, doubtless destroying many long-standing royal and ecclesiastical studs and reducing the mounted capabilities of their enemies. In fact, so important were horses to the campaigning needs of the army, that when they are described on the move, they are often termed by the chronicler as *Radhere*, a 'mounted army'.

Two men were at the head of the Great Army. Ivar the Boneless (Beinlauss) and Halfdan were the sons of Ragnar Lothbrok, a famous Viking warrior of the northern world. Legends abound on the subject of Ragnar of Sjaelland and Uppsala. It was said that in 845 his ship was blown off course and he had landed in East Anglia where he was taken to the court of the king and then finally, through political intrigue, was led to Northumbria where he was murdered in a pit of vipers. Whatever the truth of the tale, it is interesting that his sons landed first in East Anglia in 865 and then rode to Northumbria to reduce that kingdom. Perhaps they had never forgotten what had happened. Later, King Edmund of East Anglia would be brutally killed by the army. The idea that the arrival of the Great Army in England can be put down to a revenge mission on behalf of the sons of Ragnar is appealing, but has to be set against the wider picture of Viking opportunities against weak native dynasties in England and the political background of the times.

The sons of Ragnar brought with them at least one other brother and countless jarls who commanded their own sizeable retinues whose ranks were swollen by men seeking a fortune with their comrades. The army's preferred mode of operation was to build a defensive encampment, often with a river on one side (or later, as at Reading, in between two rivers) for extra security and ease of communication. From here, raids would be organised into the surrounding countryside, agricultural produce would be stolen, portable wealth carried away, tribute exacted and wealth redistributed. The Great Army consumed everything in its path. The general pattern of their campaigning year was that they would move in the late autumn in preparation for winter quartering. For a whole year East Anglia suffered until, at the end of 866, the force moved ominously on York.

The Great Army took York in November 866 and stayed there for the winter. The Northumbrians were not able to challenge them until early the following year and it is the timing of the Danish arrival on York which suggests that their leaders had prior knowledge of the political climate in Northumbria before they left East Anglia. Northumbria had been dangerously split in 866. Ælla, a man not of the royal line, had just come to power after ousting Osberht who had reigned for eighteen years and who had a loyal following of his own still at large in the kingdom. Eventually the two antagonists saw the sense in mounting a joint attack against the Danish force which had stolen their capital. Their assault upon their own city came in March 867 and it was a disaster. Both Ælla and Osberht were killed along with eight ealdormen. The fighting in the streets of York must have been bloody indeed. The leaders of the victorious Danish army now had time to choose from their many options. Real power, not just occupation, was at their fingertips. With effective opposition wiped out, they chose to adopt a policy which they would repeat again in campaigns to the south. They installed an unknown Englishman, Egbert, on the throne as an underking. Northumbrian resources would be theirs through this tributary king and, provided that Egbert behaved himself, the Great Army could be freed to move on to other areas of conquest and subjugation.

In fact, that is what they did. The winter of 867 saw the force ensconce itself at Nottingham, deep into Mercia. Alarm bells rang in Burgred's court. As king of Mercia, he had married the sister of Æthelred of Wessex and it was to the West Saxons that he sent for reinforcements. The enemy was much bigger than he had thought possible. Æthelred and the young nineteen-year-old Alfred came north to Nottingham and joined with the Mercian army outside the city. There was an uncomfortable stand-off, with the Danes firmly installed behind temporary fortifications and the English lacking the siege equipment to break it. Burgred decided to buy peace from the Danes and Æthelred and Alfred returned to Wessex, having at least had a chance to see for themselves the nature of the beast.

The army returned to York for the winter of 868, no doubt to exact tribute and check on the running of their newly acquired conquest. But they were still a force on the move, with goals to achieve elsewhere. The following winter of 869 the sons of Ragnar descended upon Thetford in East Anglia. Here the Danes unwittingly created an English martyr whom even they would come to regard with some affection in just a generation or two. The East Anglian king, Edmund, brought a force against them and was defeated. Edmund was probably murdered by the Danes shortly after the battle. Legend has it that he was brutally killed. Given the subsequent activity of the Danish army there is no real reason to doubt it. Another dynasty was eliminated. East Anglia was conquered. Monasteries were gutted and the people subjugated. Furthermore, the abbot and monks at

Peterborough were killed and the place burned down, such was the price of defeat at the hands of the Great Army.

Northumbria and East Anglia had fallen like a deck of cards. Now the army was in real striking distance of Wessex. In the winter of 870-871 it came. The army moved from Thetford to Reading, a royal manor on the Wessex/Mercia frontier, where it threw up a camp in the narrow gap between the rivers Thames and Kennet at the south of the manor. Three days later, from this camp, a detachment of two jarls and their retinues had ridden out into the open country in what was probably a reconnaissance-in-force. The long-serving Berkshire ealdorman Æthelwulf caught and defeated the force at Englefield and his fyrdsmen killed Sidroc, one of the jarls.[1] Just four days after this, Æthelred and Alfred attempted to take the Reading fortress by storm, but their experience at Nottingham had not been particularly educational. They could not take the defensive position and ealdorman Æthelwulf died in trying. There was at least some attritional value in the fight at Reading in that the Danes lost many men, but so too had the English. The Danes, it seems, were now without Ivar, who had taken some men north to Strathclyde where he destroyed the city of Dumbarton,[2] but they had many other leaders to take his place and, despite their losses, they were still formidable.

Having relieved the pressure against it at Reading, the Great Army felt assured enough in its strength to venture along the chalk ridge of Ashdown four days after the struggle at Reading. Quite what it was doing there, we may never know. Æthelred and Alfred had remained with their forces and tracked the Danes to Ashdown. There followed a famous pitched battle. The Danes stayed on the higher ground and arranged themselves in two divisions. One division was split between the commands of the two 'kings' Halfdan and Bagsecg and the other comprised the smaller units of the jarls. The English too were drawn into two main divisions, with the king facing the division of Danish kings and the young Alfred facing that of the jarls. What happened next is summarised by Asser, Alfred's biographer, and demonstrates how the young English prince, or Ætheling, won his spurs, so to speak:

> When the forces had been deployed and the Pagans were advancing fully prepared, the king remained in deep prayer. Alfred, second in command, could not hold his ground without either retreating or

going into action without his brother. Before the king appeared he ordered the Christian army forward against the enemy as planned, with the line closed up shield-to-shield, unhesitatingly leading the charge 'like a wild boar' sustained by his own courage and by 'divine resolution and the wisdom of the Holy Spirit'.

Asser, *Life of Alfred*,
Paragraph 38

Asser said that he had seen the lonely hawthorn tree where the battle had raged. And rage it did. As battles of the period go, what was remarkable about it was that Wessex won. The Danes held the higher ground and Alfred appears to have attacked in the first instance on his own. His engagement with the jarls' division, if met head on, would have left his flank vulnerable to a sweeping attack on it from the Danish kings wheeling down from the top of the hill. Æthelred, it seems, led his division up the hill just in time to prevent such a disaster. Alfred was able to rout the jarls before him and bring at least part of his division to bear against the kings with whom his brother was engaged. The victory was emphatic. Like other victories in this period the emphasis was on casualties received in the rout. It must be the case that the West Saxon forces kept back fresh mounted infantry for the chase, without which the victory could not have been properly prosecuted. The mopping-up operation was said to have gone on into the night.

Subsequent events proved the victory to be hollow, but it had shown several important things to be true. The Great Army could be defeated in the open. Not only that, the young man who was chiefly responsible for the victory had displayed a presence of mind and bravery equal to his calling. Wessex would be no Northumbria or East Anglia for the Danes.

And yet a fortnight after Ashdown, Alfred and Æthelred were defeated in open battle by the Danes at Basing. Eight weeks later, presumably after both sides had cooled their heels a little, they met once more at Meretune, a place which has not been identified. The chronicler describes the English as having held the upper hand in the fighting for most of the day, but something had given way on the English side towards the end of the battle and the Danes held the place of slaughter, and consequently, the victory. Clearly, it would take more than just a series of pitched battles to rid Wessex of the Pagan onslaught. Even the resources of Britain's richest kingdom could not sustain constant attritional warfare. The last battle had cost Wessex the life of Heahmund, the bishop of Sherborne. Although he could be replaced, Rome could not afford to lose good men in key appointments on the embattled frontier of Christendom.

In April 871, Æthelred died and Alfred, his surviving brother and natural choice in the circumstances, succeeded to the kingdom. He had no time to rest. A new fleet of Danes had landed in the summer. Their size more than compensated for the losses received by the Great Army so far in the struggle with Wessex. Alfred's troubles were mounting. While he watched his brother being buried at Wimborne, the Danes were defeating a small English force at Reading and then, to make matters worse, Alfred was defeated himself by the whole Danish army at Wilton on the River Wylye in Wiltshire.

At this time London was a Mercian town. The Great Army came from Reading to London towards the end of 871 and exacted tribute so great as to affect the lives of property owners as far away as Worcester. The bishop of that town recorded a transaction of land sold to a Mercian king's thegn that had been undertaken in order to go some way towards redressing the balance after such huge tributes had been paid to the Danes in London. Mercia was forced to buy peace from the Danes.

The Great Army appears to have been drawn north again by a crisis in 872. The puppet king Egbert of Northumbria and his archbishop, Wulfhere, had been driven out of York by a rising in favour of Ricsige, a man chosen by the Northumbrians in his stead. Egbert and Wulfhere fled to the court of Burgred of Mercia and although Wulfhere was later recalled to York, Egbert would die in exile. More important perhaps than the details of the affair is the fact that the Northumbrians appear to have chosen their own destiny. This is a characteristic that they would display countless times in the decades to come, making their choices out of a concern to maintain their independence regardless of the background of the ruling caste.

Later that winter the Danes arrived in Torksey in the ancient Mercian province of Lindsey. It is not clear if they had managed to assert their will at York before they moved on to their new Lincolnshire base. Ricsige appears to have continued ruling for a few years, but in what form of independence is unknown. From Torksey, the usual treatment was meted out to the people and, to buy time, the Mercians sued for peace from the Danes. But it did not last long. The army chose for itself a more central place from which to dominate Mercia and moved to Repton in Derbyshire in late 873. Here at the junction of the north-south roads and the trackways leading across the valley of the Trent, the Danes made camp. The choosing of the site at Repton was deliberate. The Mercian aristocracy had created for themselves a royal mausoleum at an important ecclesiastical site. The stronghold at Repton has been painstakingly excavated over the years and it is clear that the temporary fortifications erected by the army were of a formidable structure. The 3½-acre D-shaped encampment had its straight side protected by the cliffs of the river and earthworks were thrown up around it, running to both sides of St Wystan's Church, which acted as something of a fortified gateway. From Repton the Danes campaigned to an extent which is not recorded, but it resulted in the flight of King Burgred to Rome. The king of the ancient Mercian kingdom, after a reign of twenty-two years, ended his life abroad and was buried at St Mary's Church in the English quarter of the great city. It was a sad moment for Mercia. It would take three generations for English Mercian independent sentiments to reach anything like their former level of confidence, and then only after so much had changed.

The Danish appointee in Mercia was a king's thegn, known as Ceolwulf. He is described in a rare judgement by the *Anglo-Saxon* Chronicler as 'foolish'. Ceolwulf, who seems to have had a following of some note[3], had very little choice but to co-operate, but the price was high. He would have to keep his kingdom open for Danish settlement whenever the army should desire it and supply his own military forces to meet Danish needs. Foolish or not, Ceolwulf effectively paved the way for a profound change in the cultural identity of Mercia. Alfred must have looked north with alarm.

Clearly the Danish leaders had an eye for the future. They had established enough political power in Northumbria and Mercia to settle there if they wished. Late in 874, the Danish army split into two different groups each with varying objectives. The Great Army would never be as big as it had been before 874 and, in effect, a new era was born with the break up of the army. The threat, however, was hardly over. Halfdan took a force to the north and, from the area around the mouth of the Tyne, campaigned into Strathclyde and Scotland before seriously considering permanent land apportionment for his men. The other half of the Danish army left Repton for Cambridge and was led by three kings – Guthrum, Oscetel and Anund.

The first phase of Danish settlement which was organised by Halfdan in the north occurred in Northumbria. The extent of Danish place names in Yorkshire suggests that here was the densest settlement. This area, which would form the heart of the later Viking kingdom of York, from now on would have a strong Danish culture. The descendants of Halfdan's settlers of 876 would be the 'Danes within England' who gave support to the allied assault against Athelstan's English empire in 937. But, in the late 870s, and for a little while longer, power beyond the Humber was more or less in the hands of native dynasties, Danish appointments included. The kings of Stratchclyde and the Scots ruled in independence and Ricsige's successor, Egbert II, ruled at York. Meanwhile, at the independent English citadel of Bamburgh sat Eadwulf, holding the balance of power between all the competing factions. Halfdan's Danes had simply become the newest additions to the Northumbrian diaspora in this colourful northern world. Halfdan does not seem to have opted for the settled life. He was an old campaigner in the true Viking style and it may very well be that he sailed to Ireland to fight with the Norse. The *Annals of Ulster* record the death of an Albann in 877, said to have been a king of the 'dark foreigners', or the Danes.

The army that went to Cambridge from Repton was large in size. It may have included the men of the great summer army of 871 in its ranks, who, it seemed, had stayed after all. These may be the people who set up their funerary barrow complex at Heath Wood at Ingelby in Derbyshire, just a few miles up the road from Repton. It is thought that there was an ideological split between the Danish factions, which is reflected in the striking differences recognisable in the archaeology of the two places. Whoever buried their dead at Ingelby had a penchant for cremation, this being in stark contrast to the burial practice of the Danes at Repton. Also, Repton's symbolism is not shared by Ingelby. If these two places are contemporary, and if they both represent the Danish army's presence, then it is likely that they represent a difference of opinion on some scale.[4] Moreover, there are historical precedents for the manner in which Viking armies split up. The *Annals of St Bertin* record that in 861 the army of the Seine broke up in the winter, dismantling itself into constituent parts for which the term 'sodalitates' is used. Each group took up a different camp along the river and the implication is that the split was made on social grounds, groups of leaders taking away their retinues from the main force. The idea that something similar happened at the end of 874 in England seems to be suggested by both the archaeological and historical evidence.

Ceolwulf was keeping Danish options open in Mercia, but before they could consider settlement, their leaders had some unfinished business to attend to in the south. Wessex once again attracted Danish attention. The army of the three leaders moved to Wareham in Dorset late in 875. Wareham was an important port on one side of Poole harbour. The Danes devastated the surrounding countryside, but found themselves too close to a sizeable West Saxon fyrd for their menace to be a lasting one. The stand-off worked in favour of Wessex. A tribute was paid to the Danes, although hostages were given by them and oaths sworn on ancient rings. For the first time since the Great Army landed in England, the Danes had promised to leave a kingdom alone. In 876, they rode to Exeter, shadowed by Alfred's fyrdsmen, who struggled to overtake them before they reached the city. The flight from Wareham had been part mounted and part seaborne. Many Danish ships were lost at sea around Swanage in a great storm, a fact which the *Anglo-Saxon Chronicle* recorded without a glimmer of emotion. At Exeter, the depleted Danish force exchanged further hostages with Wessex and kept their peace. In the late summer or early autumn of 877, they left Exeter and set up temporary encampments at Gloucester. Now back in Mercia after a disappointing West Saxon campaign, the Danish leaders must have felt that it was time to let Ceolwulf know of their intentions to settle. Some stayed with their leaders, whilst others settled to the east of Mercia. The active campaigning army which was left comprised those men who had not had enough of the life to which they had doubtless become accustomed. Their leader was Guthrum.

It is difficult to imagine what was on Guthrum's mind on the cold winter morning early in 878 when he led his determined force from Gloucester to Chippenham. It surprised everyone. Perhaps Guthrum thought that the only way to take Wessex was by surprise, at a time of year when the West Saxon fyrd might not be ready for campaigning. The line of march he took corresponds with some of Alfred's royal possessions, which may have something to do with it. The ferocity with which Guthrum took settlements on his drive into the northern frontier of Wessex sent people running in all directions, some of them abroad.[5] Those who remained had no choice but to offer allegiance and submit immediately. It was a campaign of terror. Exacted under duress, each offer of support to Guthrum from a West Saxon landowner or minor noble, or each thegn departed for foreign shores, deprived Alfred of the military service that he as king of Wessex would have expected. It was like a domino effect. Alfred's military resource was dwindling.

To make matters worse, early in 878 a brother of Halfdan and Ivar came to Wessex from South Wales and landed with his ships at Countisbury Hill in Devon. Odda of Devon and many king's thegns were encamped in the impressive ancient fortification there when they were besieged by the new Danish force.[6] They led a dawn counter-attack against the Danes and killed their leader along with 800 of his men and forty of his immediate hearth-troop, or retainers. There is some uncertainty about numbers in the accounts of this battle and it seems that the Danes, despite their losses, had the victory. Meanwhile, Alfred was retreating into the Somerset marshes, arriving by Easter at the Isle of Athelney where he had built a fortification on this defensible island in the marshes, reachable only by a causeway fortified at both ends. A Somerset nobleman, Æthelnoth had placed a small force in a wood covering Alfred's position, which was probably stationed between Street and Illminster, to guard against an approach along the Fosse Way.[7] The frontier of Christendom, as it must have seemed to Alfred, was now reduced to no more than a small army of retainers and Somerset fyrdsmen on an island where a forge, temporary houses and a church were built. From here, Alfred's men could only harass the Danes and face the ignominy of having to plunder their enemy's supplies deep inside Alfred's own kingdom. Weapons were not the only thing forged in the fires on Athelney island. An iron determination was forged there, too. Alfred knew that there were still men who owed him service who were at large in the kingdom and had not fled over the sea. He calculated the numbers he could expect to receive if he summoned them to him, and, more importantly, how long it would take. Seven weeks after he had lit the fires on Athelney island, Alfred rode out to a place known as Egbert's Stone on the eastern part of Selwood, where he was met by his fyrd. They had come from Somerset, Wiltshire and the unaffected parts of Hampshire and, to his delight, they were pleased to see him.

The West Saxon army now moved quickly north to Iley Oak, the traditional meeting place of the Warminster and Heytesbury hundreds, where they may well have received a few more reinforcements. From here, it marched six miles to the north-east to a royal manor which Alfred had bequeathed to his queen, Ealhswith. That place was Edington, just fifteen miles south of the Danish camp at Chippenham. Here Alfred won a famous victory, of which scarcely any details s urvive. It is clear that Guthrum was utterly routed. Those of his men who were not cut down in the chase made it back to Chippenham, but Alfred had not finished with them. He seized all the stock and killed everyone he found outside the camp. For two weeks Alfred sat there refusing to lift the siege. It was enough to make Guthrum realise that the game was up. The Danes gave in. Even with Alfred seemingly on the run with no real army, Guthrum could not subjugate Wessex for more than a few weeks without receiving a hammer blow in return. Much has been written about Alfred the statesman and scholar over the centuries, but the immediate aftermath of Edington demonstrates a characteristic that he would pass to his son and his favourite grandson: a ruthless mastery of the sword.

Guthrum sought terms with Alfred. The Danish leader would take the remainder of his force away from Wessex and leave him in peace. Furthermore, Guthrum would be baptised into the Christian faith so that wherever he went and settled, he would do so as a disciple of Rome. It was no token gesture, either. Three weeks later, Guthrum came to Aller, near Athelney, for his christening ceremony. It was a highly symbolic moment. A white fillet was anointed with holy oil and tied around his head. This 'chrism', as it is called, remained on the head for a week and was taken off in a separate ceremony at Wedmore, after which a great festival took place in celebration of the new Christian king. Alfred gave gifts to Guthrum and his followers over a twelve-day period of feasting and then it was time for the Danish leader to return with his thirty chosen men to Chippenham and make preparations to leave Wessex. He would go not as Guthrum, but as Athelstan. The new name had come with the christening ceremony. As his new godfather watched him leave, he could not have imagined that this desperate year would be looked upon as the year in which English fortunes changed for the better. Nor could Alfred have imagined that his unborn grandson, his own dear Athelstan, would rise to head an English empire and become the most powerful ruler in Britain since the days of the Roman governors. Wessex had survived, just.

The troubles were far from over, of course, but Alfred's reputation was known to all who would attempt to attack his kingdom. In the winter of 878, whilst Guthrum was cooling his heels at Cirencester and making plans for settling his men, a large raiding force sailed up the Thames as far as Fulham. Whatever this Viking army was planning in England, it soon moved away and sailed to Ghent where it stayed for a year. The force fought against the Franks at Saucourt on the Somme in 881, where the victorious Vikings found themselves many horses after the battle. Now a mounted force, they caused havoc in the early 880s in Frankish lands.

Wessex was not entirely left alone, however. In 884, one part of the force had moved to Louvain, whilst the other had come to Rochester and besieged the town, setting up their own earthwork encampment. The strength and surprise of Alfred's response was too much for the force and the Vikings were coerced into leaving behind some of their recently acquired Frankish horses. They even left their own prisoners behind in the rush and took to their ships again. But an active force had remained. Their subsequent raids into Wessex were supported by the Danes of East Anglia, and so it was to East Anglia that Alfred sent a fleet which defeated sixteen shiploads of Vikings yet was itself mauled by a similar fleet on its way back from the Essex coast. In this era after Edington, East Anglia had been the first Danish area to rise again against Wessex. West Saxon control would need to be exerted in this region if there was to be an end to threat. But first, a kingdom needed to be utterly reshaped and as it turned out, renamed.

## A KINGDOM REBUILT

Before Wessex could launch anything like a counter-offensive against Danish areas, it first had to look within itself and reorganise on a vast scale. Alfred used every faculty he had. It was fortunate that he was an educated man. He showed in his reorganisation of his kingdom and its extension into English Mercian areas a consummate understanding of what was needed to secure a kingdom in the face of both a land and sea threat, whilst at the same time bringing an injection of foreign scholars into the heart of English ecclesiastical and court life. The years between the collapse of Guthrum's aggression against the West Saxons and the arrival of the next big Viking threat, the army of Hæsten in the 890s, are characterised in the *Anglo-Saxon Chronicle* by the preoccupation of the scribes with the activities of the Viking army in Francia, but there was much that was achieved at home in these important years.

Quite when the puppet king Ceolwulf died, or was deposed, we do not know. It may have been in the early 880s that the change came about, since Alfred seems to have acquired for the new 'kingdom of the Anglo-Saxons' the areas of the Thames Valley, Cotswolds and Severn Valley in a deal that was apparently unopposed. The Englishman who replaced Ceolwulf was not, however, a king. He was a leading nobleman named Æthelred who is thought to have been a distant relative of Alfred's. Æthelred, who in 889 married Alfred's redoubtable daughter Æthelflæd and who formed a ruling partnership with his new wife, would help change the face of Mercian politics under the watchful eye of Alfred. The family ties between Wessex and Mercia, which were already strong with Alfred's wife Ealhswith being the daughter of Æthelwulf, a Mercian ealdorman, were once again firmly established, perhaps not to the liking of all. Although there is evidence from a decline in the quality of Mercian silver pennies from the early ninth century onwards that the power of their kings was on the wane, this dynastic manoeuvring by Alfred was of critical importance to English Mercian survival, and it would be repeated again during the reign of his son, Edward the Elder.

Alfred still had Danish troubles, however, and at the heart of the trouble was London. London simply had to become English once again. Alfred's charters and some entries in the *Anglo-Saxon Chronicle* firmly hint at the fact that he was actively engaged in a military campaign against what some believe to be a Danish garrison in London as early as 882-3. But the traditional reduction of London and its takeover by Alfred is given as 886. However he had managed to achieve it, Alfred then gave London back to its rightful owner – Æthelred of Mercia.

Significantly, we are told that all the English who were not under Danish rule submitted to Alfred after the capture of London. It was quite an emotional moment. The retrieval of London and its surrounding territories for the English represented a real change in their outlook. With the Danes of East Anglia a very real threat, there could perhaps now be some sort of consolidation of the West Saxon and English Mercian position. But instead of opting to fortify an entire linear frontier against enemy incursion, Alfred chose a remarkable system of defence-in-depth within his own kingdom by erecting fortifications known as burhs, some in new places, others in existing settlements which dated back to Roman times. The Alfredian response to the threat of invasion was different from what went before in both the scale of construction and the administrative mechanism which was required to achieve it. As early as the late eighth century, King Offa of Mercia had made fortification building against the threat of the Viking pirate a part of the system of land tenure and military obligation and in a way Alfred was building on a known governmental mechanism. We must attribute a very great deal to the organisational and intellectual capabilities of Alfred in his approach to this problem. His was one of Europe's most remarkably successful responses in that it not only protected his kingdom, but provided the launching pad for a re-conquest of former lost territories. The claim that Alfred's building programme resulted in construction of planned towns is a little far-fetched despite the evidence of street layouts in some of the larger places. This attribute belongs more properly to the tenth century and to the laws issued by Edward the Elder and Athelstan, who brought mercantile and financial activity into many of these places.

The notion that burh building was a peculiarly English response is also misleading. The inspiration came from the Continent and Alfred, who had travelled widely, would have been only too aware of how other leaders in Christendom were preparing to meet the threat. He will have seen the papal defences of Leo IV in Rome and will have known that they were part of an integrated system on this, another embattled frontier of Christendom. He will have known of the success of Charles the Bald's fortification building programme from the late 860s which saw the defences of towns such as Angoulême, Tours, Le Mans and Dijon rebuilt according to a new organisational regime. And, most importantly, he will have learned from his experience at Nottingham how the Vikings themselves could build sound defensive walls and yet had no stomach to undertake a siege themselves.

But what of the English evidence? Listed in a document known as the 'Burghal Hideage', a sixteenth-century transcript of an eleventh-century Winchester document, are thirty-three strongholds accompanied by a note of how many hides of land are attributable to each place. Cornwall, Kent and London are missing from the list probably because at the time of its original compilation, these areas were under semi-independent jurisdiction, like Kent and Cornwall, or controlled by the English kingdom of Mercia, like London. But the areas not listed must also have had similar protective fortifications. Exeter, Bath, Winchester, Portchester, Chichester, Rochester and Canterbury form an obvious network of nodal points. The list is a simple clockwise run around the kingdom of Wessex, but, importantly, shows that the burhs were not merely concentrated on the frontiers of the kingdom, but were carefully placed within the kingdom so that no burh would be more than a day's march from another, a distance generally taken to be about twenty miles. The defences worked not only as places of refuge for the local population during times of Danish incursion, but as bases from which to dominate a territory under hostile attack. The strongholds were close enough together for each of the garrisons to support each other in the event of combined military action. The estimated garrison strength of all the burhs of Wessex was around 27,000 men. The calculation of this figure is arrived at by a remarkable piece of good fortune. A footnote on the manuscript states that:

> If every hide is represented by one man, then every pole [16 feet] of wall can be manned by four men. Then, for the maintenance of 20 poles of wall, 80 hides are required and for a furlong, 160 hides are required by the same reckoning.

This formula works remarkably well and ties in with the archaeological evidence for most burhs with the peculiar exceptions of Exeter and Chichester, where more excavation is needed to fully understand the whereabouts of the missing yardage. Alfred was not the only European monarch to be presented with the same organisational difficulties, however. Charles the Bald in 868 had looked at the twin forts at Pont de l'Arche and realised after their capture by Vikings in 865-66 that a reorganisation of service duties was required, so he carefully divided the fortifications into sections for which individual landowners would have the responsibility for manning and maintenance. But what both Alfred and Charles were trying to do was perfectly simple – a wholesale tightening-up of military organisation based on the familiar taxation and service duties which had their roots deep in the past. For both Alfred and Charles, the undertaking would probably have required a land taxation assessment survey almost on the scale of the famous Norman Domesday book to make sure that everyone knew and met their obligations. The shifting around of populations and landowners may even have resulted in the payment of compensation.

The inclusion of Buckingham, Worcester and Warwick in the Burghal Hideage list suggests that the extension of the system into Mercia had begun and perhaps points to a date of compilation of the list in the Edwardian and not Alfredian period. Eight new burhs were added to the system between 907 and 913. The burhs of northwest Mercia, which included Chester (907), Eddisbury (914), Runcorn (915), Thelwall (919), Manchester (919) and Cledmutha (Rhuddlan) built in 921, were an important part of Æthelflaed's defence system against the Norse settlers from Ireland and from the ever-present threat of Welsh incursion. But the point is this: the burghal system has both defensive and offensive capabilities. Alfred's reorganisation of the fyrd service so that his army would at once have one third on garrison duty, one third on active campaign and the remainder tilling the land, meant that the kingdom, with its deep network of fortified refuges, would be a tough nut for an invader to crack.

That the network of fortifications worked in this respect was first evidenced by the limited success of the Danish force which had returned from the Continent in 884 to arrive at Rochester. Still further proof comes from the extraordinary events of 892 when the Danish army that had been at large in France had gathered at Boulogne and sailed for the south of England with supplies and a mobile capability. The huge force arrived at the mouth of the river Lympne in east Kent. They sailed four miles up the river and found a half-finished small fortification manned only by a few peasants, which they duly took. This force had been 250 shiploads strong. But there was another at large, a detachment from the same huge continental Viking army in eighty ships under a notable leader, Hæsten. Hæsten sailed up the

Thames estuary and built a camp at Milton. Alfred's main worry was that these two forces should join hands within his kingdom. Clearly, not all of his forts were built yet and this must have been a great concern. Moreover, the Danes of Northumbria and East Anglia had heard of the new force in the south and wanted to help. Alfred managed to come to terms with Hæsten and it seems he set off to the east. Alfred took his main force and blocked the two enemy forces preventing them from coming together. The larger force raided through Berkshire and Hampshire and then turned east to meet up with its other half, with both sides recorded as sending out mounted scouting patrols day and night. Their raiding had acquired for themselves much loot, but their penetration into Wessex was limited. Both forces were probably seeking to link with their cousins in Essex, but the larger force was caught in the open by Alfred's son, the future King Edward, who defeated them at Farnham and drove them in confusion twenty miles across the Thames into Berkshire, where they took refuge at Thorney Island in the River Colne. Edward sat and watched the Thorney Island force. Meanwhile, with a combined fleet, the Northumbrian and East Anglian Danes had come to the West Country and undertook a joint attack on Exeter and north Devon. Alfred's Wessex was under threat from all directions, so he took off for Exeter. He had, however, left a force to go to London which joined with the English garrison there and which pushed out to Benfleet towards Hæsten's force, which had come from Milton to Benfleet. Edward and Æthelred of Mercia, who had joined him, retreated with the Thorney Island force and allowed them to travel east to join up with the Benfleet force.

Hæsten had gone back on his word. His children and wife had been baptised in a ceremony reminiscent of that of Guthrum and yet on the arrival of the English army at Benfleet, they found that the Viking leader had acted as an apostate on behalf of Alfred and Æthelred's godchildren by raiding the locality. The English response was emphatic. The force which they found there was overwhelmed and ships, booty, women and children were taken to London and Rochetser. Hæsten's wife and children were spared and sent back to him. Hæsten had now re-formed his force and fortified a base at Shoeburyness. But from here, despite East Anglian and Northumbrian reinforcements, he could not harm Wessex effectively, so he set out on a dangerous campaign with a still depleted force up the Thames Valley, across the Cotswolds and along the River Severn. The focus of Danish activity was shifting.

The new military organisation of Wessex was now tested. A force from all the garrisons in Mercia and from Wessex east of the river Parret was called out, and with Welsh support (who had every reason to be wary of Danish intentions), Æthelred and his combined force trapped the Danes on an island in the Severn at Buttington near Welshpool. There followed a long stand-off, with the Danes ending up having to eat some of their own horses. They attempted what seems to have been a partially successful break-out but were defeated in the ensuing pitched battle, taking many casualties. Yet they still had something of a force when they returned wearily to Shoeburyness. Here they received new reinforcements from Northumbria and, sending their women and children off to East Anglia before the end of 893, they rode to Chester and took the scarcely populated town. Æthelred's wife would learn from this mistake and later Chester would be well fortified. But for now the English had to besiege this place for two days. The temporary loss of Chester must have been something of an embarrassment to the English. Their enemy had ridden day and night across their own kingdom, overtaking them and arriving at Chester in the probable hope of uniting with some of the Norse of Dublin in the Wirral. The English response was to adopt a scorched-earth policy, razing the surrounding area of all agricultural produce and once again starving the Danes. The Danes had no stomach for a second protracted siege and fled west into Wales. What followed was a tacit admission of the growing strength of the English. After campaigning widely in Wales in 894, the Danes headed back to Essex, taking the long route through the north and Midlands, avoiding English Mercia, finally arriving at Mersea Island. Meanwhile, the force with which Alfred had been preoccupied in the west had returned through Sussex but was badly mauled by the garrison at Chichester where it lost many of its ships to the English.

The force at Mersea Island in the winter of 894-5 sailed to a point twenty miles above London up the Lea. The London garrison took them on at great cost to their leaders, many of whom were killed. Alfred, who in the autumn of 895 had come to the area to place a force in the district to protect those farmers who were harvesting, saw an opportunity to construct twin forts on either side of the river, thus blocking the Danish ships to the north, preventing them from going back the way they had come. This was a method which would be frequently employed by Edward the Elder in the early years of his campaigns against the Danes. Their response was to strike across the Midlands in a similar campaign to that which they undertook in 893, only it is likely this time that they were closely shadowed. They arrived at Bridgnorth on the Severn, taking winter quarters and staying there until the summer of 896. The Danes had reached the end of their tether by now. These remarkable campaigns, which involved long and dangerous marches around the outskirts of English territory and sometimes at great cost through the heart of it, had taken their toll. In 896, the force split up. Some chose to become another generation of settlers in the Danish areas of Northumbria, others in East Anglia. Still more found their way back to Francia where they enjoyed a successful era of campaigns. Wessex and English Mercia had survived a far greater test in the 890s than anything which the army of Guthrum had thrown at them. Alfred's new kingdom of the Anglo-Saxons had been blooded. It had suffered simultaneous attacks on its coastline at both ends of the kingdom, faced a land threat from the north and east and had the added problems of a well-documented plague and cattle fever to contend with. But Alfred's system held firm under the strongest tests imaginable.

Still the Danes came along the coasts by sea, raiding and plundering, but nearly always returning to their ships. Alfred now had to look at the naval response to the Viking threat. He did not waste time in ordering the design and construction of a new type of longship to combat the Danes at sea – it was a remarkable, though probably cumbersome, vessel, with up to sixty oars and a fighting crew twice the size of the Danish. It was neither high-sided such as the Frisian proto-cogs (although it appears that there were Frisian crews aboard some of them) or shallow-drafted like the keel-built Danish ships, but worked out exclusively to the design of a king who knew exactly what he needed. But the ships were not without their problems. What they gained in fighting manpower they lost in manoeuvrability and draft. In at least one encounter where Alfred's ships' crews attacked some beached Danish ships on the South Coast, the Danes, who fared worst in the fight, were able to float away at high tide before the English ships could catch them. One account from 896 ended with the escaped Danes running aground in Sussex and being brought to the king in

Winchester where they were hanged. So, whatever their limitations, a seaborne defence system was better than no navy at all.

It had been a remarkable re-birth. And as Alfred's kingdom was pulling itself together in the face of the external threat, a little boy was born to the young Ætheling Edward. Father and son would go on to dominate the politics of the whole island of Britain in the decades to come.

# 4

# A VISION OF ENGLAND

The Danes in England were not the same mobile offensive force that they had been a generation or two ago. The security of their boroughs and farmsteads might now depend upon who could give them the best protection, whether he be Dane or Englishman. By the early years of the tenth century, there could be no doubt that the Danes of the Midlands and Northumbria were an integral part of insular politics whether they liked it or not. At Wedmore, Alfred and Guthrum had set up by treaty the division of territory which separated the English from the Danish. From the 880s to the 890s a new political order to the south of a line which ran roughly from London along Watling Street towards Chester can be observed in the making. The king of Wessex would no longer be *Westseaxena cinge*, but *Angol Saxonum rex*, ruler of the Anglo-Saxons, commanding also the rump of English Mercia through loyal and blood-tied subordinates. A vision was forming.

What was left of English Northumbria after the Danish settlement was split into the control of minor English lords ruling it seemingly in isolation. One of these, Eadwulf of Bamburgh, ruled a territory running from the Firth of Forth to the Tees. William of Malmesbury dryly noted that Northumbria had already grown into one nation with the Danes.[1] Further west in Cumberland, Westmorland and Lancashire, the settlement pattern was still predominantly English and British though not yet

Scandinavian, but this would soon be profoundly changed. From the Welsh border across the Cheshire plain and down to Herefordshire, Worcestershire and Gloucestershire and more centrally in Oxfordshire and through most of Warwickshire ran the territory of English Mercia, including parts of Buckinghamshire, ruled by Æthelred, ably assisted by a woman who would pass into legend and who would have much to do with Athelstan's upbringing, Æthelred's wife and successor Æthelflæd.

Then there was Wessex itself, a kingdom which had grown and subsumed Sussex, Surrey, Kent and the West Country to the Tamar. In fact, it contained all of England south of the Thames at this time. Back in the days when Wessex had been listed along with other kingdoms as tributaries of the powerful Mercian kingdom, it was rated in hides, a unit of land taxation, at a colossal 100,000. Resources of manpower were also at the disposal of the West Saxon kings. They would have to use them carefully if West Saxon power was to be felt again beyond the line of the partition of England between Dane and Englishman.

## CRISIS AND VICTORY

The political climate into which Athelstan was born in around 895 was no less turbulent than it had been in previous years, but there had been a sea-change south of Watling Street. The next king of the Anglo-Saxons who succeeded Alfred in 900 was his son, Edward. He would have to decide what to do about the political geography which lay before him and he was hampered from the beginning.

Edward the Elder was the first of Alfred's sons to be crowned at Kingston upon Thames in Surrey. But soon after the coronation and for some time, his thoughts were focused on a pressing accession crisis. Æthelwold, the son of the West Saxon king Æthelred I, began a campaign to prosecute what he must have thought was a perfectly legitimate claim to Edward's throne. He gathered men and supplies and took over the royal estates at Wimborne and Christchurch (then known as Twinham). It was a credible threat indeed. The potential consequences of an alliance between Æthelwold and any of the Danish forces at large in the north were obvious for Edward to see. Edward soon fortified Badbury Rings, four miles to the north-west of

Wimborne, and made his intentions known. One night, during this stand-off, Æthelwold slipped away, neglecting to take with him the former nun he had kidnapped in defiance of the king and his churchmen. Edward's greatest fears began to unfold before him. Æthelwold fled to the Northumbrian Danes and found many friends there. There is no doubt that he was serious about his claim to Edward's throne. The Northumbrian Danes accepted him as king and although he went missing from the historical record for a year whilst he gathered a fleet and men abroad, he turned up in Essex with a force large enough to persuade the East Anglian Danes to launch an attack themselves on English Mercia and northern Wessex. We can only guess at the nature of the negotiations between Æthelwold and the East Anglian Danes, but these must have included some promise of recognition from the would-be king of the south. The *Annals of St Neots* even refer to Æthelwold as the king of the Danes, and later, as king of the Pagans. What kind of promises had Æthelwold given the Pagans? Would he really rule from Wessex as an apostate? If Æthelwold did renounce Christianity in his bid for power, he would not be the first European nobleman to do so. Pepin II, a great grandson of Charlemagne, during a dispute with Charles the Bald, had done precisely this in order to solicit Viking aid. Nevertheless, Edward's first major campaign in the long tale of the re-conquest of the Danish territories was to be against an army encouraged by the actions not of a Viking, but of another Englishman.

Edward mounted a punishment campaign which stretched from the dykes of Cambridgeshire to the River Wissey and across the Fenlands. This episode revealed something of interest in the way that a West Saxon king's army fought. It was an extraordinary encounter and the way in which the Anglo-Saxon chronicler records it is exceptional for an account of a battle in this era, for he seems to suggest to his reader that he has thought very carefully about all those who were involved:

> Here Æthelwold led the raiding army in East Anglia into hostility, so that they raided across all the land of Mercia until they came to Cricklade and there went over the Thames, and took all that they could grab, both in Braydon and thereabouts, and then turned east homewards. Then King Edward went after them as quickly as he

could gather his army, and raided across all their land between the Dykes and the Wissey, all as far north as the Fens. Then, when he wanted to go back out from there, he ordered it to be announced through all the army that they all go out together; then the Kentish remained behind there against his command and he had sent out 7 messengers to them. Then they were surrounded there by the raiding army, and they fought there. And there were killed ealdorman Sigewulf, and ealdorman Sigehelm, and Eadwold the king's thegn, and Abbot Cenwulf, and Sigeberht, son of Sigewulf, and Eadwold, son of Acca, and many others in addition to them though I have named the most distinguished. And on the Danish side were killed King Eohric [the Danish ruler of East Anglia] and the Ætheling Æthelwold, whom they had chosen as their king, and Beorhtsige, son of the Ætheling Beorthnoth, and Hold [a minor nobleman] Ysopa and Hold Oscytel, and very many others in addition to them whom we cannot name now; and on either hand there was great slaughter made, and there were more of the Danish killed although they had possession of the place of slaughter...

*Anglo-Saxon Chronicle,*
Worcester Manuscript (D) entry for 905 [904]

So, the Kentish refusal to obey the king's command almost resulted in disaster. They lost the ensuing battle, but had managed to eliminate the threat of Æthelwold and dispatched the Danish East Anglian king too, before retiring from the battlefield. For the Danes, it must have seemed the most pointless victory they had ever won. But for Edward, the message was clear. Events had proved him lucky. He would have to tighten up his command and control capabilities in the field.

There appears to have followed a treaty arrangement in the years after this affair between the Danes and King Edward. Northern chronicles[2] record that in 906 an agreement was reached at Yttingford, a place identified as being on the River Ousel near Leighton Buzzard in what would surely have been frontier territory.[3] The terms and conditions of the treaty are not known, but there is an interesting characteristic to Edward's policy over the next few years between 906 and 909 and one wonders if this treaty might have had something to do with it. Land in Danish Mercia was bought by the West Saxon authorities from Danish owners and given to chosen men. This policy, as far as can be ascertained from the charters of the reign of Athelstan which confirm the English ownership of various manors, was enforced across a region stretching from Derbyshire in the north to Bedfordshire in the south. There is a sense of deliberation about this policy which suggests that it may have been executed with strategic concerns in mind. These little islands of English interest in Danish Mercia might be joined together by systematic campaigning. Military consolidation of newly won territories might be achieved through a programme of fortress building. Furthermore, this approach to the problem of Danish possessions beyond the frontier was not just an Edwardian concern. Æthelred, ealdorman of the Mercians, gave his full administrative support to the policy.[4] Furthermore, the switch of land from Dane to Englishman continued at least into the reign of Edmund, who in 942 awarded land to Wulfsige the Black in south Derbyshire which had just been 'recovered' from the Danes.

The gradual exchange of land for silver across the border must have left Edward in a position to choose his starting lines for a reduction of Danish Mercia and for a gradual expansion of the landed resources of the kingdom of the Anglo-Saxons. By 909 he was ready. He chose for his first campaign to attack the Danes in their Northumbrian homes. The campaign lasted five weeks and involved a reduction of the countryside of Northumbria and clearly surprised the population living there. The Danes negotiated a peace under duress, winning for themselves a reprieve from aggression. The campaign seems to have left an impression on the Northumbrian victims: in the next year, the Danish army launched a revenge attack deep into the heart of English Mercia, a campaign from which a significant number of them would not return. At the time of the Danish offensive into Mercia, Edward was in Kent, putting together a fleet for campaigns along the east coast whilst no doubt reminding the Kentish men of their obligations to their king. The news of the large-scale invasion must have come as a surprise to him and there is a suggestion that the timing of the attack – initiated while Edward was otherwise engaged – had some degree of military intelligence behind it. The Danes raided right down to the Avon near Bristol and then along the banks of the Severn. Edward's reaction was to raise a force from Wessex and English Mercia to challenge the enemy in his own kingdom. The force he raised was, after some time, able to shadow the raiding army eastwards across the country and it is described as finally overtaking it on 5 August 910 at Wednesfield, a few miles to the east of Tettenhall, in Staffordshire, the place after which the subsequent battle is named. Given that any army of the pre-industrial era moves at the pace of its slowest components, this statement must indicate the widespread use of mounted infantry in Edward's armies. Little is known of the battle itself save one important fact: it was a crushing victory for the English. Three of the main Northumbrian Danish leaders were killed and the English held the field.

The problem with winning such a spectacular victory was that by eliminating the Danish leaders of Northumbria, Edward created something of a power vacuum in the north. The Northumbrian Dane was virtually neutralised as a military threat in the short term. The Scandinavians based in Ireland would shortly see their chance to pour forth into the vacuum which Tettenhall had created. Edward might not have been able to foresee the events of the future, but there may be some strength in the argument that a negotiated peace would have preserved the balance of power in the north.

### THE LADY OF THE MERCIANS

Æthelred of Mercia, who had been a co-operative ally in the early years of Edward's reign, died in 911. His wife Æthelflæd came to power in his stead, but had effectively been ruling English Mercia throughout her husband's long illness. She seems to have begun her part in the great Anglo-Saxon combined fortress building programme as early as 910, building the unidentified fort at Bremesburh.[5] To this were added the forts at Scergeat and Bridgnorth (912), then Tamworth and Stafford (913), Eddisbury and Warwick (914) and Chirbury, Weardburh and Runcorn in 915. Some of these places extended a long way into Danish territories and were essentially frontier forts along the more traditional limits of Mercian domination.

Æthelflæd, Edward's sister, has her activities recorded in the 'Mercian Register', a document incorporated into the *Anglo-Saxon Chronicle*. There is also some descriptive material in the much-maligned Irish document known as the 'Three Fragments', which records events in

England with a refreshing and amusing neutrality. But it is nothing short of a national tragedy that her life has not passed into popular legend and has subsequently been lost in the mists of time. Described by William of Malmesbury as a 'woman of great determination', she was a redoubtable character, a leader who accompanied her army in the field and who certainly directed military operations from the saddle. She had decided after the difficult birth of Ælfwyn, her only child and daughter, to abstain from sexual relations with her husband, preferring it seems, to dedicate her energies to matters of state. One wonders to what extent she devoted herself not just to the upbringing of Ælfwyn but also to the creation of a vision in her young charge the Ætheling Athelstan, who was brought up at her court. What had she told him of her struggles in the north and of the Pagan threat to the English, and how had this ambitious young man responded?

The profound silence of the West Saxon-based sources for her period in office speaks louder than a thousand words. To them, although Æthelflæd was a fellow Anglo-Saxon in this era of re-conquest, there was always a danger that the ghost of Mercian independence would haunt Wessex at a time when unity was crucial. But there were some historians who remembered her with justifiable affection, even if their words may sound strange to modern ears. Henry of Huntingdon included a Latin poem of praise – a panegyric – to her in his work, a translation of which was made by Francis Peck, the rector of Godeby, Melton Mowbray, in his *History of Stanford* [sic] of 1727:

> *O potent Elfleda! Maid, men's terror!*
> *You did conquer nature's self; worthy*
> *The name of man! More beauteous nature's form of*
> *A woman; but your valour shall secure*
> *Man's higher name. For name you only need*
> *Not sex to change: unconquerable queen,*
> *King rather, who such trophies have obtained!*
> *O virgin and virago both farewell!*
> *No Ceasar yet such triumphs hath deserv'd*
> *As you, than any, all, the Ceasars more renown'd!*

Fine praise indeed for a worthy woman. But why had she been known to some as a queen when her technical title was something different?

Erroneously styled as 'Queen of the Saxons' by the writer of the Irish Three Fragments, there is every reason to believe that such a title might have been used of her in places where the proper term for a wife of an ealdorman was unknown or likely to be misinterpreted, for she was the kind of woman who inspired her followers to great deeds and she had an impeccable royal pedigree. She was, in fact, Æthelflæd, the Lady of the Mercians. This proper title is more explicit than it sounds. Roughly contemporary with the elevation of the West Saxon king to the title of king of the Anglo-Saxons, her husband, Æthelred, had been made Lord of the Mercians (*Myrcna Hlaford*) and she was his Lady (*Myrcna Hlæfdige*). She was the first-born child of Alfred the Great, but on her mother's side she had a Mercian noble heritage. During this period of English Mercian co-operation with Wessex in the face of the threat from the Dane, the humiliation of the days of Ceolwulf was set aside. Under Æthelred and Æthelflæd there was a new era of English Mercian confidence and, indeed, aspiration. The two English courts were close: Athelstan would be brought up under the watchful eye of Æthelred and Æthelflæd. But still the spectre of Mercian separatism stalked the halls at Winchester. We need not necessarily assume that the two allied commanders, Edward and Æthelflæd, saw eye-to-eye on military and political issues, as anyone who has read about the struggles between Dwight D. Eisenhower and Field Marshal Montgomery will be aware. However, it was the way in which Edward dealt with the threat of Mercian independence after his sister's death which explains the silence of the sources for Mercian matters in this period.

In 911 Edward took over London and Oxford, presumably for strategic reasons and with the support of his sister. That same year he built a burh on the north bank of the Lea at Hertford, a carefully chosen and naturally well-protected site. In 912 the stage was set for a campaign into Essex against the Danish force of Colchester. Edward's march to Maldon was probably accompanied by a combined naval operation as was often the custom in hostile territories, re-supply of provisions and fresh troops being a pressing concern. Edward had a fortification constructed at Witham on the Roman road from Colchester to London to prevent a westward advance of the enemy. We are told that this much was enough to bring many of the English people of the old East Saxon kingdom under the wing of Edward, as people flocked to the king in hope of his protection. Meanwhile, a detachment from Edward's army was building a second fortification at Hertford on the south side of the Lea in the first of many such twin fortification systems designed to deny the enemy river access. Æthelflæd, for her part, is recorded as building in the summer of 913 fortifications at Tamworth and Stafford. The next year fortifications were established at Eddisbury (re-utilising the ancient Iron-Age hillfort there) and Warwick. Again in 915 the forts at Chirbury in Shropshire and Weardbyrig are recorded as being erected. The Lady of the Mercians had clearly been keeping her side of the bargain.

The year 913 was unusually quiet, but there was one incident of note. After Easter, two mounted Danish forces from Northampton and Leicester 'broke the peace' and killed many men around the Hook Norton area. Another mounted band of Danes rode against Luton but the local people attacked it successfully and took their enemy's horses and weapons into the bargain. This remarkable local achievement may reflect a growing confidence and high morale among people who had for two generations been living under fear of such raids. Æthelflæd's fortifications at Tamworth and Stafford were probably built as a response to this incident. The next year, this morale was put to the test by a Scandinavian force which had sailed from Brittany and which entered the Severn, raiding into Wales and Mercia as far as Archenfield. A garrison force from Hereford and Gloucester (which had been established by Æthelred and his wife before 914) was called out together with men 'from the nearest strongholds' and the invader was driven by this force after a battle in which the jarl Hroald [sic] was killed, to a place where they were unable to offer battle and had instead to give hostages to the West Saxon king and promise to leave the kingdom. They seem to have attempted to call Edward's bluff by subsequently raiding on the Somerset coastline, the very land which they had promised to leave alone, but the chronicles recall that wherever they landed there was someone waiting for them. In the end they ran out of food. Finally, they left for southern Wales and then for Ireland and their immediate threat to Edward passed.

The king now started to pick the pace up with his campaign against the Danes. After the affair with the Viking fleet from Brittany, he wasted no time in building a double fortress on either side of the River Ouse at Buckingham with the intention of denying the Danes at Bedford any room for campaign manoeuvre. The intimidating effects of his stranglehold on the routes of communication for the Danish brought Edward the submission of Thurkytel, a leading Dane, the men of Bedford and some of those from Northampton. Bedford itself would soon be occupied and fortified by Edward, an operation which, like that at Buckingham, appears to have taken about a month.

The sequence of events is difficult to pick up in the chronicles of the time because some are dated incorrectly, but it is clear that a great deal happened in a few short years between 916 and 920. An English army took up quarters at Towcester, the Old Roman fortress on the River Tove known as *Lactodurum*. This was on the southern border of the Northampton Danish forces. Shortly after this, Edward had the same army fortify a place called *Wigingamere*.[6] Clearly, the English frontier was creeping into Danish areas and the consequence was that the Danish forces gathered themselves at Leicester and Northampton and took men from areas to the north of these bases and set out to attack Edward's force at Towcester. The Danes failed to take the stronghold, which is mentioned as being supported after a while by a relieving force and instead turned to raiding across the king's lands in the countryside around Aylesbury. But if the English forces could work in co-ordination, so it seems could the Danish, even on a wide scale. At about this time, the armies from Huntingdon and East Anglia moved to Tempsford and built a new camp there. From this new base it would be possible to launch offensives against the areas of Bedfordshire which Edward had gained in the previous years. So the Danes set out to attack English Bedford itself, but were met in the open field by a force from there and were defeated. The fortification at Wigingamere was not spared an assault either. An East Anglian force combined with others from Danish Mercia and attacked the fortification, but had no joy there, turning instead to cattle raiding after an unsuccessful siege.

The effectiveness of the fortification building programme was clearly demonstrated by the events of the wars against the Danish Mercians. Not only could garrisons work in co-operation with one another, supporting and relieving as needs be, but also the Danes, who themselves saw the merit in fortifications, did not have the wherewithal to undertake protracted sieges. Once a fort had failed to be taken, the attackers melted into the countryside again. The combined resources of two English rulers working in close association with each other in an integrated fashion eventually overwhelmed the Danes, whose multiple leadership structure may have had something to do with their defeat. Æthelflæd took the stronghold at Derby by force whilst the wars were being conducted to the south. Derby, as we have seen, is the most westerly and isolated of the Danish Five Boroughs and although she lost some thegns dear to her in the struggle at Derby, it was clear now that Danish Mercia was being attacked on two fronts and being squeezed by the fortifications in the north. It would prove too much for its defenders. Meanwhile, at Tempsford, the new Danish defenders were under a siege that they could not withstand. Edward's forces, drawn from local strongholds, slaughtered the camp's inhabitants, killing some senior men in the Danish army including the Danish king of East Anglia, an office which was proving a most dangerous one to hold.

The English advance would not stop at Tempsford. Edward drew a force from the whole of Kent, Sussex and Essex and attacked Colchester, taking it and delivering the same treatment to its defenders as he had to those at Tempsford. The southern territory of the Danish East Anglian kingdom was disappearing before its defenders' eyes, but there were enough well organised Danes to launch a counter-offensive which saw a huge army reinforced by mercenaries – pirates – from overseas who attacked the English stronghold at Maldon in the Blackwater Estuary. Once again a Danish force was unable to take one of Edward's forts and once again the fort was relieved by a separate field army which combined with the garrison force and overwhelmed the retreating Danes. This was a clear example of the effectiveness of Edward's military policy.

Later, Edward headed an army drawn from Wessex and made a base at Passenham where Watling Street on its way from Towcester crosses the Tove. At Towcester he had the walls of the fortification built in stone and this, among other threats, seems to have been enough to gain the submission of jarl Thurferth and the Northampton army. Edward now had control of the country up to the river Welland. In true Alfredian fashion, the Passenham fyrdsmen were relieved by a new force on its tour of duty, which duly occupied Huntingdon and made repairs to its defences. Further submissions and pleas of protection were received there from people in the surrounding landscape. With

Huntingdon secure, Edward turned to Colchester once again, sending a force which repaired the walls that had been broken earlier in the year. Submission followed submission. First East Saxon and then East Anglian men came to him with great willingness. Many of them had known nothing but Danish rule for thirty years. The Danish army of East Anglia, still a strong but demoralised force, gave up the ghost. They promised him support against his enemies by land and by sea (a notable offering which characterises many agreements between victor and vanquished during this period) and soon the independent Cambridge army would follow with its own offering of peace. The chronicles are careful to point out that the Danes chose Edward as their lord and protector. This has an important bearing for the future. Edward would have more resources at his disposal in his expanded kingdom, but more responsibility towards an increased number of subjects from various cultural backgrounds in this colourful kingdom.

The remaining Danish forces not yet under Edward's control were based at Nottingham, Leicester, Stamford and Lincoln. It must have been early in 918 that Æthelflæd took Leicester, apparently without bloodshed, for she is known to have passed away on 12 June of that year. But as Edward was preparing to move beyond the Welland, a new threat appeared in the north which would effect the security of all who held power there.

### THE KINGDOM OF YORK

The danger to stability in the north of England would be the concern of every political power. Both the king of the Scots and Æthelflæd of the Mercians were well aware of what the wind from the west had brought with it. The inhabitants of the kingdom of Strathclyde, the 'Britons' of the many histories, would feel the brunt of the assaults too, at least in the beginning. A new order would soon establish itself in ancient Northumbria and it came from Ireland. For the king of Wessex, now the king of the Anglo-Saxons, a very old and traditional northern enemy would reappear wearing new clothes.

From at least 902, there had been significant Norse settlement in the north-west of England, along the coastal regions between the Dee and the Solway. The Norse had been expelled from Ireland in that year and what followed has passed into the realm of legend. Archaeology and place name studies have made it clear that not only was there Scandinavian settlement in these areas of England, but it was Irish influenced, too. Place names such as Aspatria demonstrate the hybrid Norse-Irish nature of the settlement. There were plenty of Irishmen who had found something appealing in the Viking way of life. The legend of the arrival into the north-west of England of the Norse from Dublin is told in the disputed source *The Annals of Ireland, The Three Fragments*,[7] the sole preserver of the full tale of Ingimund, a Norse leader who is supposed to have come from Ireland with his fellow exiles, seeking first to settle in Angelsey. Here he was soundly rebuffed[8] and sought the permission of Æthelflæd to settle in north-west Mercia. Her response was predictable. She fortified Chester with a great host and there followed a failed Norse attempt to take the town, which is recalled in the text of *The Three Fragments*. Its tone is one of the main reasons for the unreliability of the source, as some authorities say that sieges were unlikely to have gone in this manner, but as an example of measure versus counter-measure in Dark-Age warfare, it has something to recommend it:

> ...the Norsemen, were under the hurdles piercing the walls. What the Saxons and the Irishmen who were among them did was to throw large rocks so that they destroyed the hurdles over them. What they did in the face of this was to place large posts under the hurdles. What the Saxons did was to put all the ale and water of the town in the cauldrons of the town, to boil them and pour them over those who were under the hurdles so that the skins were stripped from them. The answer which the Norsemen gave to this was to spread hides on the hurdles. What the Saxons did was to let loose on the attacking force all the beehives of the town, so that they could not move their legs or hands from the great number of bees stinging them. Afterwards, they left the city and abandoned it.

The important matter, regardless of the doubts surrounding the validity of the account in this amusing legend, is that there was large-scale Scandinavian settlement in the north-west of England in the first few years of the tenth century. Before even a generation had passed, York and Dublin would be linked in a giant corridor of power across the British Isles and the policies of the ruler of the kingdom south of the Humber would be governed not by the threat from the now Christianised Dane, but by the greater problem posed by the Norse kingdom of York.

The Scandinavians did not enter into a vacuum when they arrived in numbers in the north. The kings of Strathclyde, whose capital at Dumbarton (*Ail – Cluathe*) had felt the force of Viking attack just a generation earlier, were every bit as aware of the new threat as the Scottish king (who briefly held sway over Strathclyde in the early tenth century) and the Lords of the independent English enclave at Bamburgh. In fact, there is some evidence to suggest that the kingdom of Strathclyde had expanded into Northumbria from the north perhaps in an attempt to repel invasions from Ireland. In reality Strathclyde was taking advantage of Northumbrian weakness and reclaiming the old British lands along the Solway which had been ruled by Anglian Northumbrian kings for 300 years. This much might appear to be confirmed by the fact that when King Athelstan chose to meet his enemies at Eamont in 927, he did so at what must have been the borders of his new empire, recognising that any gains he expected to the north of this area would have to be achieved through coercion or the threat of military action. But recent excavations at Doomster Hill in Govan, which have shown that this place was rising in importance as Dumbarton was declining, have also shown that the kingdom of Strathclyde quickly became something of a hybrid kingdom, with Scandinavian influence from the Isle of Man.[9]

## RÆGNALD AND THE BATTLES OF CORBRIDGE

The sequence of events which brought Rægnald, grandson of Ivar, to power at York are very confused since the different sources appear to conflict with each other. It is possible to make some sense of matters, however, and what little light we can shed on the background to the establishment of the Norse power block at York reveals a land of patchwork polities each with a vested interest in keeping out the Norseman. The main sticking point in putting together a history of this brief period centres around the reliable establishment of how many battles were actually fought by Rægnald in his Northumbrian campaigns and whether they were fought, as some authorities suggest, at Corbridge.

The anonymous author of the *Historia de Sancto Cuthberto* provides us with some extremely partisan, though useful, material. His story is written with a view to pointing out the significance of the struggles to his bishop, Cutheard, who lost some powerful English tenants in the two battles which are supposed to have taken place in 914 and 918 at Corbridge. Rægnald is described as arriving in Northumbria at the time of King Edward and seizing the lands of Ealdred, son of Eadulf, ruler of the English independent state of Bamburgh. Ealdred's subsequent flight to the court of Constantine, king of the Scots, resulted, it seems, in the combined forces of Ealdred and Constantine giving battle to Rægnald and being beaten. Constantine fled back to Scotland and quite a few Englishmen from Bamburgh were killed along with one rather unfortunate noblemen called Alfred, who had fled from the east to escape the 'pirates' in the first place. This was probably the first of the two battles at Corbridge and it took place in all likelihood in 914.[10] Lands in Northumbria were subsequently shared out by the Norse leadership, probably the same lands lost by those Englishmen who had died at the first battle of Corbridge. One such Norseman died almost immediately after he had rudely interrupted a church service being given by Cutheard. This event, like so many others in the age of Athelstan, was seen as an example of divine justice.

Three to four years after the first battle of Corbridge Rægnald came again to the same place. He had been in Waterford in Ireland in 917 and probably had raided East Lothian in the region of Dunblane early in 918. This time, the Englishman Eadred, another son of Eadulf (who had died in 913), and a tenant of bishop Cutheard, was killed in the battle at Corbridge, although the Scots, present once again, appear to have achieved a great deal in the battle, accounting for the lives of two Scandinavian jarls Ottir and Graggabai.[11] Rægnald himself, having kept his division in reserve, made a timely interception to balance matters once again. Night-time, we are told, decided the outcome as something of a draw. With important men on both sides dead, both Rægnald and the Scots could claim victory. After the battle, it seems that Rægnald granted the land of Eadred to his sons, who had also fought at the second battle of Corbridge, perhaps as a way of acknowledging the politically inconclusive nature of the battle.

Keeping a close eye on these affairs from the south was Æthelflæd, Lady of the Mercians. It is unfortunate that she died at Tamworth on 12 June 918, because her interest in the events of the north had been more than passive. In 914 she had built the fortification at Eddisbury as a clear response to the immediate threat from the new Scandinavian Irish exiles who were settling in the north-east. From *The Three Fragments*, we can glean some important facts. It records Ottir's death in the battle and has the Anglo-Scottish force as victorious, but it suggests that the action had the guiding hand of the Mercian 'Queen' behind it. It goes on to say that Æthelflæd concluded the affair by negotiating a treaty between Strathclyde and the Scots whereby each would support the other in the event of Norse attack, something which they both subsequently did. There is no reason at all to doubt the nature of this involvement. It is given further credence by the fact that the people of York came to Æthelflæd for her protection in 918, clearly seeking the most powerful ally they could find in a time of great upheaval. Rægnald, however, after Æthelflæd's death, swept into York, and the famous Norse kingdom that was to cause such a headache to the sons of Edward was born.

### A CURIOUS ABDUCTION

Edward now launched an offensive designed to reduce the last remaining Danish opposition beyond the Welland in the Midlands in 918. Derby and Leicester had already fallen to Æthelflæd and now Stamford would be the first of Edward's targets. He built an opposing fortress on high ground to the south of the river, chopping off any hope of Danish manoeuvre. The Danish submission quickly followed, leaving only Nottingham and Lincoln to conquer. The news of his sister's death must have come as a great blow to Edward for both political and personal reasons. This remarkable woman had led Mercian armies in the field, received the submission of Danish forces at Derby and Leicester and brokered peace deals across the north. Whatever her differences with her brother, she had contributed to one of the most comprehensive strategic military campaigns in early medieval European history.

Edward's work was far from completed however, and it became obvious that he needed to secure English Mercian co-operation after Æthelflæd's death, lest there be a resurgence of Mercian political independent sentiment among the senior nobles of the region, now that they were clearly in the ascendancy against a common enemy. Edward's subsequent actions seem very much like those of a man who thought on his feet quickly. Æthelflæd's daughter, Ælfwynn, we often assume was given some nominal recognition by Edward as the new ruler of English Mercia, for it is not until 919 that the *Mercian Register* of the *Anglo-Saxon Chronicle* records an event of great significance – Edward had his niece removed from power and carried away into Wessex:

> Here also, the daughter of Æthelred, Lord of the Mercians, was deprived of all control in Mercia, and was led into Wessex three weeks before Christmas; she was called Ælfwynn.

Had this drama unfolded before Athelstan's eyes? What impression must it have left upon him? Would the Mercians now look to the first-born son of Edward, brought up as a Mercian prince, as their candidate for power south of Watling Street? It remains a distinct possibility that Athelstan was destined to become the Lord of the Mercians from an early age and that it was this position which won him support in the crisis which followed his father's death.

Before the end of 918, the Danes of Nottingham and Lincoln knew that their best interests lay with offering Edward their submission. But they were faced with a dilemma. The Norse pressure on the Danes and English of Northumbria showed no signs of waning and, with a most formidable Anglo-Saxon military machine in the south, the surrender of these two towns was something of a mere formality. Edward even received the submission of the Welsh kingdoms of Gwynedd, Dyfed and the area between Merioneth and Gower. What is extraordinary about the Ælfwynn affair is not that Edward had ordered an abduction of his niece, but the time it appears to have taken him. The *Mercian Register*, which is usually reliable for its dates, has one important word in the opening sentence of the 919 entry: the word 'also', which in Old English is 'eac'. Usually 'eac' is employed to continue a chronicle from the previous section of the same year, something like 'also, in this year something else happened besides that which we have already mentioned'. But here it is used at the beginning of an entry for a new year. It remains a possibility that this scribal slip indicates that Ælfwynn's abduction took place within weeks or months of Edward hearing of Æthelflæd's death in 918. This would be in keeping with the style of his leadership and the necessity to quickly sort out what was surely a crisis.[12] This single event might even explain the politics of the next fifty years. The West Saxon royal line was in the ascendancy and the Mercian focus of attention and support for a future leader would now surely turn to the young prince brought up at the Mercian court. But it would not be that simple. Edward's son Ælfweard, from his second and more legitimate marriage, would have a claim to his father's throne too. Athelstan's accession would be fraught with difficulties.

## THE SUBMISSION TO EDWARD

The Mercian frontier, now under the care of Edward the Elder, was restored to the Humber once more. Edward knew that he had to look again at the provision of fortifications along the frontier. In 919, he had Thelwall (ten miles upstream from Runcorn, commanding the crossing of the Mersey at Latchford) built and garrisoned, and also directly ordered a Mercian force to occupy and repair the Roman fortifications at Manchester, much as he had done at Towcester. Similar works were constructed in the Peak District in the region of Bakewell. Nottingham's defences were strengthened with large-scale ditches and ramparts, linking the English with the Danish sections of this new key strategic fortification. The attention of its garrison would be focused now not on the south, but on the roads to the kingdom of York. It is not known how many frontier fortifications were built along the borders of the Northumbrian and Mercian Kingdoms, and it must be borne in mind that many of the small ones will have gone unrecorded. Their presence was vital, but still sometimes not enough to prevent invasion. Sihtric, Rægnald's cousin, for example invaded and devastated the area of Davenport in Cheshire in 920. But the military reaction from other garrisons and a field army in the south would inevitably follow. The forts of the crucial area to the west of Doncaster, which included Mexborough, Barnborough, Spotisborough and Doncaster itself, were built on a landscape which became the stage for the greatest military encounter in the whole of Anglo-Saxon history during the age of Athelstan.

One more thing remained for Edward to do. It had seemed an inexorable climb to ascendancy for the son of Alfred, but in reality it had been a mixture of fortune, military might and clever leadership that had taken Edward's domain to the border with Northumbria. An entry in the *Anglo-Saxon Chronicle* dated to 924, but which is thought to represent the year 920, describes a submission of a range of rulers to Edward:

> ... And then the king of Scots and all the nation of Scots chose him as father and lord; and [so also did] Rægnald and Eadwulf's sons and all those who live in Northumbria, both English and Danish and Norwegians and others; and also the king of the Strathclyde Britons and all the Strathclyde Britons.

So, Edward had secured the submission of Constantine, the king of the Scots; Rægnald, king of the newly founded kingdom of York; the Englishmen, Danes and Norwegians of that dependency; the sons of Eadwulf of Bamburgh; and Ywain, the king of Strathclyde. In return for recognising Edward as their ultimate lord, each polity would, on the face of it at least, stand to be recognised itself. So much would be an achievement for each of the leaders in an age of migration, settlement and warfare. Rægnald's York was now a reality despite the best efforts of Edward and Æthelflæd. The English enclave of Bamburgh would at least feel protected having its southern cousin's might at its disposal. Stratchclyde, which had encroached upon lands previously held by Anglian Northumbria, would have its territory legally recognised. The Scots king would temporarily be spared the wrath of Rægnald. The way that this important piece of power-broking worked was that each party would attack the enemies of Edward. But would the former antagonists keep their hands off each other for long? What now would be the obvious solution for all these powers – save perhaps for the Englishmen of Bamburgh – to throw off the South-Humbrian yoke? Beneath the triumphalism of the *Anglo-Saxon Chronicle*'s account of the submission to Edward runs a cold vein of reality as subsequent events would show. The men of the north simply did not like the idea of southern overlordship, yet saw it as a temporary political understanding. This had bothered them intensely ever since the great days of the competing Bretwaldas in early Saxon times, where the rulers of Northumbria, Wessex, Sussex, Mercia, East Anglia, Essex and Kent had jockeyed for the position of king over kings in Britain. Over the years, some historians have wrongly seen the submission to Edward as a form of feudal subjection to England (Edward I even used the submission as an excuse for his campaigns in Scotland in the late thirteenth century). But it should be clear that from the relationships outlined above, nobody was in fact reduced to the feudal notion of vassalage. What happened next in the north would still have to be decided at sword's edge.

# 5

# THE THUNDERBOLT

Athelstan, intent on not disappointing the hopes of his countrymen
and falling below their expectations, brought the whole of England
entirely under his rule by the mere terror of his name, with the sole
exception of the Northumbrians… His subjects, who admired his
courage and modesty, loved him dearly; on rebels, invincible and
unsleeping, he descended like a flash of lightning.[1]

William of Malmesbury,
*Gesta Regum Anglorum*, 134

## ACCESSION

Edward the Elder died in the summer of 924 at Farndon-on-Dee. He
had been campaigning in the region of Chester to quell what seems
to have been an uprising which involved the Chester men. William of
Malmesbury tells of the 'rebellious spirit of the City of Legions' and
mentions that Welsh aid was solicited in quelling the rebellion. It was
after suppressing the rebels and installing a garrison there that Edward
died. Just fifteen days later his son Ælfweard died at Oxford and both
were buried at Winchester. Edward had died on 17 July and Ælfweard
on 1 August 924. There followed something of an accession crisis, the
nature of which has led to much speculation. Ælfweard almost certainly

had been nominated by Edward as his successor whilst the king was still alive. Inevitably, Ælfweard would have his supporters. Athelstan was one of two children (the other being a sister) of Edward's early liaison with Ecgwynn, a beautiful noblewoman sometimes referred to as Edward's concubine. Edward's first legitimate marriage to Ælfflæd had brought Ælfweard (the eldest legitimate son), Edwin and several beautiful sisters into the world. Edward's next marriage to Eadgifu produced, along with another sister, Edmund and Eadred with whom Athelstan would get on much better than he had with Ælfweard and Edwin. Leading West Saxon figures were of a mind to favour Edwin as a legitimate successor to the unfortunate Ælfweard, but the Mercian camp pressed its claim for Athelstan by electing him at Tamworth. The man who had been brought up under their protection as a Mercian prince, the man who had campaigned with his aunt in the north and who may have seen at first-hand the abduction of his cousin, would become an extraordinary king.

But what was it about this man that brought such unparalleled fame in his own lifetime and for centuries afterwards? There are numerous sources which can help us paint a picture of what Athelstan was like as both a person and a monarch. We can form a physical image of Athelstan better than we can for most kings of this period. William of Malmesbury, to whom we owe a very great deal in this respect, describes him as being of no more than average height, of slim build, with flaxen hair.[2] Sometimes the accounts leave us in no doubt as to the character of the man, whereas at other times the references are somewhat obscure, recording incidents which perhaps ought to have received more attention at the time. One such incident is recorded by a rather glib entry in the *Anglo-Saxon Chronicle* for 933, which simply stated that in that year King Athelstan's brother Edwin was drowned at sea, an event which was loaded with profound meaning.[3] Clearly, Athelstan took his grip on power seriously. The legends which grew about the man lead one to believe that he was a consummate leader of men, a man who was almost mesmeric in the intensity of his gaze and his steadfast resolve, pious, courteous, and yet ruthless with his enemies. We shall discover that there was more to his character than those features which the dutiful recorders of history wrote down. But for now, the description that we have here will serve to explain many of his successes in the first few years of his kingship.

Quite why the men of the City of Legions had been in revolt is an unresolved question, as indeed is Athelstan's role in all this politicking. Idwal the Bald of Gwynedd was clearly involved in the uprising, but what happened between 1 August 924 and the September of the following year when Athelstan was crowned, may remain a mystery. If William of Malmesbury, who quotes the king's own words on the matter, is to be believed, then there was a twist in the tale. A certain Alfred, who he says the king describes as 'always jealous of my prosperity and of my life and was party to the wickedness of my enemies when they tried after my father's death to blind me in the city of Winchester', was a prime mover in an attempt to deny Athelstan the throne. Alfred, a man who is described by William as 'of overweening insolence', was sent to Rome after the attempt to blind the king and had to defend himself on oath in front of Pope John, but he was stricken at the altar and carried away to the Schola Anglorum, where he died two nights later, eventually being giving a Christian burial after lengthy negotiations between Athelstan and the pope. The story is described by William as a reliable one, since he quotes it from a charter in which the king granted to the monastic community at Malmesbury lands which the jealous Alfred had forfeited to the king on account of his sedition, a grant which had the approval of the pope. Athelstan had made a point, he said, of granting to the Church the lands which he had acquired legitimately and not through robbery, handing back to God that which God had granted him:

> All this I have set down in writing that so long as Christianity endures it may not be forgotten how it came about that the possessions aforesaid, which I have given to God and St Peter, were made over to me. And I know no more just course of action than to give them to God and St Peter, who caused my enemy's downfall in the sight of all men and have given me a prosperous reign.
>
> William of Malmesbury,
> *Gesta Regum Anglorum*, 137

Careless talk at Athelstan's court would soon implicate his brother Edwin in the plot, with profound consequences for the unfortunate prince and for Athelstan's long-term reputation. Whoever Alfred was, he seems to have backed the wrong horse. Alfred is described as having his own supporters and may have brought them into the fray at Winchester against Athelstan. He might have been supporting Ælfweard, transferring his allegiance to Edwin on the death of the former. With lands around Malmesbury, Alfred might have been suspicious of Athelstan's intentions to give gifts and land to the community at Malmesbury. William, however, attributes the source of the opposition to the contested legitimacy of Athelstan's birth.

Notwithstanding the Winchester conspiracy, Athelstan was elected there with the overwhelming support of the nobility. He was thirty years old. His coronation service, which did not take place until 4 September 925 at Kingston upon Thames, has been preserved in a document at the National Library in Paris. In it we can observe that his consecration was as 'king of the Anglo-Saxons' and not as would later be the claim 'king of all Britain'. Clearly at the beginning of his reign there was still much work to be done in the building of a famous empire, the foundations for which had been laid by his father and aunt. The anointing with holy oil at the service was of great significance in the eyes of its contemporary audience. More so with Athelstan, who needed people to see how God had granted him his role, bearing in mind the troubles of his accession. The keeping of the peace, prevention of crime and robbery and the promotion of the king's justice were the three promises which Athelstan made on that day at Kingston. Furthermore, he would have meant them. Soon after the ceremony, the new king immediately performed some of his kingly duties. He restored to Canterbury the area of Thanet which had been taken from them at a time of emergency during the Danish wars. This was also a way of acknowledging Canterbury's help in the accession crisis, no doubt. In an ostentatious display of compassion, the king freed a slave called Eadhelm and his children before a large audience.

The seeds had been sewn for Athelstan's grand vision of a unified English kingdom in his youth. He had probably been educated at Worcester under the watchful eye of Æthelflæd. His aunt had seen it all. She had set herself in the saddle and commanded forces in the field after her husband's death and was probably equally active during his long illness. The young Ætheling, or prince, had been with her. The vision of a united England under an Anglo-Saxon king was as much hers as it was her father's. She had taken responsibility for the young Ætheling's education and would have spoken to him at great length about the things he might expect in the future.

It seems that Athelstan was groomed from an early age to aspire to greatness. His grandfather clearly regarded the fair-haired boy as his favourite and gave him a purple cloak, a bejewelled belt and a 'Saxon' sword with gilded scabbard. The symbolic significance of the gift is variously interpreted but it does seem to recall a similar experience which Alfred underwent at the hands of the pope (see page 198).

Throughout his reign Athelstan appears to have been celibate. This has puzzled historians for centuries and has led to speculation as to why he should have remained so. Some have suggested that it may be an indicator of homosexuality, whilst others point to the prevailing conditions at the time of accession and the fact that the king was acting as a 'caretaker' for the young Æthelings, Edmund and Edred. Athelstan certainly dedicated himself to the protection of the two princes, both of whom would go on to rule the kingdom in turn. Also, at his accession, he already had – by courtesy of his father's relationships with three different women – several beautiful sisters with which to play the game of national and international diplomacy. One might argue that Athelstan did not need to marry and sire children since the tools of the trade were already there in the form of heirs to the throne and unmarried princesses who could be used in effective marriage alliances at home and abroad. The two young princes acted almost as sons to the king. And yet there are some curious and troubling references to Athelstan's marriage and childlessness, some more reliable than others. It might be that if Athelstan decided not to sire a legitimate heir, this fact would help dispel some of the disquiet surrounding his accession.[4] But what of illegitimate children? The late twelfth century *Liber Eliensis* (III.50) has an enigmatic reference to 'Æðida filia regis Ædelstani'. It might be a scribal error, or it might be true. Could Athelstan have, like his father had done before him, fathered a child whose legitimacy was not recognised? If so, who was the mother? We may never know the answer, but it remains an interesting fact that at Malmesbury in 1380 it was recorded that prayers were to be said for the soul of a Maud, Athelstan's wife, at St John the Baptist Chapel, set up by the burgesses in *c.*1180.[5]

## FOREIGN RELATIONS

And what of the opinion held of Athelstan abroad? By this measure we might more clearly judge an early medieval monarch since we are likely to be freer from the hyperbole and bias of domestic accounts. The answer to this question is in fact very revealing. Athelstan was well known on the Continent and used his political skills and contacts better than perhaps any monarch of his age. To some extent Athelstan owed his continental connections to his grandfather, Alfred the Great, who had married his daughter Ælf to Count Baldwin II of Flanders. This marriage had taken place presumably to strengthen ties between two states constantly at the mercy of Danish raiders.[6] It was through the blood ties with Flanders that the kings of the Anglo-Saxons became interested in continental affairs. But Flanders was not the only house to marry into the old West Saxon line. Between 917-919 Charles the Simple of France married Eadgifu, Edward the Elder's daughter. Charles was unfortunate in politics and his supporters left him in 922 to support Robert, count of Paris, as king. Robert was killed in 923 and his son claimed no higher rank than 'Duke of the Franks'. Robert's supporters chose Rudolf, duke of Burgundy, as king and Charles was captured and died later in prison in 929. His son, Louis, was brought to England by his mother and for a while lived at the court of Athelstan until such time as he could go back to France. However, in 926 Hugh had the foresight to propose an alliance through marriage with the king. His deputation to England was led by none other than Adelulf, Count of Flanders and son of the English princess Ælfthryth. This meeting, held at Abingdon, was where Athelstan acquired great riches from the deputation, including gems, horses, perfumes 'hitherto unknown in England', the Lance of Charlemagne (which had supposedly been used to pierce the side of Christ by a Roman centurion), a crown of thorns in crystal and the sword of Constantine the Great with a nail from the true cross imbedded in its hilt and probably the banner of St Maurice. Hugh's gifts echoed Byzantine diplomatic practice, but there is every reason to believe that Athelstan rightly thought he was being confirmed as a western monarch second to none in Christendom, as the gifts very much suited him as the protector of the heir to the Carolingian throne. Soon, Hugh was married to Eadhild, one of Athelstan's sisters.

The whole arrangement made sense because the young Louis, who was under Athelstan's protection in England, could hardly be expected to launch a bid for the French throne without the support of the Duke of the Franks and now he would have just that through a blood tie with the house of Wessex.

It seems Athelstan held the cards in a number of continental political relationships, with leaders across Europe seeing him as an ideal figure to make friends with. Henry the Fowler, in Germany, a Saxon by birth, had used Charles the Simple's incarceration to acquire for himself Lotharingia in 925. Fearing an uprising which might be inspired from Athelstan's court by the heir to the West Frankish state himself, Henry attempted an alliance in 928 by asking that his eldest son Otto be given the hand of one of Athelstan's sisters. Two sisters were in fact sent, Edith becoming Otto's wife and the other sister marrying another obscure prince, possibly Conrad the Peaceable, king of Burgundy. Although Edith died in 946 and her son in 957, the period nevertheless opened up an era of cultural and political contact between England and Germany. There followed a great deal of traffic of princesses and books, of marriage alliances and the immigration into England of clerics of some note. In 929 the wedding of Edith and Otto took place in Quedlingburg and it seems to have been associated with an embassy of some influence. Athelstan's diplomatic party was led by Cenwald, bishop of Worcester. It was sent to 'all Churches' in Germany in that year. They brought precious gifts with them when they came and stories of saintly connections linking Otto's new wife with St Oswald on her maternal side. In fact, the mission may well have been a recruiting one. Athelstan needed clerics to run aspects of his Anglo-Saxon empire, and the fact that he recruited from Germany is given obvious strength by the activities of Theodred, bishop of London, who in the 930s surrounded himself with German helpers and had the job of setting straight the rather ragged church of East Anglia which had suffered so greatly over the last two generations. There was clearly more to Edith's wedding to Otto than meets the eye. Its cultural impact would last for generations.

Meanwhile, King Rudolf died in 936 and once again Hugh showed no sign of ambitions to take the throne. Instead, he sent for Louis in England. Athelstan, we are told, heard the plea in York and subsequently sent Oda, bishop of Ramsbury, with an armed escort to secure safety for the heir to the French throne. Louis d'Outremer was crowned king on 19 June of that year. The subsequent reign of Louis was fraught with difficulties, but there exists the probability that England sent a military expedition at least once in his support.[7] Athelstan, again at the centre of continental politics, found himself in a difficult position when Henry the Fowler's son, Otto, king of the Germans, invaded the disputed Lotharingia. The English king in 939 sent a fleet in support of Louis and does not appear to have had much difficulty in making the decision quickly. The campaign was utterly ineffective however, with the English fleet failing even to turn up at the right place, preferring instead to raid along the continental coast. The point is, nevertheless, that this was an example of Athelstan's direct involvement in continental affairs. King Edmund I, Athelstan's brother and successor, early in 946 also attempted to intervene in events abroad, despite some very pressing domestic difficulties in the north-east of Mercia. Once again, his nephew King Louis d'Outremer was the subject of his attempts. Louis had been taken prisoner by the Scandinavians of Rouen, but had been 'rescued' by the Duke of the Franks who handed him into the custody of an ally. Edmund had gathered together a mission to firmly express support for the king in his attempts to claim back the French throne, but within a matter of months Edmund had been murdered in an infamous incident (see page 171).

And yet it is in Scandinavia where we find Athelstan's reputation at its most respectful. Harold Fairhair, the Norwegian king of Westfold, was as much threatened by pirate activity as the English and Flemish leaders were. So, a Norwegian mission was sent to the English king in the form of a glorious ship with purple sail, golden prow and shields, befitting any western monarch. But this had come from a land where the name of the English king was remembered as 'Athelstan the Victorious'. Leading the deputation were two men, Helgrim and Osfrid. We cannot be sure what arrangements were made between the two men, because sources are silent on the matter, but it is true to say that many northern sources, when mentioning Harold's son Hakon, term him as *Athalstein's Fóstri*, the implication being that, like Louis of the West Franks, Hakon benefited from the protection and education of the English king.

## BRITTANY

It was not always intermarriage which formed the basis for Athelstan's continental interests. The case with Brittany, for example, is quite complex. Athelstan saw Brittany as a rich source of books, relics and religious men which could help him in his task of strengthening Church teaching and culture in England. But Brittany was suffering too. The arrival in 919 of a huge Scandinavian host in Brittany led to the migration of a number of Bretons into England. Edward the Elder had close contacts with the Bretons during his reign and this fact may have made the flight of the Bretons an apparently appropriate move to make.[8] One immigrant, Mathedoi, count of Poher, who had married a daughter of Alan the Great (the last ruler of all Brittany), raised and had baptised a son, Alan, in England. In fact, the Bretons spent the years between 919 and 936 in England. As a prince, Athelstan had stood godfather to Alan and took the role with the sort of seriousness one would expect. Alan (known as 'the one with the twisted beard') tried hard to turn his countrymen in Brittany against the northmen of the Loire Valley who had caused such destruction, but the campaign of 931 in which he took part was a complete failure. He seems to have been recalled to Brittany, perhaps at the request of John, the abbot of the important community at Landévennec. This time, Alan seems to have had Athelstan's direct military help and in 936 he once again managed to secure a foothold in his family's ancestral Breton Lands. *Les Annales de Flodoard* recorded the campaign in a short account but one which leaves us in no doubt as to Athelstan's involvement:

> … the Bretons, coming back from overseas, with the support of King Alstanus, regained their land.

There was every reason for this military intervention. Athelstan needed the help of Brittany's clergy for his own purposes at a time when the religious houses of Brittany were fleeing from the Viking onslaught. In fact, during this difficult time the monks of Redon fled to Poitou, those of Landévennec to Montreuil-sur-mer, Saint Malo to Orléans and Lehon to Paris. Clearly, there was a scramble for the rescue of relics, a religious campaign in which Athelstan showed himself not to be wanting. William of Malmesbury said that he had found a letter among some relics at Milton Abbas addressed to King Athelstan, written by Radbod, prior to the community of St Samson of Dol, in which the king is reminded that his father had been a subject of the community's prayers and had always assured them of his support. The letter bemoaned the fate of the community, who were living now in exile. The shrine in which the relics were housed bore a legend celebrating the Breton connection:

> King Athelstan, emperor of all Britain and of many peoples round-about, ordered this, which deserved to receive these relics from land across the sea, to be made in honour of St Paternus.

But the Breton influence hardly stops there. Added to a Breton gospel book probably written at Landévennec is a list of relics given to the monastery of SS Mary and Peter at Exeter which also included a reference to the systematic use by Athelstan of official relic hunters who were sent abroad for the purpose. The relics of the saints in the extensive list are those of Winwaloe, Wennal, Conocan, Melanius, Withenoc, Machutus (St Malo), Tudval, Wigenoc and St Impotemius. Exeter was not alone in the celebration of Breton saints. Winchester too became a centre for such things, even before the reign of Athelstan with the bones of Iudoc at New Minster (which arrived in the early tenth century) and the adoption at Winchester of St Machutus. Furthermore, the Winchester calendars of the eleventh century are rich in the names of Breton saints days.[9] There is some evidence too, that a few inscriptions at a Wareham church may also represent a displaced Breton community and that the dedication of a church to St Samson at Cricklade may indicate a similar phenomenon.[10]

And yet the most fascinating story combines aspects of both the military and religious Breton connections. A badly fire-damaged letter in the British Library[11] introduces a warrior who has adopted the lifestyle of a hermit during a time of peace in Brittany. He has already visited King Athelstan, perhaps as one of the soldiers of Alan, and had been installed by him at Cen, a place which has yet to be identified. The hermit wishes to go on another pilgrimage and the author of the letter is beseeching its Christian recipients to aid him on his way. The wording is of significance:

By permission of the most Christian King Athelstan, having become an anchorite, he led his life religiously… for no few days. By his [Athelstan's] advice and permission he comes on this pilgrimage also…

We do not know where the one-time soldier who had changed his military cloak for that of an anchorite was going, but what we can deduce is the power of the king in his authorisation of the pilgrimage and his piety in making it possible.

This story further emphasises the role of relics in Anglo-Saxon life. The huge increase in Breton relics in England in Athelstan's reign must have been a welcome boost to this, the most popular aspect of medieval tourism. Each English house containing such relics would receive countless visitors and would consequently profit from them. It can be no accident that Athelstan's own foundation at Milton Abbas was dedicated to SS Samson and Branwalator.

### LAND, LAW, MONEY AND GOVERNMENT IN ATHELSTAN'S EMPIRE

Any empire has at its heart a fundamental and defining dynamic: it expands. Much of the work of government is taken up with making sure that the expansion runs smoothly. That the military machine which protects existing land and dominates new territory remains efficient and numerically strong is always important. As the main strength of the English army came from the thegnly class, tied to its superiors by the bond of lordship through land holding, the 930s saw an expansion of this class of semi-professional warriors and many of the king's law codes represented measures that were designed to keep this army as a well organised and professional force.

The holding of land in Athelstan's time meant that the holder usually owed military service. There is no surprise in the fact that the land grants of the 930s reflected a growing need to enlarge the resources from existing military estates and to create new ones. The more land you granted, the greater the service you could expect in return. In Athelstan's time, every plough would provide two mounted men for military expeditions, giving the lie once again to the notion of the Anglo-Saxon warrior having to travel about on foot. But in the peace of the few short years after Brunanburh before Olaf Guthfrithson swept back into England on hearing of the king's death, there were a few occasions when Athelstan had felt able to let some of these obligations go unfulfilled. So during these incredible two years, between 937–939, this new empire must have seemed like a utopia in comparison to the dark years of Danish invasion.

The style of government at this time was essentially mobile. We talk of royal itineraries – a government on the move. If there was ever a reflection of a monarch in the process of running an empire then it would be in the itinerary of Athelstan. The king was very energetic. He held court at Exeter, Lifton, Frome, Dorchester, Wilton, Chippenham, Wellow, Amesbury, Winchester, King's Worthy, Grateley, Abingdon, Lyminster, Hamsey, Thunderfield, King's Milton and Faversham as well as York, Tamworth, Buckingham, Whittlebury, Colchester and London. A king's subjects needed to see him on a regular basis. Also, those who he controlled by coercion or threat of force beyond his natural territory were likely to become forgetful or downright recalcitrant. This is not to say that the king did not spend time on his own favourite estates in the Wessex heartlands tending to more parochial affairs. In fact, Wessex features most heavily in Athelstan's itinerary, but it is still the case that in this age, the more he was seen to be doing, the more he was doing. So the English king and his court, his thegns, his curia and clerical advisors, archbishops, bodyguard, senior earls and their retainers, and even at times his subject kings, would take to the saddle and travel around the domain of the monarch, providing him with support and protection in the governing of his kingdom. On hearing of the intended arrival of the king at a certain royal tun or estate, the reeve responsible for the management of that place would have to make provision for accommodation space for probably over 1,000 people, many of them armed men. The year 931 for example, coming as it did after the submission at Eamont Bridge of a multitude of northern and Celtic kings, saw the court in its imperial glory travel across southern Britain taking residence at Colchester, Winchester, the royal estates of Hampshire, Kingston upon Thames and then to Devon in November and the small royal vill at Lifton, where among other duties, Athelstan rewarded a loyal official known as Wulfgar of Inkpen with a grant of land. With Athelstan on the journey to Lifton were the archbishops of York and Canterbury, King Hywel Dda of Dyfed and

King Idwal Foel (the Bald) of Gwynedd, seventeen bishops, fifteen earls (mainly from the Danish territories who would play such a vital part in the politics of the next few decades), five abbots and fifty-nine thegns. They would nearly all have been mounted or in carts forming a train of impressive size.[12]

The issuing of law codes and the rewarding of men with land were two of the key aspects of the court. Anglo-Saxon law has occupied historians for years, and has often been misunderstood, especially where the famous trial by ordeals are concerned. Athelstan's law codes have often attracted comment. He issued six codes inside just fifteen years, a keenness for legislation which has been unfairly interpreted as indicating a government unable to crush lawlessness and disorder.[13] Clearly, there was great concern for the observance of law and order. Athelstan is known to have complained about the state of the king's peace and said that his advisors had told him that he had put up with it for too long. Mercantile activity at England's burgeoning urban centres such as burhs and ports was very much on the increase in the tenth century and this is where a lot of crime such as cattle rustling and major theft or fraud must have taken place. In fact, cattle rustling seems to have dominated Edward the Elder's mind when he demanded that all buying and selling should be undertaken at a port with the port reeve as a witness. The fact that Athelstan had to modify this law to include only goods worth more than 20 pence shows that royal legislation sometimes had to be tried out before it was known whether it could be properly worked. Another of Athelstan's measures against the thief was the provision for the organisation of mounted posses to chase down thieves and those who harboured them. This measure comes from the law code known as VI Athelstan, which tells us of the provisions made to enforce the law in London, sometimes known as the London 'Peace Guild'. London, although urban, clearly had a legal responsibility for a wide area and the arrangements described in this code for the division of freemen into groups of nine with one superior (these groups being known as tithings) which combined into a group of a hundred, mark the beginnings of the recognisable later Anglo-Saxon judicial system. Soon, these groups of a hundred men would be given powers of jurisdiction. For now, they would be bound by a joint responsibility for the control and prosecution of the king's law: meeting together, dining together and, in all probability, getting drunk together. It is likely that this sort of community spirit was exactly what Athelstan was looking for in his people. Small wonder that the king was remembered as a fair and just ruler. The social consequences of Athelstan's laws cannot be underestimated. It was a dangerous time and the grouping together of people against criminals and Pagans would have seemed a vital form of self-protection for the subjects of the king. Modern Freemasons claim that their origins lie in the measures that Athelstan took to protect traders and, although there is no evidence in written form to corroborate their claim, their insistence is strong.

Towards the end of his reign, Athelstan's compassion and leniency is observed in one of his laws where he exempted all persons under fifteen from the death penalty, unless they resisted arrest. He even made the comment that he felt such punishment to be too cruel. It may not seem much of a gesture to us, but it was one of the reasons why the king was later remembered for his justice and wisdom.

But there are several laws of Athelstan which do not often attract comment, for they seem to be short and to the point. The laws under consideration here have explicit military overtones. Firstly, let us consider '...that no man part with a horse over sea, unless he wish to give it' (II Athelstan 18). Most historians have assigned to this law the meaning that the king was clearly concerned with the preservation of a valuable resource, the horse. This is perfectly true. Few, however, have gone on to examine the implications of the law. It is accepted that the phrase 'unless he wish to give it' allows for the practice of including horses in important gift-giving arrangements, perhaps as part of a dowry or 'bribe' in proposed marriage arrangements, and that the essence of Athelstan's concern here was that no trade should be carried out by Englishmen taking their mounts to foreign markets. Clearly, horse breeding was now to be under tight royal control.

The implications are profound. If horse breeding in Athelstan's England was royally controlled, then we must presume that there were royal studs and officials who undertook the task. There is an explicit reference in the *Anglo-Saxon Chronicle* in an entry for 896 to two horse-thegns, whose rank was high enough for them to be included in a list of important people who had recently lost their lives:

> ... [the English Race] were a great deal more crushed in those three
> years with pestilence among cattle and men, most of all by the fact

that many of the best of the king's thegns there were in the land passed away in those three years. Of these one was Swithwulf, bishop in Rochester, and Ceolmund, ealdorman in Kent, and Beorhtwulf, ealdorman in Essex, and Wulfred, ealdorman in Hampshire, and Ealhheard, bishop at Dorchester, and Eadwulf, the king's thegn in Sussex, and Beornwulf, town-reeve in Winchester, and Ecgwulf, the king's horse-thegn, and many in addition to them, though I have named the most distinguished...

The same year, Wulfric, the king's horse-thegn passed away; he was also the Welsh reeve.

*Anglo-Saxon Chronicle* entry for 897 [896]
Winchester Manuscript (A)

It seems that there had been royal officials, perhaps similar to the French Marshalls (*Marescales*) in Wessex before Athelstan's reign. Their job is unknown, but is likely to have involved the organisation of horse management and breeding in their areas and for the provision of horse fodder, particularly over the winter months when foals and mares would need nutrition to avoid stunted growth. It should not be any great surprise that one Englishman was given a Welsh base for his work since Wales was a fine breeding area for horses. But why were horses so important to Athelstan that he had to issue laws to ensure that they stayed in England? What type of horse was being bred in Athelstan's England?

To examine this notion, we must first show how horse breeding in early medieval Europe was usually carried out. Running a stud is a delicate affair. The native horse of north-west Europe at the time was not much more than a Shetland pony. Anything else that we have evidence for is almost certainly the product either of human horse management or the result of cross-breeding caused by escaped horses. But a breed can be lost much quicker than it was created if the programme of segregation of chosen stallions from the mares is physically broken down at any stage, or if a common male is allowed to get into the mares' compound. That is just one of the concerns of the royal stud manager. The selection of the right stallion is of paramount importance. The qualities from a horse which might be required in Athelstan's England may include endurance, speed and strength whilst on campaign. The selection of mares is important too, for much the same reasons. The idea is to breed-in or breed-out certain qualities, which is done by choosing the offspring who most openly display the characteristics needed and selecting them for the next generation of breeding. A serious regression of the breed will result if this selection is disrupted. It could happen that in just a few generations a breed will be all but gone and that is exactly what must have happened in England and France during the ninth century when the Viking attacks were at their height, as the invaders are known not only to have horsed themselves on a great scale, but to have demanded horses as part of their tribute payments from religious communities.

The concerns of the Carolingian monarchs in France for the care of their horses have been well documented.[14] The emperor Charlemagne was especially anxious that proper arrangements were made at the royal studs as the following section of the Capitulare de Villis, dating from the end of the eighth century, demonstrates:

> 13. take good care of the stallions, and under no circumstances allow them to stay in one pasture, lest it be spoiled. And if any of them is no good, too old or dead, the stewards are to see to it that we are informed at the proper time, before the season comes for sending them in among the mares.

> 14. look after our mares well and separate them from the colts at the proper time. And if the fillies increase in number, let them be separated so that they can form a new herd by themselves.

> 15. have our foals at the winter palace at Martinmas.

It would appear that the most crucial aspects of horse breeding were being catered for in the Frankish empire under Charlemagne. There is an implication that if any stallions were not up to scratch at the studs, then the Emperor himself would take direct responsibility, perhaps through the offices of his Marshalls (whose principal job was horse management), to have them replaced by quality horses.

In Frankia, it is argued,[15] the most desired stallions were obtained from Spain where, since the Arab conquest of the eighth century, both Arabs and Barbs could be found. A trade in these horses had grown by the ninth century and they were sought far and wide by the wealthy.[16]

Frankish protection of their acquisitions is reflected in the royal concern shown in the Capitulary of Mantua of 781 in which Charlemagne forbade the export of stallions, and again in the Edict of Pîtres of 864 where the embattled Charles the Bald made clear that the giving of horses as ransom to the Vikings and their sale even for a 'small price' would meet with royal disapproval.

But what of England? The Frankish royal concern seems no different than that of Athelstan. So what was he trying to protect? It seems most unreasonable to suppose that the studs of England were involved exclusively with the limitations of breeding-in and breeding-out equine characteristics by concentrating only on indigenous or feral males. If the English king was not already dealing in the acquisition of stallions such as Arabs and Barbs through his horse-thegns, or indeed through the advice of the Breton military presence at both his and his father's court between 919-936, then there may be a clue in the gift of Hugh, the duke of the Franks, who, as we have seen, brought treasures to the English court in 926 fit for a Carolingian Emperor, a package which of course included horses. From the wording of William of Malmesbury's account of the gift, the horses were both numerous and extraordinary. Although we must be cautious with the reference to Virgil and the general 'talking-up' of the gift, it remains reasonable to suppose that a gift of horses would soon have practical benefits for the king. The wording of Malmesbury's statement is as follows:

> ... he [Adelulf, the leader of Hugh's mission] produced gifts [at Abingdon] on a truly munificent scale, such as might instantly satisfy the desires of a recipient however greedy: the fragrance of spices that had never before been seen in England; noble jewels (emeralds especially, from whose green depths reflected sunlight lit up the eyes of the bystanders with their enchanting radiance); many swift horses with their trappings, 'champing at their teeth' as Virgil says...[17]

Many of these gifts were transferred from Abingdon, where they were received, to Malmesbury in Wiltshire. Here, Athelstan granted the land which became known as the King's Heath 'near my vill at Norton', towards the end of his reign, 'for their help in my struggle with the Danes'. We are only at the beginning of understanding the nature of horse management in England in the Anglo-Saxon period, but it remains a possibility that this was a reward for stud management on the royal estate as well as for military service.

In Frankia, it seems royal estates, and quite often monasteries, bred horses. The best land for horse breeding, it is suggested, is an area of limestone or chalk which will produce grass rich in calcium which is, of course, good for the horses' bones. Also, a forest nearby is required for the keeping of the mares.[18] This is not the only place to breed horses, but it is interesting that the Malmesbury landscape is conducive in most respects to these requirements. The problem is that we simply do not have enough evidence yet to support the idea that there was a royal programme of horse breeding in Athelstan's England on the same scale as in Frankia, despite the fact that so many other aspects of Athelstan's reign have Carolingian overtones to them. In fact, we are poorly off for evidence of studs as a whole across the entire Anglo-Saxon period, having only one at Colungahrycg and Ongar in Essex listed in the wills, or heriots, of the eleventh century.

If Hugh's horses were indeed Arabs or Barbs, the practical benefits would be recognised in a short space of time if properly managed. Hugh's horses are likely to have been quick to breed, strong and durable. Suitable mares would of course have to be found in England unless the package included them, but it would not have been impossible. By the time of the first great pan-British expedition of 934 when Athelstan took his imperial army as far as Scotland, many of the horses he used may have been descended from the stallions in the gift. By the time of Brunanburh in 937, the gift will have realised its practical benefit on the battlefield itself. One cannot help but recall the lines in the poem describing the English pursuit of the vanquished northerners:

*All day long*
*the West Saxons with elite cavalry*[19]
*pressed in the tracks of the hateful nation*
*with mill-sharp blades severely hacked from behind*
*those who fled battle.*

Argument has raged for centuries over the question as to whether the Anglo-Saxons used cavalry. The only reason that the question remains unresolved is that it is the wrong question to be asking. It is not a question of whether one culture or another had or did not have cavalry. The question should be 'how did the Anglo-Saxons use their horses?' The problem has been compounded by the insistence of many authorities on comparing the English mounted warrior with that of the Normans at the time of Hastings. This is not comparing like with like. There were few mounted forces in Western Europe who fought in the same way as the Normans, who trained and bred their horses to charge-home instead of wheel and turn like others. The ferocity of the Norman cavalry charge was legendary and in many ways unusual, attracting comment from Anna Comnena, the eleventh-century Byzantine writer, who stated that a Norman cavalry charge could 'break the walls of Babylon'. We must not think that the later Anglo-Saxon armies fought in the same way. In fact, when Ralph the Timid, earl of Hereford, demanded that his English fyrdsmen fight in the Norman style, theirs was a conspicuous failure. William of Poitiers too, said of the English that they were unaccustomed to fighting on horseback, and there is no good reason to doubt him. The English tradition of fighting on foot must be recognised, but there is one important caveat which has led to the confusion which currently reigns supreme over the issue. The English armies of late Saxon England made extensive, and perhaps even universal use of the mounted infantryman, an armoured warrior on horseback armed with spear, sword and shield. Any group of such fyrdsmen will seem to the casual observer to be cavalrymen, the only difference being that when they arrived at the battlefield most of them would dismount to fight in the traditional style. At Brunanburh, the so-called 'elite cavalry' will have been mounted units deliberately kept in reserve to prosecute the rout, hacking at the heels of infantrymen who had little chance of escaping. Most medieval battles saw the infliction of the greatest casualties at this stage of the struggle. At Stamford Bridge in 1066, where the thirteenth-century writer Snorri Sturluson described the English army as using cavalry, the curious echo of events at the batle of Hastings may have had some foundation in actuality. Most people take this reference to Anglo-Saxon cavalry to be an anachronism, suggesting that Snorri was simply referring to the mounted tactics of his own day, but he may have been referring to what many Scandinavians had known the English to use: mounted infantry. The

English armies are frequently described as overtaking their enemies in strategic manoeuvres in the field in the tenth century and it is this benefit for which English horses would have been bred. The qualities of stamina, fast breeding and greater offspring of the Arab would provide the ideal chemistry for a mounted arm of which Athelstan could be justly proud. How else could the king descend upon his enemies like a 'flash of lightning'?

Athelstan had built an English empire by 927. He had just received a gift of horses which meant that he could once again bring new blood into the breeding programmes of a countryside wrecked by the depredations of the Vikings. And in another law code, he had demanded that every landowner should provide two well-mounted men for every plough in his possession (II Athelstan, 16).

Another of Athelstan's laws which seems to have either baffled historians or been ignored by them, states: '…that no shieldwright cover a shield with sheepskin; and if he do so, let him pay thirty shillings'. What could possibly be the reason for such a punitive fine? Some have sought the answer in the desire of the monarchy to protect sheep. This is an unlikely reason, since England was swimming with sheep at this time. The reason is more likely to be practical. In earlier Saxon times, some shields had been covered with sheepskin to an impressive visual effect. The problem in Athelstan's day was that everything needed to be accounted for in his military machine. The wood which was used by a shieldwright must be openly displayed and not hidden by a fleece. In this way, a thegn or ealdorman could see if his men were properly equipped. A shield made from poor quality wood had the unnerving capacity to splinter in the face of its handler when struck by an opponent. Certain types of wood do not do this. Lime wood, or Linden wood, is one type and it was by far the most popular wood for shields in the tenth century, as the poem of Brunanburh shows:

> *Here King Athelstan, leader of warriors,*
> *Ring-giver of men, and also his brother,*
> *the aetheling Edmund, struck life-long glory*
> *in strife around Brunanburh, clove the shield-wall,*
> *hacked the war-lime, with hammers' leavings.*

It would not matter if the shield was painted. The nature of the wood would still be on display. The intent here was to make sure that deception was not being practised for the sake of expediency by the shieldwright. The Anglo-Saxon fyrdsman of Athelstan's empire would have a strong shield and that was that.

Of great concern to Athelstan also was money. His reign is the first in which we have a numismatic portrayal of a crowned head. The English silver penny acts for us as an indicator of the fortunes of monarch after monarch and the successes or otherwise of their political and economic measures. The Danes were quick to emulate the designs of Alfredian coins, even leaving the West Saxon king's name on them in some cases. Athelstan was determined that there should be one coinage over his dominion, where there had previously been many. His law code (II) was a propaganda statement which at the same time represented a real desire to see things done well. Moneyers should now mint only at a port or a burh, and risk losing their hand if they produced fake coins. The moneyer could accept a trial of ordeal by hot iron if he felt brave enough to defend himself.

So, one kingdom, one coinage. Athelstan had a new arrangement to the existing mint structure which he decreed as follows:

> In Canterbury seven moneyers; four the king's, and two the bishop's, one the abbot's. At Rochester three; two the king's, and one the bishop's. At London eight. At Winchester six. At Lewes two. At Hastings one. Another at Chichester. At Hampton two. At Wareham two. At Exeter two. At Shaftesbury two. Else, at the other burhs one.

We have seen the way in which Athelstan exercised the tremendous power that he came to wield. We can see it in the style of government, the laws for the catching of thieves and the promotion of order in society. We see it too in the measures taken to produce one centrally controlled coinage over the whole kingdom. Now we must return to the big question for this period of history. What had made Athelstan so great? How had he risen above all other leaders in Britain to be able to style himself *Rex Totius Britanniæ*? Was it the self-confidence generated by the submission of northern rulers at Eamont in 927, or the successful punitive campaign into Scotland of 934? Something else happened towards the end of Athelstan's reign which effectively bought his place in history. We must now understand what led to the greatest showdown in Anglo-Saxon times. We must understand the meaning of the Great War of 937.

# 6

# BRUNANBURH
# THE GREAT WAR

A great, lamentable and horrible battle was cruelly fought between the Saxons and the Norsemen, in which several thousands of Norsemen, who are uncounted, fell, but their king, Olaf, escaped with a few followers. A large number of Saxons fell on the other side, but Æthelstan, king of the Saxons, enjoyed a great victory.

The *Annals of Ulster*

The Anglo-Saxon chroniclers rarely took to poetry for an explanation of events. In fact, it was only when something remarkable, glorious or sad happened that they felt compelled to express themselves in such a way. The reasons for so doing were not merely artistic. There were a number of instances throughout the tenth century where poetry was employed like this and the greatest inspiration for such efforts was the battle of Brunanburh. Wherever an historic event needed to be 'legitimised' instead of merely recorded, the genre of heroic poetry seems to have been the most powerful form of justification to adopt. Brunanburh had been the battle which Æthelweard, writing later in the century, said that the Englishman in the street recalled as 'the Great War'. Clearly, what happened on this battlefield somewhere in the north of England was of great significance. In short, Athelstan, by securing a military victory over an alliance of Dublin Norse, Western Isles Vikings, Man Vikings, Orkney Vikings and Scots, through force of arms confirmed himself in a position which years of treaties had sought to establish; *Rex Totius Britanniæ* was becoming a reality.

For a battle of such importance, we have very little physical or historical evidence to go on. We do not know for sure where it took place. There have been a number of historians who have endeavoured to pinpoint this great battlefield, many at variance in their views with others. Some have laboured on the place name evidence whilst others have sought a more historical route, yet no one is in complete agreement with anyone else. The efforts to locate the battlefield are discussed below. But first, we need to examine why the confrontation came about and conclude with an analysis of its importance in Anglo-Saxon and later history.

### THE ROAD TO BRUNANBURH

The political process which ultimately led to the great confrontation at Brunanburh had its immediate origins in the 920s when Rægnald, the Scandinavian leader from Ireland, had conquered the Danes of York, the Scots and the English of Bamburgh. He had also submitted to Edward the Elder in that year. On Rægnald's death in 921 he was succeeded by his cousin Sihtric, who had invaded north-west Mercia in 920 despite its frontier defences. At first, he appears to have offered no submission to the king in the way that Rægnald had done. Athelstan quickly took the opportunity for an alliance by marrying his sister to Sihtric in 925 at Tamworth on 30 January. There is some evidence that the agreement was as much sought after by Sihtric as it was by Athelstan. The marriage ceremony included Sihtric's conversion to Christianity and it must have satisfied Athelstan that, for the time-being, potential trouble in the north had been smoothed over with this familiar form of statecraft. In the spring of the following year however, under pressure from his followers, Sihtric returned to a conspicuous Pagan life, parting this world, we are told, as a miserable apostate and apparently meeting with a violent death.[1] Sihtric's son by a former marriage, Olaf, was elected king of York and soon an alliance with the king of the Scots was cemented with the offering of the hand of the daughter of Constantine to Olaf Sihtricson.[2] The potential for a great northern anti-English alliance was becoming clear to Athelstan and the news that Guthfrith, the Viking king of Dublin had sent an army to York in support of Olaf Sihtricson, must have sent alarm bells ringing around the halls of Winchester. What it would mean in practice would be that a giant corridor of power would open up between York and Dublin, and if it had the combined weight of the forces of the kings of Strathclyde and Scotland behind it, it would spell great danger.

Athelstan had no choice but to move hard and fast on York. This he did with good effect. In a lightning campaign, he scattered the Norse of York, the result being that Guthfrith fled to Scotland and Olaf Sihtricson to Ireland. With his enemies expelled, but not out of the picture, Athelstan seems to have wasted no time in affirming his new power in the north. In another speedy campaign into Cumbria and Strathclyde, he summoned a meeting of submission from all the leaders of the northern powers. No southern English king had ruled directly in York before and it was a profound moment which northerners did not fail to recognise. Ealdred of Bamburgh, too, did not escape the coercion of Athelstan before his submission. The agreement reached between Athelstan and Ealdred probably included the involvement of this ancient northern English citadel in the proposed governance of Athelstan's new acquisitions. The meeting, which took place *aet Eamotum* ('at the meeting of the waters'), was set against the backdrop of a significant Roman fortification (Brocavum), much of which was still standing at the confluence of the Lowther and Eamont rivers, at the site which became Brougham Castle, two miles south-east of Penrith. The Roman fortification had guarded the junction of the roads to Carlisle and the cross-Pennine route. This place represented the limit of Athelstan's empire in terms of direct government and so, in time-honoured style, he was meeting his subjects on the borders of his kingdom.[3]

*Æt Eamotum*, Athelstan, in imperial style, accepted the submission of Constantine of Scotland and stood godfather to his son. Owain of Strathclyde and Ealdred, the ruler of the independent English state of Bamburgh, gave their pledges too. There was one notable absence. Guthfrith had managed to 'escape' from Constantine's care at around about the time Athelstan had ordered the Scottish king to hand him over. The fugitive – if that is what we should call him – found his way to York with another Viking leader and started to drum-up support amongst the men there.

Once again, York was the thorn in Athelstan's side. He headed south to deal with the threat and again the strength of his abilities as a strategic commander seem to have given him the element of surprise and Guthfrith's forces were scattered at York after an unsuccessful attempt at persuading the men of York to ally with him. This time the king had his man. Guthfrith was taken prisoner and brought to Athelstan and, in the custom of the times, he was entertained for four days before being sent back to Ireland where he died in 934. York for a short time would now attract Athelstan's attention. The strongly defended Danish enclosure there needed to be weakened to prevent and discourage further defiance against him. Athelstan had the city's Scandinavian defences, built earlier in the ninth century, levelled by his forces who delighted in sharing out a large hoard of silver whilst they were at it.

The momentum of Athelstan's wide-ranging campaign was about to pick up speed. The north Welsh had clearly come out in open defiance at the end of Edward's reign. It was whilst he was campaigning in that area that Athelstan's father had died. Idwal Foel of Gwynedd seems to have been at the centre of the anti-English sentiment. He was the highly praised subject of much vitriolic Welsh poetry of the time which pointedly promised revenge upon the English aggressor. Athelstan's campaign, although we know little about it, was clearly successful. He systematically broke the resistance of Dyfed, Gwynedd, Morgannwg, Gwent and Brycheiniog, ordering their kings to meet with him at Hereford. Here, a massive tribute was arranged to be paid to the English king which took the form of 20 pounds of gold, 300 pounds of silver, an impressive 25,000 oxen and numerous hounds and hawks. The River Wye was set to become the new boundary between the English and the Welsh. But if we dare take history at face value, we might think that everyone in Wales was anti-English at this time. Not every Welsh king was anti-Athelstan however, as the remarkable reign of Hywel Dda demonstrates, and yet there is something menacing in the notion expressed in Welsh poetry that the northmen would be welcomed if they were to ally with the Welsh against the over-proud English.

At about the same time as the Welsh wars, the west Welsh of Cornwall were sending defiant signals from Exeter. The king succeeded in expelling them from Exeter and setting them up again west of the Tamar, even giving them their own new bishopric at St Germans. Athelstan's

rebuilding of Exeter was a wholesale affair. Its church would benefit greatly from the gifts of the king and it would be here at Exeter
that Athelstan would hold his Great Court in 928 and again in 935.
Remnants of the old Cornish dynasty which had ruled here for so
long can still be traced in the names of those present at the witnessing
of charters and in the stone monuments around the ancient kingdom,
but Athelstan had now clearly added much of Cornwall to his expanding empire. We are told by William of Malmesbury that numerous
reminders of the king were to be seen in Exeter and its surrounding
district, but that the 'natives' of that area could give us a better account
of it than he could with his pen.

Throughout the early 930s, the new Britain of Athelstan was being
ruled with a firm hand. We can be left in no doubt as to how the king
saw himself. Not only are there coins demonstrating his imperialistic aspirations, but there are charters of land grants too, which tell a
revealing story of the developing notion which Athelstan had of
himself. In 930 Athelstan granted lands in Amounderness, north
of Preston, to the archbishopric of York in a charter that was witnessed at Nottingham by the archbishops of York and Canterbury,
three Welsh sub-kings, seven English ealdormen, six Danish jarls, ten
king's thegns and thirteen others, revealing the cosmopolitan nature
of Athelstan's court and the wide range of his power. In this charter,
Athelstan has moved away from styling himself as *Angul Saxonum Rex*
or *Rex Anglorum* and instead chooses a strikingly imperial definition of
himself:

> ... king of the English, elevated by the right hand of the Almighty,
> which is Christ, to the throne of the whole kingdom of Britain

At about the same time as Olaf, son of Guthfrith, came to power in
Dublin, something of great significance appears to have happened in
the far north. From the end of May 934 until the autumn, Athelstan's
year would be taken up with the largest campaign he had yet mounted.
Constantine had broken his word. Perhaps Athelstan had heard that
tribute was not forthcoming in the way it was promised, or perhaps
he was told of open defiance from Scotland, we will never know. The
result was the pulling together of the first imperial army of Britain since
the days of the last Roman governors. It was described as being 'drawn

from the whole of Britain', a grand expedition. At Winchester on Whit Sunday the West Saxon fyrd were gathered together. They were joined there by contingents from the four subject kings of Wales each under separate command. Athelstan took this combined force to Nottingham, the most central of the former Danish strongholds and there collected a sizeable Anglo-Danish force from the surrounding territories. Through friendly York and Ripon and on to Chester-Le-Street the vast army marched. Athelstan took his own private detour to Beverley where he visited the church of St John and gave prayers for a victory. Here he laid his knife on the altar so that he could come to reclaim it after his successful campaign. According to legend, he left Beverley with the banner of St John to add to the others of his army, which probably included the banner of St Maurice. At Chester-Le-Street the king paused and gave more prayers and great gifts to the shrine of St Cuthbert, whose community had found a new home here since the Viking attacks on the Holy Island in years gone by. Some of his gifts can still be seen today at the shrine now in Durham Cathedral. Athelstan is thought to have requested that he be buried with the saint if all went wrong on the campaign.

As Edward had done before him, Athelstan organised a supporting fleet of fighting men and supply ships which sailed up the east coast of Britain and which raided as far north as Caithness. Dunnotar was as far into Scotland as the giant combined force went, but clearly it was enough. It must have seemed to observers that wherever it went, the fields were left bare, since Athelstan took much stock as recompense for the breaking of tribute. There is some evidence for a battle taking place on this campaign – an encounter which came after the king had seen a vision of St John which told him to advance and conquer the enemy. The Scottish king retreated beyond the Solway and was followed and defeated by Athelstan. The activity in Scotland in 934 has lead some historians to mistake Scottish sites for the lost site of Brunanburh, which was a different campaign entirely. Whatever happened in 934, Constantine realised that he could not face Athelstan's army in the open. Not, at least, without support from allies. But who would possibly join him against such a force?

Along with Owain of Strathclyde, Constantine met Athelstan and had to renew his promises. Once more, he was Athelstan's 'underking' and he gave as assurance his own son over to the English court. The

1 The Three Towns Pageant of 1951 involved the people of Kingston, Surbiton and New Malden. Here, in front of a thrilled audience, Athelstan is crowned on a replica coronation stone. *Photograph courtesy of Kingston Museum and Heritage Service*

2 In 1975, the millenary of the crowning of Edward, king and martyr, was celebrated with the coronation stone at Kingston being re-employed once again. *Photograph courtesy of Kingston Museum and Heritage Service*

3 In the grounds of All Saints' church at Kingston can be seen the foundations of the Saxon chapel of St Mary. Here the walls are outlined in tape, shortly after their excavation in the late 1920s. *Photograph courtesy of Kingston Museum and Heritage Service*

ÆLFRED REX HA
NC URBEM FECIT·
ANNO DOMINIC
AE INCARNATIO
NIS DCCCLXXX
REGNI SUI VIII

4  *Above left:* W.E. St Lawrence Finny single-handedly elevated Kingston's Anglo-Saxon kings to a position of local pride in the town. The notice of his lecture and of the millenary pageant was given in 1924. The Saxons, incidentally, won the game of football.

5  *Above:* Esther Hammerton, Sexton of Kingston, d.1745-6. A truly remarkable woman, she survived the collapse of the Saxon chapel of St Mary beneath which both she and her father were excavating at the time. He was not so lucky. She inherited her father's office but, due to her injuries, could only wear men's clothes. *Photograph courtesy of Kingston Museum and Heritage Service*

6  *Left, top:* This fragment of a plaque from Shaftesbury commemorated the founding of the burh by King Alfred in 880. It is the same plaque which William of Malmesbury claimed to have seen in his visit there in the twelfth century.

7  *Left, centre:* On one side of a memorial stone from Lindisfarne thought to depict the coming of the Day of Judgement, are seven Scandinavian warriors, probably Viking pirates brandishing their characteristic weapons. The punishment for the sins of the people would come in the form of pagan raiders for centuries to come.

8  *Left, below:* Sword pommel from the River Seine at Paris, perhaps dropped by a member of the Viking force of 885 which wintered there. Almost certainly an English sword of Anglo-Saxon manufacture, this discovery demonstrates the extent of looting and travelling of the Scandinavians in the late ninth century.

9 When the English Midlands were transformed by the treaty of Alfred and Guthrum into the Danelaw, the peoples of England became increasingly culturally diverse. Today, the streets of Alfred's own Wantage bear testimony to the continuation of old and new in English culture.

10 The statue of King Alfred rightfully stands tall in the centre of the market town of Wantage, a much-loved home. Yet for much of the medieval period, Alfred's favourite grandson, Athelstan, was as widely acknowledged as he was.

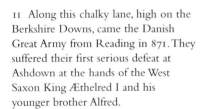

11 Along this chalky lane, high on the Berkshire Downs, came the Danish Great Army from Reading in 871. They suffered their first serious defeat at Ashdown at the hands of the West Saxon King Æthelred I and his younger brother Alfred.

12 Just another field? The hedges which outline the strips of land awarded to the townsfolk of Malmesbury in Wiltshire by King Athelstan after 937 are still visible today. The strips of land were continually farmed and are still administered by the Old Corporation.

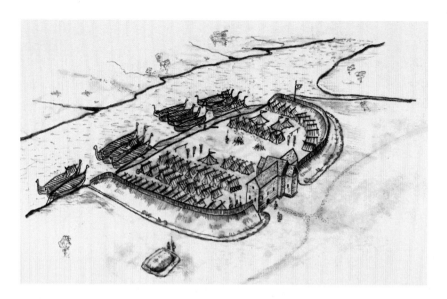

13 The Danish camp at Repton was built in 873 and utilised St Wystan's church as a fortified gateway. It had a perimeter of around 200m. From here the Great Army dominated Mercian politics for a year.

14 The Alfredian burghal system was a masterpiece of military organisation. Essentially places of refuge for a frightened populace, these fortified settlements were placed twenty miles apart (a day's march) and garrisoned accordingly. Danish armies found it hard to campaign in Wessex after their construction since, wherever they went, they were threatened by the fortified landscape.

15 A 'Saxon' arch forming a gateway leading to the abbot's house at Malmesbury, Wiltshire. Athelstan had a real affection for St Aldhelm, his kinsman, and for the community at Malmesbury. Drawing based on an original of 1801.

16 *Above left:* Tamworth's Millenary celebrations in 1913 included a parade by local people dressed in costume. Here, Lady Æthelflead caresses her nephew, the young Prince Athelstan. She brought him up in her court and may have encouraged his vision of a united kingdom. *Photograph courtesy of Tamworth Castle Museum*

17 *Above right:* A tenth-century thegn in the army of Athelstan. The king's army that went into Scotland in 934 was drawn from the whole of England and contained many professional warriors. Modern re-enactors are increasingly authentic in their recreation of warriors' costume.

18 *Below:* The Shire Moot deliberates. Many of Athelstan's law codes protected his military machine, whilst others were concerned with the preservation of law and order. They would have been known to every man in every area of the realm. From a Victorian painting.

19 'Athelstan orders Scriptures to be translated into Saxon' from a Victorian drawing. *Picture courtesy of Kingston Museum and Heritage Service*

20 King Edmund is killed during a feast at Pucklechurch by the outlaw Leofa. From a Victorian print. *Picture courtesy of Kingston Museum and Heritage Service*

21 The young King Edwy at his coronation banquet in Kingston. His early retirement from the feast in search of the caresses of the two women pictured here cost him his reputation and St Dunstan was exiled for daring to intervene. Edwy, however, was probably a victim of later propaganda. *Picture courtesy of Kingston Museum and Heritage Service*

22 *Left:* The Battle Stone at Mereclough, near Burnley, Lancashire. One of the many claimants in the north-west of England for the site of the battle of Brunanburh. In reality, the stone probably commemorates a much later struggle during the English Civil War.

23 *Below left:* These tombstones or grave markers from Brompton in North Yorkshire represent bow-sided buildings with bears at either end. Whatever their meaning, their presence in Cumbria and North Yorkshire speak of Scandinavian settlement across the whole of the north of England from coast to coast.

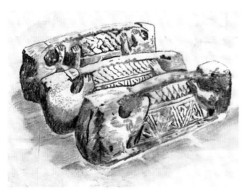

925    940

**ATHELSTAN,**

SON OF EDWARD THE ELDER.

Conspiracy of Alfred the Etheling.
Invasion by Anlaf the Dane.
Defeat of the Danes at Brunsbury 937.
Peace during the remainder of the reign.
Revival of commerce.
Scriptures translated into Saxon.

24 *Above:* The mighty King Athelstan, from a Victorian drawing, demonstrating the curious notion of what a Saxon king should look like. *Picture courtesy of Kingston Museum and Heritage Service*

25 *Left:* The murder of Edward the Martyr at Corfe Castle, from a drawing in Baring-Gould's *Lives of the Saints*, 1897. *Picture courtesy of Kingston Museum and Heritage Service*

The Coronation Stone, Kingston

26 The Coronation Stone in Kingston in around 1900. Today it occupies a less conspicuous site near the modern police station next to the Guildhall, just 50 yards from where it is depicted in this print. *Photograph courtesy of Kingston Museum and Heritage Service*

27 Athelstan's coinage soon developed an imperial tone. After the meeting at Eamont in 927, where the king received the submission of northern rulers, coins bearing the legend *Rex Tot Brit* (*Rex Totius Britanniæ*) became more prevalent and a similar title appeared in the charters of the king. The ancient Roman province was ruled again by one man. *Photograph courtesy of Kingston Museum and Heritage Service*

28 In the modern age, Kingston's love affair with the Saxon kings remains strong. Here in 1995, Athelstan is crowned once again at the site of the Coronation Stone. *Photograph courtesy of Kingston Museum and Heritage Service*

29 The Abingdon sword, in the Ashmolean Museum, Oxford, ninth century. No other discovery symbolises the crusading nature of the English struggle with the pagan Danes more than this piece. Captured in the silver niello cartouches on the upper and lower hilt guards are the symbols of Matthew, Mark, Luke and John. It would be as important for Rome as it was for Wessex that the north should be recovered. *Photograph courtesy of the Ashmolean Museum, Oxford*

30 Seven tenth-century English kings are thought to have been crowned at Kingston upon Thames. The Coronation Stone stands in that town as a monument to its royal history. *Photograph courtesy of Kingston Museum and Heritage Service*

**England became a Kingdom, Anno Domini 819.**
**England in 1850 is ruled by a Descendant of her first King.**

# Kingston-on-Thames.

## THE INAUGURATION

OF THE

# CORONATION STONE

OF THE

# ANGLO SAXON KINGS,

### THE ANCESTORS OF OUR

# ILLUSTRIOUS QUEEN,

#### WILL TAKE PLACE ON

## THURSDAY, the 19th of SEPTEMBER,

# WITH MASONIC HONOURS.

### AT ONE O'CLOCK,

The Right Worshipful the PROVINCIAL GRAND MASTER of the FREEMASONS of Surrey attended by the Brethren of the Province and other Masons, will meet his WORSHIP THE MAYOR, attended by the Corporation and Burgesses and Visitors at the TOWN HALL, and go in procession to the MONUMENT.

### AT TWO O'CLOCK,

A Public Dejeuner for LADIES AND GENTLEMEN will be provided in the Grounds of CHARLES ROWLLS, ESQ., kindly granted for the occasion.

### AT HALF-PAST FOUR O'CLOCK,

The CHILDREN of the SCHOOLS will sing the NATIONAL ANTHEM, and be presented at the Monument with Books and Medals.

### AT HALF-PAST FIVE,

A series of AQUATIC SPORTS will take place at Town's-End.

### AT SEVEN O'CLOCK,

# A GRAND DISPLAY of FIREWORKS on the Thames

### By Southby, WILL CONCLUDE THE FESTIVITIES OF THE DAY.

## MILITARY BANDS WILL ATTEND.

TICKETS for the Dejeuner at 7s. 6d. each, including Wine and a Medal may be obtained on or before Monday, the 16th instant, of Messrs. Shrubsole, Ranyard, Gould, Hollingdale, E. Phillips, and Henry H. Young, Esq., Town's-End, Kingston; Mr. Furze, Greyhound Hotel, Richmond; Mr. Henry Lamb, Chertsey; Messrs. Russell, Guildford; Mr. J. White, Dorking; Mr. Wigsell, Epsom; G. Morrison, Esq., Reigate; and in London of Mr. Taylor, Medalist, 33, Little Queen Street; Mr. S. Sainsbury, 177, Strand; Messrs. Eastman and Yeo, 100, Cheapside; and Messrs. Barclay & Son, 170, Regent Street.

*The beautiful Medal by Taylor, and the Genealogical Chart of the Queen's descent from the Anglo Saxon Kings will be ready for Sale on the day of inauguration.*

H. J. FRICKER, PRINTER, MARKET-PLACE, KINGSTON.

31 The Coronation Stone in Kingston went through something of a major marketing re-branding exercise in 1850. The Victorians made sure that Queen Victoria herself was legitimised through the events of the day. Athelstan's connection with the Masons was not forgotten, either. *Photograph courtesy of Kingston Museum and Heritage Service*

32 The standard of St Maurice is likely to have been amongst the many gifts given to Athelstan by Hugh, Duke of the Franks, in 926. This, along with the golden dragon of Wessex and individual unit banners, would have made Athelstan's army a resplendent sight in the field.

33 The battle of Ashdown was fought between the Great Army and the West Saxons some time early in 871. King Æthelred's division was late in lining-up against the Danish king's division, whilst Alfred led his men up the hill against the Danish Jarls. Æthelred's arrival on his brother's flank came just in time. *Illustration: Paul Hill and Julie Wileman*

34 According to legend, the battle of Brunanburh was fought in a hazelled field, marked with poles to denote the fighting area. Here, with a river on one flank and the woods on the other, is the Vinhiethr of *Egil's Saga*. Mercians (bottom) are aligned against the Scots. The West Saxons (top right) are against the Norse of Olaf. Viking mercenaries prepare to charge the allied lines, while Egil waits at the rear. In the distance is the fort of Brunanburh. *Illustration: Paul Hill and Julie Wileman*

35 The Statue of Ethelfleda (Æthelflæd), Lady of the Mercians, at Tamworth. She clutches her young nephew Athelstan to her side. The son of a West Saxon king, Athelstan would learn much about northern England during his youth here in Mercia. His formidable aunt, who fought the Vikings herself, was a perfect tutor. *Photograph by Paul Barber*

36 The tomb of Athelstan in Malmesbury Abbey contains no bones and dates from the thirteenth to fourteenth centuries. Even the head on the effigy has been removed and replaced at a later date by one from another monument. There is, however, something of an aura around the tomb, which attracts visitors to this day.

37 Malmesbury Abbey, Wiltshire. The twelfth-century historian, William of Malmesbury, provides us with much essential information about Athelstan's reign. William, who saw the king in his tomb and spoke of his popular legend, was in a better position than most to speak knowledgeably of Athelstan.

eadweard the elder 900 | athelstan 925 | eadmund 940 | eadred 946 | eadweard the martyr 975 selfthryth | aethelred the unready 979

38 This mural in Eden Street, Kingston upon Thames, is over nine feet long and was made in the mid-1980s by ceramic artist Maggie Humphry. It commemorates the lives of each of the seven kings thought to have been crowned at Kingston and there are some scenes from the town's vibrant local history along the bottom. *Photograph courtesy of Kingston Museum and Heritage Service*

39 At the foot of a remarkably beautiful eighth-century gospel page is inserted a laudatory poem about King Athelstan. Written in Latin in the tenth century, it tells of a united England and of a king made glorious through his deeds. *Photograph courtesy of Durham Cathedral. MS. AII.17 f31v*

40 The age of Athelstan was a period of great craft and trading activity in both the Viking and Anglo-Saxon worlds. Here a re-enactor produces goods at his portable workshop. Like clerics, craftsmen were rotated on a regular basis at Athelstan's court. *Photograph: Lise Farquhar*

41 Storytellers and musicians in tenth-century dress. The role of popular song in promoting the legend of King Athelstan was noted by the medieval historian William of Malmesbury. *Photograph courtesy of West Stow Anglo-Saxon Village*

42  Athelstan is one of the few English kings of the period for whom we have a description. William of
Malmesbury tells us that he had shoulder-length blond hair and was no taller than other men. This
reconstruction is on display at Kingston Museum in Surrey. *Photograph courtesy of Kingston Museum and
Heritage Service*

triumphant army returned to the south having achieved its objectives. It had been an impressive display of military might and coercive state-craft. It also demonstrated that the empire was not just a theory or an idea. It was a military reality. An army could be drawn from 'all over Britain' by the southern king and it would be big, too. As Athelstan pushed on southwards, stopping at Buckingham to reward some of his men for their performance on the campaign, the Scottish king, who was with the English army, must have suffered these ceremonies with a tight lip. The hardened, grey-haired old northern warrior would not forget this spectacle and would have grimaced at every overt display of English pride.

In the following year, the emperor held an assembly at Cirencester. This ancient Roman town had for some time been the traditional regional taxation point and Athelstan chose it for its powerful symbolism. Here presided the hated 'Stewards of Cirencester' who had stirred so much anger in Welsh hearts. The town had many surviving Roman features which clearly stood as symbols in the urban landscape and also had a huge church to rival that at Brixworth. Constantine was there again, observing and remembering what he saw. There may even have been a ceremony here along the lines of that which took place later in the reign of King Edgar – where subject kings in front of a huge and influential audience rowed the English king along the river with their lord at the rudder. Such a scene would certainly have been in keeping with the style of Athelstan, and it is inconceivable that no ceremony took place at all in front of this ostentatious assembly.

Sooner or later a coalition would have to come against Athelstan. Olaf Guthfrithson wanted York back. So too did Olaf Sihtricson, whose political career was to be one of the most extraordinarily long ones of the tenth century. The Scandinavian power block of the north was still an ambition of theirs. Most of all, after having to observe the indignity of subordination and punishing tribute, Constantine wanted revenge. The self-styled *Rex Totius Britanniæ* was too powerful and must be taken down a peg or two. But in which places would the attack on Athelstan's England be prepared? Who would mastermind it? Where was it intended to fall? And upon whose support would the success of the operation depend?

## SHIPS, CAMPAIGNS, TACTICS AND LOGISTICS
## IN THE AGE OF ATHELSTAN

There is little point in addressing the issue of the whereabouts of the battle of Brunanburh without first trying to understand the capabilities of armies of the period. Once we are able to identify such factors as logistics, sailing capabilities, campaigning seasons and supply needs, then we can measure these facts against what we know of the campaigns of the period from historical sources.

Campaigns such as that at Brunanburh took months to organise. From Athelstan's point of view, he will have had to send messages ahead through a network of royal officials as he had done in 934 for the great expedition into Scotland. These officials will have been detailed with numbers they were required to summon and the mustering places would have been well known. The logistical concerns of supply were paramount. Although Athelstan's army of 934 took a great deal of stock from the Scots in revenge for Constantine's apparent duplicity, it will have had its own huge baggage train, whose contents were carefully planned to last the expected duration of the campaign. The logistical support which the army received during these long campaigns was vital. Athelstan, like his father before him, simply could not contemplate such a far-reaching exercise without fresh supplies coming from a supporting fleet. It is no surprise that when the young King Edmund later handed parts of Strathclyde over to Malcolm, king of the Scots, in 946, he did so in return for the Scots king's support at both land and sea. It simply will not do to suggest, as so many Anglo-Saxon military historians have in the past suggested, that armies lived solely off the land whilst on campaign. Of course, scouting and foraging took place, but this was as a supplement to the materials already in the baggage train. It also meant that sections of the army would need to disperse in order to forage. This was always a danger and it cost the Kentish men dearly in the early years of Edward's reign when on campaign in East Anglia. It is the case which proves the point: the army that Edward had summoned to chase Æthelwold was intended to raze parts of East Anglia as a punishment. It was very quickly recruited, and when the king gave orders for it to return, the Kentish element was presumably dispersed and foraging. Seven king's messengers could not get word to the disparate force before they were set upon by the Danes. The fact that the force managed to kill Æthelwold in the ensuing struggle is a matter of pure luck. The English were caught out by poor logistical planning.

From the point of view of the allied force (this being the Viking and Scottish side), the practical considerations would have been just the same. The Brunanburh campaign was to take place inside an enemy kingdom. No amount of foraging would sustain an army the size of Olaf and Constantine's for long. The tradition that this combined force entered the Humber with 615 ships is one of the linchpins for the Yorkshire argument for the site of the battle, but here, just the mention of these numbers is an important clue. There has been a remarkable tendency to presume that all of these ships were crammed with armed warriors. This would make the allied army around 20,000 strong if we assign a not unreasonable thirty men to a ship. But anything up to half of these ships, if not more, will have been given over to logistical support, carrying tents, cooking equipment, fodder, weapons, armour, food and water for the army. The question of the size of the non-combatant 'tail' of early medieval armies is seldom looked into since people have rarely given the commanders of the period the benefit of the doubt in terms of their logistical capabilities.

On the subject of the navigation of the Viking fleets, or for any fleet of the era for that matter, mention is rarely given of William of Malmesbury's account of King Edgar's patrol fleets of the later tenth century. The island of Britain could be sailed around by large fleets keeping formation and maintaining their strength. There is no reason why in 937 Olaf's fleet could not have sailed around the top of the island to come down its eastern side and enter England via the Humber, there being no need to restrict his fleet to a short hop from Dublin to Man and then to the Ribble or Mersey estuaries. Here is how Edgar organised his patrols:

> … every summer, immediately after the Easter festival, he used to order a gathering of the ships on every coast, his custom being to go with the eastern fleet to the western part of the island, and when that had been patrolled, to make with the western fleet for the northern, and then with the northern fleet for the eastern, his virtuous purpose to find out whether pirates were giving any trouble.[4]

Recruitment is another issue. When we look at the list of allied casualties at Brunanburh recorded in the surviving copy of the *Annals of Clonmacnoise*, it should be apparent to us what a huge undertaking it must have been for Olaf and Constantine to gather what seems to have been a disparate force. Olaf had been recruiting and coercing warriors in Ireland as late as August 937, showing that some came from a sense of allegiance whilst others were virtually press-ganged. In fact, there was good reason for Olaf's aggressive approach to his fellow Scandinavians in Ireland. By knocking out the Limerick Vikings, Olaf had secured himself in Ireland to the extent that his dynasty was free for the first time in fifteen years to turn its attention to a full-scale military campaign designed to retrieve territories lost in England to the king of the Anglo-Saxons. Guthfrith had not watched his back in Dublin and paid the price in 927.[5] Nevertheless, the seventeenth-century translation of the annal for 931 (really 937) contains strange-sounding names of Norse-Irish and other Viking islanders:

> The Danes of Loghrie arrived att [sic] Dublin. Awley [Olaf] with all the Danes of Dublin and north part of Ireland, departed and went over Seas. The Danes that departed from Dublin arrived in England, and by the help of the Danes of that kingdom gave battle to the Saxons on the plaines of othlyn [the lands beyond the Irish sea], where there was greate slaughter of Normans [Northmen] and Danes; amongst whom these ensueinge Captaines were slaine Sithfrey and Oisle the two sonnes of Sittricke Galey, Awley Froit and Moilmorrey y^e son of Cossewara, Moyle Issa Gibeachan king of y^e islands. Ceallagh Prince of Scottland [Constantine's son] with thirty thousand, together with eight hundred Captaines about Awley m^c Godfrey [Olaf Guthfrithson] and about Aricke m^cBrithe, Iloa, Decke, Imer the kinge of Denmarkes owne son with fower thousand soldiers in his guard were all slaine.

Few of these names can be confidently identified as truly historical, but the fact that Olaf Guthfrithson and the son of Constantine are among them, lends some authenticity to the list. Moreover, Cossewara, whose son is included in the list, is thought to have sacked Munster in 915, and the 'king of the Islands', which probably means the Hebrides, is a title which Eric Bloodaxe is later supposed to have held. These islands were a great recruiting ground for the Vikings, containing a mixture of Scandinavians and Irishmen who had gone over to the Scandinavian way of life. But the point is that there was a very wide geographical base from which these troops were drawn, stretching from the Hebrides to the west of Ireland. It seems that Olaf's recruiting style required his personal presence. If this is the case, then it would be reasonable to assume that he would sail to Man after leaving Dublin with his fleet and then sail north to the recruiting grounds of the Western Isles and Hebrides. From here it might seem that he would have a choice – to sail south again to Dumbarton soliciting a fleet from Scotland and Strathclyde and enter Athelstan's England from the west, or head north to the Orkneys and Shetlands gaining further recruits and travel down the east coast of Scotland seeking Constantine's aid and enter England through the time-honoured and obvious route of the Humber estuary. This latter trip would be one of 600 miles through difficult, but not impossible, seas. But there is another model for the recruitment campaign yet to explore. It has been argued that it is possible to travel from Dublin Bay to the walls of York by a route which involves sailing up the Firth of Clyde, then travelling across land to the east coast and continuing the journey under new sail from the Firth of Forth.[6] The logistics surrounding this route would of course be immense, but not beyond the capabilities of the time. The allies of Olaf would have to organise a huge fleet on the east coast to pick up their partner marching across land from Dumbarton with his own numerous recruits. Olaf's march would be just a day long, this being the narrowest part of the British Isles when measured from west to east coasts. From here, an allied fleet containing Vikings recruited from the Western Isles and Hebrides – either at Dumbarton or more likely by Olaf on his travels in the west – and the forces of the kings of the Scots and of Strathclyde, would sail down the east coasts of Scotland and Northumbria to the mouth of the Humber, a distance of some 240 miles. This would make sense of the northern tradition surrounding Brunanburh that not only was there an allied invasion which came up the Humber, but that it was organised by Constantine. The latter part of the logistical operation would indeed have been in Scottish hands.

Despite this most plausible model, which eliminates the thorny issue of a round-the-top of Britain approach while still arguing for an east coast entry, passionate arguments have raged for centuries. As is the case with most historical conundrums, the fact that the answer has not been found is the fault of those who pose the questions. The question has produced two polarised camps: west coast and east coast. We have seen how logistically capable the forces were in this period and we know that an allied force was perfectly able to sail into England from both sides of the island. But here in lowland Scotland, along the line of the old Roman Antonine Wall, we have a probable route to Brunanburh. The remains of the old wall itself may have aided the march by acting as something of a road.

Now we must examine the history of the various claimants to the field of Brunanburh and assess the likelihood in each case of the argument being the correct one. There can only have been one battle of Brunanburh and this means that a majority of the theories which have aroused such emotion and prompted such lengthy research and debate are red herrings.

# 7

# OF MYSTERY
# AND MEANING

… After this they sent messengers to king Olaf, giving out this as their errand, that king Athelstan would fain enhazel him a field and offer battle on Vin-heath by Vin-wood; meanwhile he would have them forbear to harry his land; but of the twain he should rule England who should conquer in the battle. He appointed a week hence for the conflict, and whichever first came on the ground should wait a week for the other. Now this was then the custom, that so soon as a king had enhazelled a field, it was a shameful act to harry before the battle was ended. Accordingly King Olaf halted and harried not, but waited till the appointed day, when he moved his army to Vin-heath.

… North of the heath stood a town. There in the town king Olaf quartered him, and there he had the greatest part of his force, because there was a wide district around which seemed to him convenient for the bringing in of such provisions as the army needed. But he sent men of his own up to the heath where the battlefield was appointed; these were to take camping-ground, and make all ready before the army came. But when the men came to the place where the field was enhazelled, there were all the hazel-poles set up to mark the ground where the battle should be.

The place ought to be chosen level, and whereon a large host might be set in array. And such was this; for in the place where the battle was to be the heath was level, with a river flowing on one side, on the other a large wood. But where the distance between the wood and the river was least (though this was a good long stretch), there King Athelstan's men had pitched, and their tents quite filled the space between wood and river. They had so pitched that in every third tent there were no men at all, and in one of every three but few. Yet when King Olaf's men came to them, they had then numbers swarming before all the tents, and the others could not get to go inside. Athelstan's men said that their tents were all full, so full that their people had not nearly enough room. But the front line of tents stood so high that it could not be seen over them whether they stood many or few in depth. Olaf's men imagined a vast host must be there. King Olaf's men pitched north of the hazel-poles, toward which side the ground sloped a little.

Chapter LII, *Egil's Saga*

The mystery surrounding the whereabouts of the battle of Brunanburh has occupied many a northern local historian for centuries. It should, in fairness, have occupied national historians too and it is unfortunate that, generally speaking, it has not.[1] Contemporary descriptions of the battle are few and far between. The *Anglo-Saxon Chronicle* gives the most glorious account of it, but it is the much later *Egil's Saga* which records topographical features that might prove useful for the battlefield detective. But we must be careful what we do with our scanty descriptions of battles when we are trying to hunt for a site. It would be easy to take any short description of a battle anywhere in Western Europe and find a hill that fitted an account, or a marsh adjacent to a river with a fortification in the rear that would fit a contemporary description of the battle and then place it in a landscape by matching these features to existing terrain. The result invariably would be that we would end up hundreds of miles away from the truth in most cases.

The descriptions of the battle that are in any way useable come down to us from William of Malmesbury's lengthy account (which states that the Olaf in question was in fact Olaf Sihtricson and makes no mention of Guthrifthson), *Egil's Saga* and the chronicles of Ingulf (an abbot of Croyland in Lincolnshire who died in 1109). William's account, for all its faults, may be based on a lost manuscript which he saw called *bella Etheltani regis* ('the wars of King Athelstan'). Listed in 1247 along with other texts as a manuscript at Glastonbury Abbey, this important piece of evidence is now lost.

The descriptions are at slight variance with each other and Ingulf has less respect paid to it than Egil, who similarly is not held to be as reliable as Malmesbury, whom many would say has his own failings. The order of battle which they strive to record can be summed up quite simply and is set out below. First of all, we should look at what is generally accepted to be the tradition of the encounter, including the preamble to the battle which is largely based on William of Malmesbury, with some insertions from the other traditions, since so many Brunanburh hunters have used snippets of information here and there to back up their claims.

Athelstan's army had not all arrived at the battlefield, or so the tradition goes. He encouraged Olaf to come deeper into England so that his own victory would be all the more glorious, and decided to buy time by striking a deal with the northerners that there would be no more ravaging of his kingdom until a decision was made on the battlefield, a place which would be specially enhazelled, or ring-fenced. The delay surrounding these negotiations while Olaf ravaged Athelstan's northern domains attracted some accusations of negligence towards the English king. Meanwhile, Athelstan had cleverly pitched his tents on the slope of a hill to make it look like there were a great deal more men present than there really were. The Strathclyde king suggested a night attack on Athelstan's camp, which was defended by Thorolf and Alfgar, whose job it seems was the protection of northern Mercia. Olaf subsequently disguised himself as a harper and entered the English camp to establish the whereabouts of Athelstan's tent. Indeed, Olaf performed as a minstrel at the court of Athelstan and was rewarded with gifts by the unsuspecting king. As he left the camp, Olaf discarded the gift and buried it in the sand. A member of Athelstan's army, perhaps a mercenary, spotted Olaf and, recognising him, rushed to tell the king who he had seen. Athelstan greatly chastised the man for not apprehending Olaf, but the man defended himself by saying that he could not betray a man whom he had once given vows to himself. The warrior wisely advised Athelstan that he had better move his tent lest the weight of a surprise attack fall on this most important quarter. This the king did and his spot was replaced with the tent of the bishop of Sherborne and his warriors when they arrived at the field of battle. At night, the two Viking leaders of Olaf's army, Adils and Hryngr, advanced on the English camp and attacked the unfortunate bishop of Sherborne. Alfgar and Thorolf rose to the sound of commotion and headed toward the battle. Adils' unit assaulted the warriors of Alfgar and Hryngr's unit fought against the men of Thorolf. Alfgar seems to have been soundly rebuffed in the fight and he withdrew from the field and eventually fled the country in disgrace. Adils then brought his forces to bear upon the struggling Thorolf, who called upon his brother Egil to help. Egil's men were strong but relatively few in number. They were ordered to stand firm or head to the woods if they had to. Thorolf somehow managed to fight his way to the enemy standard beneath which he dispatched Hyrngr. Adils, on seeing this, ordered his retreat and the battle was won for the mercenaries of Athelstan.

There followed a night of rest. On hearing of the struggle, Athelstan then began to arrange his forces in order of battle. Egil, with his small troop of brave warriors, was set in the front of the main battle lines ready for swift deployment to areas of decision on the battlefield. Thorolf's Vikings, with some Englishmen, were set against the forces of Olaf, as were the whole West Saxon division under Athelstan. Olaf's division expanded to match the size of Athelstan's division, an evolution which gives the impression of a high degree of tactical organisation, but which must have thinned his line considerably. On the other side of the battlefield, the Mercians and Londoners under Turketyl were formed up against the forces of the Scottish king, Constantine.

Thorolf's mercenaries were very near a wood which was on their flank and they advanced quickly to give battle to the Irish contingents in Olaf's division who opposed them. As Thorolf advanced, his men were hit in the flank by a cleverly deployed ambush commanded by Adils, who rushed from the wood with his men. Egil's independent unit rushed to the rescue of his brother, joining in with what had become a battle within a battle.

Meanwhile, Turketyl advanced against the Scots with his large division and detailed the leader Singin to take the men of London and

Worcester, who advanced and crashed into the Picts and Orkneymen. Soon, Constantine's son got into trouble and was unhorsed. The main division of the Scots and Cumbrians under Constantine advanced on Turketyl, putting him under great pressure, so much so that he had to release his grip on the son of the Scottish king. At a critical moment, Singin fell upon the young prince with a blow that killed him. The main Scottish and Cumbrian division began to withdraw, releasing Turketyl and the wandering Egil to fall with their men on the rear of Olaf's division which was heavily engaged to the front with the West Saxons of Athelstan and his brother Edmund. Athelstan broke his sword in the struggle at this stage and had it immediately, almost magically, replaced. Now there was no way out for Olaf and here was the greatest slaughter in the battle. What remained of his division squeezed itself to the rear and escaped. The victory was emphatically Athelstan's.

What are we to make of this concocted miscellany of semi-legends? A great deal, in fact. There is much here that makes sense. In fact, a clear picture emerges of the nature of the battlefield and the course of the battle. The enhazelled field need not worry us, unusual as it may appear. This was an ultimate showdown and Olaf, Athelstan and Constantine knew it. So, it seems, preparations were made for the battle to commence at *Vin-Heithr* a week after the message had been sent to Olaf to this effect.[2]

As for the appearance of the battlefield itself, we will no longer be able to see the hazel poles or the remains of Athelstan's cleverly placed tents, or, indeed, the small fortification which has variously been described as a 'town' or 'city' down the years, but we may just be able to see similarities in the modern landscape. The dangers of this approach are outlined above, but for the sake of argument, we should be looking for a battlefield with a river on one side and a wood on another with open heath ground in the middle which is gently sloping to the north. This hardly narrows down the options and has unfortunately provided a misleading blueprint for Brunanburh hunters for over a century.

On the matter of the great hunt to solve the mystery of Brunanburh, the story is full of oddities and intrigues and a great many local legends. People in the north of England have come to jealously guard their claims to the battle site, knowing full well how significant it was. This, of course, has lead to competing schools of thought. It makes sense to list the known historical spellings of Brunanburh in the sources, since so many of the competing claims are based on the simple fact that the name of a place sounds like the word. It soon becomes apparent that the etymologists have their work cut out in the quest for Brunanburh.

The historical sources give a variety of names to the battle. They are as follows:

BURH — A FORTIFIED PLACE

*Brunesburh / Bruneburh / Brunesburith* — Henry of Huntingdon.
*Brunanburh / Brunannburh / Brunanbyrig / Brunanbyri* —
   The *Anglo-Saxon Chronicle*
*Brimanburh* — Higden
*Banborow* — Capgrave
*Brunnanbyrg / Brunnanburch / Brumenburh / Brunebergh / Bruneberih /*
   *Brumanburgh* — Roger of Hoveden
*Brunanburgh / Brunesburgh* — Langtoft (a Humber protagonist)
*Brunenburh / Brunnenburh* — Matthew of Westminster
   (a Humber protagonist)
*Bruneberih* — Roger of Wendover (a Humber protagonist)
*Brunnanburch* — Chronicles of Melrose (a Humber protagonist)
*Brunneburgh* — Brompton
*Brunesberich* — Bart. Cotton


WEORC — FORTIFICATION

*Æt Brunanwerc / Brunnanwerc* — Simeon of Durham
   (a Humber protagonist)
*Bruneswerc / Burneswest (corruption of -werc) / Brunewerche* —
   Geffrei Gaimar


DUN — HILL (FORT)

*Brunandune* — Æthelweard
*Brunesdown* — Leland
*Weondune / Wendune* — Simeon of Durham
*Duinbrunde / Dunbrunde* — Chronicle of the Picts and Scots

FELD — OPEN GROUND
*Brunefeld/Brenefeld/Bruneveld* — William of Malmesbury
*Bruningafeld* — Charter B.C.S. 727 (dubious)

FORD — PASSAGE OVER A STREAM
*Bruneford* — William of Malmesbury
*Bruneford* — Ingulf (who adds 'In Northumbria')
*Brumford/Brymford/Brunfort* — Ralph Higden of Chester
   (a Humber protagonist)
*Brumford* — Camden

MISC.
*Broninis* — Aeddius, Vita S. Wilfridi
*Brun* — Brut y Twysogion
*Bellum Brune* — Annales Cambriæ
*othlyn* [sic] — *Annals of Clonmacnoise*
*Vinheiði/Vinheath* — Egil's Saga

The fact that the battle site has not been confidently identified has led people to make some claims for it in places which have ranged from the reasonable to the ridiculous. There are in fact, over thirty claimants to the site of the battle. Most of the candidates are listed below, with a brief explanation of the strengths or weaknesses of their claim, after which we examine a few of the more likely candidates in detail.

1. Axminster, Devon — Camden tells us that there were tombs here of Saxon noblemen who were killed in the battle. Their presence may well point to an involvement of Devonshire thegns in the battle, but hardly points to the place being the actual site of the battle, just as Malmesbury (where two princes were also buried after the battle) does not pretend to be Brunanburh.
2. Banbury, Oxfordshire — included only on the grounds that the name sounds similar. It is geographically too far away from the known theatre of war in the 930s.
3. Bromfield, Somerset — same argument as for 2, above. Also, wildly at variance with the theatre of war described by the sources.
4. Dunbar, near the Firth of Forth — at, or near, Dunbar, Athelstan is said to have prayed for success in his war with the Scots. This is

almost certainly the campaign of the great expedition of 934 which entered Scotland and not that of Brunanburh in 937.

5. Brumford, Northumberland – in the right theatre, but possibly too far from the Humber, if we accept that the Humber was used by the allies.

6. Bamburgh, Northumberland – similar argument to 5, above.

7. Kirkburn, near Driffield, Yorkshire – case examined below.

8. Burnham, Thornton Curtis – case examined below.

9. Brumby, near Scunthorpe, Lincolnshire – same argument as 2, above.

10. Bourne, South Lincolnshire – possibly derived from the name Brunne, but no other evidence.

11. Bourne, near Poulton, Lancashire – same argument as 10, above.

12. Bromfield/Brunefeld, Cumberland – five miles from the Solway Firth. Good etymological argument, but not far enough into Athelstan's domains to be in agreement with many of the sources.

13. Brindle, near Preston, Lancashire – same argument as 2, above.

14. Bamber/Bamford, near Rochdale – Cuerdale hoard of c.902 not good enough corroborating evidence.

15. Burnley (Mereclough), Lancashire – case examined below.

16. Elslack, near Skipton, Yorkshire – claim based loosely on the nearby Otley being the 'Plaines of othlyn' [sic], from the Irish sources.

17. Bromborough on the Wirral peninsula – case examined below.

18. Burnswork, Dumfriesshire – case examined below.

19. Aldborough, near Boroughbridge, sixteen miles from York – a Roman road network converges here and there are known to have been fourteenth-century battles in the area, but there is no evidence for Brunanburh.

20. Barnborough, near Conisbrough in southern Northumbria – an attractive theory with a name that means 'Barni's fortification', but its case is eclipsed by the case for nearby Brinsworth.

21. Brinsworth, near Rotherham – case examined below.

Clearly, some candidates have better qualifications than others. Bromborough in the Wirral has been one of the more abiding ones. The peninsular had been put forward as a possible location before Dodgson undertook his examination of the etymology of Bromborough,[4] but central to his argument[5] was the expertly presented sequence of name changes which he says led from the Old

English Brunanburh to the modern place name of Bromborough. The sequence runs thus: Brunanburh leads to Bruneburgh which leads to Brunburgh. This can give rise to Brumburgh which itself leads to the modern name Bromborough. No one has really challenged this philological exercise. It is lauded as a fairly sound argument, even though the later medieval versions and variants of the name do not necessarily chronologically occur in the order in which the philologist suggests in his analysis of the sequence.

So, if Bromborough is identified as the historical Brunanburh, then surely we have the battle site? Not necessarily. The philological argument, although sound, simply gives us a fairly reliable basis for concluding that here near the base of the Wirral peninsular was a place called Brunanburh. What sort of a place was it? Where is the evidence for it being a fortification of the type we expect to find from so many other sources that mention the battle? We have seen that this area was a vital one in the early tenth century and it was here that the legendary Ingimund had come from Ireland and sought permission from Æthelflæd to settle. A war had followed and a siege of Chester too. The theory deserves exploration. This area was clearly a frontier area in the early years of the tenth century. But was it such a place in 937 after all Athelstan had done to push his frontier to Eamont and the line of the Duddon and could a Norse-Irish invasion have taken place right into the flank of his new empire? There is no good reason why it should not have done. The Mersey would be perfectly navigable and the Wirral peninsular would provide an admirable natural defence for an invasion force, having water on three sides. All the invader had to do would be to meet Athelstan at the neck of the peninsula, without over-stretching his supply lines, win the battle, and England was open to him. In fact, in 1066, this is precisely what happened, but not in the Wirral peninsula. William the Conqueror had landed at Pevensey, then he had camped at Hastings, an area which at the time represented more of a peninsula than it does today, having large river estuaries on two sides of William's camp and the English Channel to the rear. The distance from the coast to the battlefield site at Senlac ridge is just seven miles. Senlac ridge occupies the central sector in a narrow stretch of land which it can be argued forms the neck of a peninsula. William had fought a battle within reach of his supply lines. So, there are similarities. But Olaf lost his battle and William won his. For William the hinterland was opened up, even though he wisely chose a coastal route on his journey north. For Olaf, it would have been a dangerous sea journey and a chance to think again.

There is a great attractiveness about the Bromborough bid. Notwithstanding the place name evidence, the very fact that a fleet from Dublin, meeting up perhaps with a fleet from the Isle of Man and the Western Isles, could land in the Wirral peninsula is a patently obvious and historically proven phenomenon. But what of the Scots and the men of Strathclyde? How would they rendezvous with the Vikings? The obvious answer to that would be that a combined fleet came by sea to the Wirral. It has been argued that Bromborough, despite the strength of the etymological argument, is an unlikely place for the battle of Brunanburh since the site is walkable from the shore. This would make a mockery of the Brunanburh poem which states that all night long, mounted companies chased the Vikings until they reached their ships. Whatever the etymological case, the historical argument sits uncomfortably at Bromborough.

Barton in Lincolnshire has been a claimant, too. A Mr Hesleden fixed the site at Barton, placing Olaf's camp at Barrow and Athelstan's at Burnham, stating that Burnham was formerly spelled *Brunnum*.[6] Here, at Brunnum, was an eminence known as 'Black Hold', where Hesleden believed the actual battle was fought. Lincolnshire's claims are based on a number of places which sound similar to Brunanburh. Brinkburn, for example is another candidate and was called *Brincaburh* by John of Hexham in 1154.[7]

Some base their claim on the possession of a place name that merely sounds right coupled with a general argument that the site in question lies within the territory of one of the antagonists. This is usually tied in with a brief survey of terrain features and names which might fit. *Burnswork* in Ecclesham, Dumfriesshire, is a case in point.[8] The author of this theory bases his identification on the interpretation of Geffrei Gaimar's *Brunswerce* with Burnswork. Furthermore, he goes on to point out that just 3½ miles to the south of the site is a hill known as Brown Moor which matches the description of *Vinheithr*. A farm on the western slope is called Whins, which would match Simeon of Durham's *Weondune*, and the name of the farm at the foot of the hill is Pennersaughs, possibly derived from Penrsax ('Hill of the Saxons') as it was described in 1194-1214. We are told that there are other 'Pensax' derivatives in both Worcestershire and Dorset. But most significantly, we learn that Brown Moor was once called Dumbretton – 'Hill of the Britons'. Quite where this leaves the earnest researcher is anyone's guess. It is the sort of approach that has confused the issue for centuries. That is not to say that there is no significance at all to any of these place names from the Scottish camp. As we have seen, Athelstan is known to have campaigned in Scotland in 934, but then so had many southern English and Northumbrian English monarchs before him. Also, it seems odd that what was clearly a fight for power over the control of the area of the kingdom of York, should take place in Dumfriesshire.

Lancashire and Yorkshire are clearly the most likely areas for the battle. Simeon of Durham stated that the allies came up the Humber with 615 ships, and Florence of Worcester stated that it was a combined fleet which landed in the Humber and that Constantine had been the instigator of the campaign.[9] All this provides us with strong evidence for the Yorkshire case. Lancashire, as we shall see, was also no stranger to Viking traffic from Ireland. The Lancashire story appears to have started with the work of two authors. Thomas Turner Wilkinson published a paper on his interpretation of the site in 1857.[10] Charles Hardwick, working independently from Wilkinson, later published a book, a chapter of which argued for a Lancashire site.[11] Thomas Booth, in a series of newspaper articles written for the 'Literary Corner' of the *Burnley Express* in the 1890s, stirred up something of a hornet's nest for a while, arguing for the area around Burnley being the site of the battle, dismissing most of Hardwick's efforts in favour of the much earlier work by T. T. Wilkinson.

Hardwick's arguments, it seems, were based on the nomenclature of places in the district around Cuerden, near Preston, and his only corroborating evidence was the Cuerdale hoard of silver coins and hack-silver found in the banks of the Ribble in 1840. The Cuerdale hoard is an impressive discovery. It is doubtless the treasure chest of a Scandinavian army, but close examination of the chronology of its coins forbids a date to be assigned to it later than *c*.902. This was the year that the Norse were temporarily expelled from Ireland by a powerful native uprising and there followed a generation of settlement in the north-west of England, fundamentally altering the demographics there. Despite the fact that the Cuerdale hoard cannot be used as evidence for the Norse-Irish army in the Brunanburh campaign, it remains an intriguing find. Clearly, the Ribble was used as a thoroughfare into Northumbria from Ireland in the generation before Brunanburh, and the notion that Lancashire conceals the famous battle of 937 should not be entirely discarded. In fact, another Lancashire argument bases itself around the idea that Athelstan had granted land in the north of the county whilst on campaign. Hardwick wrote 'In the early part of the seventeenth century lived one William Elston who placed the following on record':

> It was once told to me by Mr Alexander Elston, who was uncle to my father and sonne of Ralph Elston, my great-grandfather, that the said Ralph Elston had a deede or coppice of a deede in the Saxon tongue where it did appear that King Athelstan lying in camp in the county upon the occassion of warres gave the land of Ethelston unto one who himself Belsyred.[12]

Elston, he says, which is a settlement in the parish of Preston, was formerly *Ethelston*. There are several Elstons and Altons situated alongside the main Roman road between Ribchester and Kirkham, including a place known as Athelston Fold. Lancashire is full of these intriguing and seductive stories and there may be much to recommend them.

Citing the term 'Bellum Brune', used by the *Annales Cambriae*, Thomas Booth claims that this means, in effect 'the Battle of the Brun' and so goes on to look for the site along the banks of that river. Brunanburh, he suggests, means 'the place of the springs', a popular misconception at the time. Booth launches into a pinpoint identification of the site, fixing it at Mereclough, a few miles south-east of Burnley, at a place known locally as the 'Battle Spot'. The geography of this place does indeed fit the description of the battlefield given in *Egil's Saga*, as doubtless many others do. The River Brun rises here (so here is our 'place of springs') and there is at this field a great stone known through local lore as 'the Battle Stone'. Nearby, it is claimed, is a hill which would surely do for Brunandene. An admirable attempt to justify all these thought processes is emphasised by Booth's quotation of a Mr Weddle of Warrington, who wrote an essay on the matter in 1857. If only history would be so kind as to follow Weddle's reason. He had said that the:

> … uncertainty of the whereabouts of the battlefield is a good reason
> why it should be sought in some place half forgotten.

The Mereclough bid clearly has some strength. But how are we to reconcile the fact that not every source gives Brunanburh the name which we have come to expect. Simeon of Durham, as has been noted, supplies us with the name Weondune or Wendune. Booth gives us an answer. Wendune and Swinden are one and the same, he says. There is a Swinden (which, incidentally, means 'hill of pigs'), just a short distance from Mereclough. The strength of the Mereclough bid is given greater muscle by the legend that there were five kings buried in a green hollow on the hillside near the stone and that a chest of gold lies buried somewhere on Worsthorne Moor. Could these be the five kings who were slain by the English at Brunanburh? One can be seduced by such legends and, at the same time, be undone by them. Booth himself stated that he walked across the battlefield with an old local man of some considerable knowledge and asked him why he thought the place was called 'the Battle Spot'. The answer he got did not help him:

> Aw don't know, but aw hev yerd it said that cock battles used to be
> fought here upon this spot an' that's heaw it geet it name.

Booth had made some interesting points in his series of writings. Principal amongst these was his insistence that the battle was a frontier encounter and that we should be looking for it around an area that was at the time conspicuously fortified. His attempts to follow this line of reasoning by tracing what he thought was a line of forts over a nine-mile stretch of countryside were hampered by a misunderstanding of the archaeological period of each of his monuments, but the reasoning was laudable.

All we have to do is reconcile ourselves with the notion that the Norse-Irish fleet with its Scottish allies came into England via the Humber and not from the west. This may seem odd when there are so many navigable rivers on the west coast, such as the Ribble, Mersey, Dee, Lune and Wyre. In fact, in the banks of the Wyre a local historian discovered hundreds of human bones at Burnaze, between Thornton and Fleetwood Burnaze. The latter had once been called 'Brune'. We know that these routeways into Northumbria were used by the Norse from Ireland, too. But why should we disbelieve our sources which say that the fleet entered England via the Humber? There is no reason to challenge the Durham tradition, or the statement of Florence of Worcester. There had, in fact, been other Norse-Irish invasions which had come down the east coast.[13]

And so we turn from the Lancashire argument to the equally passionate Yorkshire one which bases itself on the matter of an eastern seaboard point of entry into Athelstan's England. In 1892 a notice appeared in the *Bulmer's History and Directory of East Yorkshire* stating the following:

> It is contended on very strong evidence that the famous Battle of Brunanburh was fought at Battleburn, a few miles to the west of Driffield, and that the Army of Anlaf [Olaf] was encamped at Elmswell in this parish. A series of earthworks at this place points to such a conclusion. By the side of an entrenchment near the supposed site of the battle, Mr Mortimer opened sixty graves, all apparently Anglo-Saxon. In a distinct portion of an adjacent burial ground, the bodies were found to have been cremated or partially so, from which circumstance it is inferred they were those of Scandinavians, amongst whom the practice of burning their dead still existed. Mr Holderness of Driffield has written an exhaustive pamphlet on Brunanburh and its site, and those of our readers who wish to go more deeply into the question cannot do better than study that work.

The graves were almost certainly those of early migration-period Saxons practising a mixed-rite method of burying their dead, but Thomas Holderness's argument[14] did not pivot upon this extraordinary discovery, although he was keen to mention it at the end of his discourse. Holderness was a proud and emotional gentleman who frequently paid what he called 'pilgrimages' to the spot near Kirkburn where he believed the battle was fought. There are many misunderstandings in his argument and he displayed only a poor grasp of the tricky subject of etymology, but there are aspects of his case which are worth consideration. First of all, Holderness had to explain why the East Riding of Yorkshire should be the favoured area for the battle. He does this by pinning his argument on the widely reported fact that the allies came with their ships up the Humber estuary. Simeon of Durham, Florence of Worcester, Roger of Hoveden and the chronicle of Melrose all state this fact, he claims. Local fishermen told him that the Humber is a dangerous and choppy place and that the allies would surely not have considered it appropriate to anchor there. Instead, they would have sailed north as far up the River Hull as possible to set themselves up for an attack on York from the east. The Hull was navigable up to a place called Emmotland, which he identifies with the Ea motum of the chronicle. The advance of the allies would have taken them through Driffield and then they would have set up camp at Elmswell, whilst Athelstan set his camp at Kirkburn. The heathland between these places was where the battle was fought. Elmswell, he tells us, is a compound of the Old Norse words 'Hjalmr', meaning battle and 'Velli', meaning field. Hjalmr is equally likely to have been a personal name however, and when it appears in the ancient literature it does so very often as a poetic device.

There are plentiful springs at the Kirkburn site and Holderness argued that if Brunanburh meant 'the place of springs', then this was surely it. The burns of Battleburn, Eastburn and Southburn were all places of streams and surrounded the battlefield. Coneygarth field nearby has a name derived from the Scandinavian for king (Konungr) and enclosure (garðr), he says. This must be the place where Olaf and Constantine camped. Holderness refuted suggestions made to him at the time that the term 'Coney' meant 'Rabbit' and that the field name was consistent with hundreds of other later field names in England. In his defence he stated that Coney Street in York became King's Street, and not Rabbit Street as one might expect. Besides, the place to which he was referring was once called Konyng garth.

Just as Thomas Booth of Lancashire had done, Thomas Holderness brought folklore into the tale. The words of local wise men, he assumed, must surely be based on something other than mere conjecture:

> I was agreeably surprised by being informed, by Mr Johnson, of Southburn, a trustworthy but educated man, that an old gentleman named Harrison, now dead, had informed him, many years ago, that a battle was fought here. I will give his statement in his own words, 'Yis, there was a battle there. Battleburn was thick o'battle, an when

Danes was bet they went up ti Ga'tan. They we' campt at Ga'tan an Elmswell'.

One final enigmatic statement is made by Holderness. Horseshoes were found on his battlefield. They cannot be traced today, but Holderness insists that those which were found around the area of Athelstan's camp were much larger than those found at Coneygarth field and that this would be consistent with what we should expect of Athelstan's army. It is an argument without any hope of proof, but it does at least tell us that Holderness was earnest in his endeavours and clearly sought to get close to the spirit of Athelstan's imperial army.

A historical line of argument not yet promoted by any of our protagonists is that taken in recent years by both Michael Wood and Alfred Smyth.[15] It bases itself on a comparison of the events of 937 and those of 940, when Olaf had his second chance to repeat his assault on England and did so this time with more success. Both arguments agree on a Humber entry but Wood, following Cockburn, places the site in the region of Brinsworth. Smyth, however, controversially suggests that Olaf in 937 would have done what he did in 940 and penetrate deep into England right to the boundary of the Danelaw in the south Midlands. In this latter campaign, the centre of activity had been the southern limits of the Five Boroughs of the Danelaw and the English Mercian frontier where Æthelflæd and her husband had built their forts. The first phase of the 937 campaign, he argues, would have been exactly the same as it was in 940 – Olaf must have taken York. This is not mentioned in the sources, but is taken to be of singular importance in the argument. After the invasion force had gathered in York, it would have taken the Roman roads south into northern Mercia and then pushed south into the heartland of the Five Boroughs. This would certainly make sense of William of Malmesbury's statement that Athelstan delayed his response and allowed the enemy to come deep into England. And so Smyth suggests that the battle of Brunanburh took place in the region of a forested area known as Bruneswald to the north of Watling Street on the borders of Northampton and Huntingdonshire, but brings only historical circumstance into the argument and precious little of the etymology required to pinpoint the site. There are a number of other problems with the argument. It assumes that in 940 Athelstan's brother, Edmund, had no idea that history was about to repeat itself. He had even fought at Brunanburh in 937 and must surely have been aware of how the enemy had conducted its campaign and how it had arrived at the field of Brunanburh. If, in 940, Olaf simply repeated the exercise, Edmund would surely have been waiting for him, but all the evidence points to the fact that in 940 Edmund was taken by surprise and Olaf was able to campaign deeper into England than he had ever been before. In 937 Olaf was soundly rebuffed. He had managed to get far enough into England to cause great concern to Athelstan, but Malmesbury's 'Thunderbolt' had met him and defeated him. In 940 Olaf tried again, but this time went further. The southern Danelaw case remains, however, an interesting argument. If it could be proved, it would explain why the history of the search for Brunanburh has been so fruitless: because people have been looking in the wrong place. Smyth's is the southernmost argument for the battle and does at least have a little historical strength.

But the argument which has the greatest weight by virtue of the exhaustive nature of the research which has gone into it, is John Henry Cockburn's case for Templeborough in Brinsworth near Rotherham. Michael Wood gave this case fresh impetus over recent years.[16] Cockburn's approach is largely etymological, but it is almost overwhelming in its detail. The place names of Yorkshire, he says, are teeming with references to the period of Brunanburh.[17] Ulley is named after Olaf Cuaran and Herringthorpe and Gilthwaite are named after Hring and Egil who feature as Scandinavian leaders in *Egil's Saga*. Alston and Olavesness also have particular relevance to the site of the battle of Brunanburh. The argument is that Brunanburh was fought at the frontier of Mercia and Northumbria near the famous Whitwell's Gate, or 'Gap' mentioned in the poem of the recapture of the Five Boroughs. This area has profound historical significance and is also an area where further dramas would unfold in the years after Brunanburh. Æthelflæd, it is argued, had conspicuously fortified this frontier against the Scandinavian threat from York. Cockburn argues that she built Brunesburh (which is in fact the missing Bremesburh fort), Scergate (Worksop), Ciresburh and Weardburh (near Osward Bec) along the Sheffield–Rotherham–Worksop frontier. Brunesburh would therefore be the fortification established at Templeborough on the site of the old Roman camp at Brinsford, which he says means 'ford of the

Brigantes', but which others suggest means 'Bryni's ford'. Wincobank (which he identifies as the lost Wigingamere) and Templeborough have apparently left their mark on the memory of folk in that area. There is an old Yorkshire proverb which goes:

*When all the world shall be aloft*
*Then Hallamshire will be God's croft,*
*Wincobank and Templeborough*
*Will buy all England through and through.*

Castleford, to the north of this site, is where Olaf would have been based before the battle. Here five wapentakes (hundreds) converge and it is the place where Ricknild Street crosses the Aire. Athelstan would have been at Aston. The battle took place, says Cockburn, around Brunesburh and was finally decided at Morthen (which means 'slaughter field'), after which the pursuit (which took all day) was to Maltby and Balby and the escape was up the Aire to the Humber.

Michael Wood argued that the battle took place on a hill, the Weondun of Simeon, or the Brunandun of Æthelweard. Also, he drew attention to the fact that the submission of Rægnald to Edward had taken place in 920 after the building of the fort at Bakewell and that this region was the general theatre of the war in 937. South of the confluence of the rivers Don and Rother was a strategic fort on White Hill, called Brynesford in the Domesday survey. There was later a ditched manor house here. As for the Vinheithr of *Egil's Saga*, it is suggested by Wood that the word could well be a literal translation of the Latin Wendun.[18] Furthermore, a much later Scandinavian scribe is noted as describing as the Vina, a tributary of the Humber.[19] Weondun is a term which very probably means 'Holy Hill' and is one which is rarely used by northerners. It must be a southern term, comparable to Weedon in Buckinghamshire, for example. White Hill may have once been Weondun, although the early forms of the name which date from the fifteenth century suggest Wiht (a bend in the river) as opposed to Wih, meaning 'holy'. Furthermore, the landscape around the Brinsworth site can be seen to match that of the *Egil's Saga* description.

The site of the battle of Brunanburh is still not firmly established. Nobody seems to have been able to reconcile the two opposing camps.

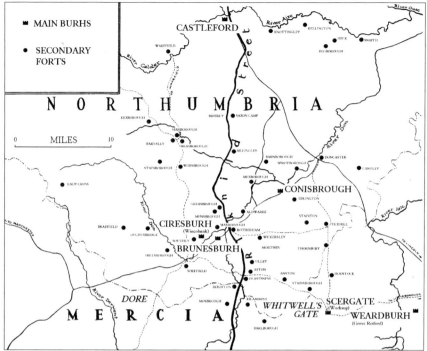

The region of the Brunanburh campaign. After Cockburn 1931, Brunesburh is marked as one of the central forts. This is one of two strong possible locations for the battle of Brunanburh, fought in 937. The Mercian-Northumbrian border was constantly disputed in this period.

The suggestion in this volume is that we can at least consider halting the tendency to pose the east or west coast argument. It seems that the entrance of the allies via the Humber is much harder to refute than to accept. Accepting that the battle was fought on the frontier of Mercia and Northumbria means that we have to accept the compelling but incomplete arguments of Cockburn and Wood. And, by association, we must reject Bromborough on the Wirral, the only place which has been confidently identified as once bearing the name of Brunanburh. It is a complex debate for which we still need more evidence, but the weight of the Yorkshire argument may yet prove Bromborough to be one of history's great red herrings. Let us leave the argument with the notion that wherever it was fought, the legacy of Brunanburh meant more to people at the time than its location somewhere in a half-forgotten northern field.

## THE LEGACY OF BRUNANBURH

... the barbarian force... held the superiority no more... the king drove them off the shores of the ocean... the fields of Britain were consolidated into one, there was peace everywhere.

The Chronicle of Æthelweard

Æthelweard's words sound triumphant. They are matched, of course, by the *Anglo-Saxon Chronicle*'s poetic summary of events, but there is one important difference. Æthelweard states that the fields of Britain were at last a single unit again. Perhaps he can be forgiven for his optimism. Writing over fifty years after the event, he shows how the battle of Brunanburh had a galvanising effect across the whole region of the country settled by the descendants of the Angelcynn of yesteryear. They were English, and they knew it.

Political reality, however, was somewhat different. Although the 'fields of Britain', whether settled by Englishmen, Dane, Scot or Welshman, were once again under the wing of a single authority, Æthelweard would have known how soon the political impact of Brunanburh had faded away. He was aware of Olaf's resurgence and of the saga of the subsequent capture and subjugation of the Five Boroughs, but he recognised, as many others did throughout the tenth century, that Brunanburh had meant something more than just another military victory. The following modern translation of the famous poem in the *Anglo-Saxon Chronicle* demonstrates the lengths to which contemporaries went in order to justify the carnage at Brunanburh:

> *Here King Athelstan, leader of warriors,*
> *Ring-giver of men, and also his brother,*
> *the aetheling Edmund, struck life-long glory*
> *in strife around Brunanburh, clove the shield-wall,*
> *hacked the war-lime, with hammers' leavings.*
> *Edward's offspring, as was natural to them*
> *by ancestry, that in frequent conflict*
> *they defend land, treasures and homes*
> *Against every foe. The antagonists succumbed,*
> *The nation of Scots and seamen*
> *Fell doomed. The field darkened*

*with soldiers blood after in the morning time*
*the sun, that glorious star,*
*bright candle of God, the Lord Eternal,*
*glided over the depths, until the noble creature*
*sank to rest. There lay many a soldier*
*of the men of the North, shot over shield,*
*taken by spears; likewise Scottish also,*
*sated, weary of war. All day long*
*the West Saxons with elite cavalry* [20]
*pressed in the tracks of the hateful nation,*
*with mill-sharp blades severely hacked from behind*
*those who fled battle. The Mercians refused*
*hard hand-play to none of the heroes*
*who with Olaf, over the mingling of waves,*
*doomed in fight, sought out land*
*in the bosom of a ship. Five young*
*kings lay on the battlefield,*
*put to sleep by swords; likewise also seven*
*of Olaf's jarls, countless of the raiding-army*
*of seamen and Scots. There the ruler of*
*Northmen, compelled by necessity,*
*Was put to flight, to ship's prow,*
*With a small troop. The boat*
*was pushed afloat; the king withdrew,*
*saved life, over the fallow flood.*
*There also likewise, the aged Constantine*
*came north to his kith by flight.*
*The hoary man of war had no cause to exult*
*In the clash of blades; he was shorn of his kinsmen,*
*deprived of friends, on the meeting-place of peoples,*
*cut-off in strife, and left his son*
*on the place of slaughter, mangled by wounds,*
*young in battle. The grey-haired warrior,*
*old crafty one, had no cause to boast*
*in that clash of blades – no more had Olaf –*
*cause to laugh, with the remnants of their raiding-army,*
*that they were better in works of war*
*on the battlefield, in the conflict of standards,*

*the meeting of spears, the mixing of weapons,*
*the encounter of men, when they played*
*against Edward's sons on the field of slaughter.*
*Then, the Northmen, bloody survivors of darts,*
*Disgraced in spirit, departed on Ding's Mere,*
*In nailed boats over deep water,*
*To seek-out Dublin and their [own] land again.*
*Likewise the brothers both together,*
*king and aetheling, exultant in war,*
*sought kith. The land of Wessex.*
*They left behind to divide the corpses,*
*To enjoy the carrion, the dusky-coated,*
*Horny-beaked black raven,*
*And the grey-coated eagle, white rumped,*
*Greedy war-hawk, and the wolf,*
*Grey beast in the forest. Never yet in this island*
*Was there a greater slaughter*
*Of people felled by the sword's edges,*
*Before this, as books tell us,*
*Old authorities, since Angles and Saxons*
*came here from the east,*
*sought out Britain over the broad ocean,*
*warriors eager for fame, proud war-smiths,*
*overcame the Welsh, seized the country.*

The *Anglo-Saxon Chronicle* entry for 937,
Winchester Manuscript (A)

Henry of Huntingdon said of this great poem that although it was 'full of strange words and figurative language', it did at least allow us to 'learn from the majesty of the language about the majesty of this nation's deeds and courage.'[21] Naturally, we must be careful how we view such a statement, which comes from a later medieval historian, but the bombast and bellicosity is still there whichever way we look at it. But the poem of Brunanburh, remarkable though it is, is not alone in Europe as a work in praise of a Christian king who conquered on the battlefield: the Old High German *Ludwigslied* celebrated Louis III's victory at Saucourt in 881 in a similar way.

But in this English example, it is the choice of the method of commemoration in the *Anglo-Saxon Chronicle* which gives the game away if we are looking for a lasting legacy to Brunanburh. Throughout the medieval period, the dominant power groups across Christendom sought to justify and legitimise their positions through various means. The poem of Brunanburh can be seen in a similar light – as an attempt to justify something which was becoming increasingly apparent through-out the tenth century – that the English were becoming a nation. The dominance of this nation would extend to the far reaches of the north, as Egil had portrayed in his poem to Athelstan sung after the battle of Brunanburh:

> *Reindeer-trod hills obey*
> *Bold Athelstan's high sway.*

Alfred had been styled as 'king over all England except that which was under Danish domination' at his death. Already the loose confederation of Angelcynn was being observed as having a geographical dimension to it. And so it would continue as the relentless campaigns in the north went on. Athelstan's own *Rex Totius Britanniæ* legend explicitly stated his aspira-tions, which were something more than ruler of just England; for he was an emperor, ruler of the whole Roman province of Britannia. But behind this imperial veneer England was taking shape. His successors would be increasingly described as the kings of England: 'Eadmund Cyning, Engla þeoden' in 942 and 'Eadgar, Engla cyning' in 975 are examples.[22] The length of time that the Anglo-Saxons have been present in Britain is not missed by the poet of Brunanburh either. Their arrival and subsequent conquest of the Britons is recalled in heroic style and, just in case we thought that it was all made up, we are told that these are the things which the ancient books tell us. Further legitimisation is given to us by the often repeated refrain that there had never been greater slaughter than this since the English first came to Britain. This is not an unusual occurrence in Anglo-Saxon literature as it is designed to stress the historical importance of the battle to the reader. This was a big one. Nothing like it has hap-pened before. Our side achieved a spectacular victory and, like us, you should sing the praises of our royal line.

So, the poem of the battle of Brunanburh is a celebration of a new-found sense of Englishness gained by the mighty Athelstan? Yes, in a way it is, but to leave our interpretation of it here would be to miss the point entirely. Scholars of literature have looked at this most unusual of the five poems in the *Anglo-Saxon Chronicle* very carefully. The inescapable conclusion about it is that whilst it contains some obvious Anglo-Saxon traits such as the statement that there had never been a greater slaughter than this since the English first came to Britain, there is also a distinct Scandinavian ring to the poet's tone and in at least five cases the poet adopts known Scandinavian literary devices or terms.[23]

As John Niles has pointed out, the poem shares more in common with the poem of the battle of Hafsfjord (where Harald Fairhair defeated a coalition against him in 872) than it does with other Anglo-Saxon poems. Here there are clashing swords and crashing shields. Here also, the king is lauded by the poet and his impeccable lineage used to justify his victory. But this is not the only Scandinavian clue. An Anglo-Saxon, for example, is unlikely in the tenth century to refer to Ireland as Iraland, for this is the Old Norse term for that country. The English at the time appear to have referred to it as Scotta ealand or used the Latin form *Hibernia*, although it makes an appearence as Iraland in 918 (*Anglo-Saxon Chronicle* version A). It could be argued that the English were familiar enough with the term by the mid-tenth century to have used it comfortably in a work such as this, but it is pointed out that in version A of the *Anglo-Saxon Chronicle* the scribe who is copying the poem was confused enough by the term to have substituted the phrase 'hira land' (their land) for the word Iraland. This would have made more sense to him.[24]

The word *cnear* is used for 'warship' in the poem. A Knorr, to give it its Scandinavian term, was not in fact a warship, but a trading vessel, but it is used here in preference to an English term. The real clues are there in the use of kennings. Instead of describing a battle as a battle, Anglo-Saxon and Scandinavian poets and skalds might choose to use a kenning, describing it as a 'spear-meeting' or 'weapon-exchange'. Both of these examples, which are used in the poem, are thought to be strikingly original and Scandinavian in origin. The whole tone of the poem, which revels in violence and destruction and has the very ground 'resounding' with blood, is also thought to be a skaldic technique.[25]

Do these revelations change the way we see the real battle of Brunanburh? The poem is written in Old English and is clearly a piece of English literature. But the tenth century was a dynamic and cosmopolitan century and there were at the court of Athelstan poets and scholars from all over Europe. In particular there were Scandinavians. There were the jarls of the Danelaw in the English army. There had been Scandinavian mercenaries in Athelstan's army and one of them was himself a poet. What we are seeing here in the poem of the battle of Brunanburh is the influence of Old Norse techniques in Old English poetry, an influence which makes the latter all the stronger and more versatile. But how are we to imagine that this particular instance came about? Let us permit ourselves to envisage a scene in a half-empty timber hall somewhere in the north of England not long after the great battle. A well-educated English scribe is sitting down with a Scandinavian skald who is reciting a heroic tale about the battle in the manner of his kind. The scribe copies down what he can and checks his material with other English poets and literary specialists. The skald knows that he had better get this right, for in a few days his work will be recited in front of the king and his court. The flavour must suit the taste of everyone there, Englishman or Dane, but most of all the king must like it.

Nor is this great celebration confined to the Anglo-Saxon period. Englishmen would not forget the true meaning of the struggle on that bloody field. Tennyson famously translated the poem and had it published in *Ballads and Other Poems* in 1880. He based his version on his own son's prose translation of the poem which had been published in 1876 in the *Contemporary Review*. Hallam, Tennyson's son, spoke of his father's love for the rush of the alliterative verse and Tennyson's predictable keeping with the feel of the original poem won him praise. But the point is this: Tennyson's version was preceded by the following words which left his reader in no doubt as to what he thought of the small matter of interpreting history:

> Constantinus, King of the Scots, after having sworn allegiance to Athelstan allied himself with the Danes of Ireland under Anlaf, and invading England, was defeated by Athelstan and his brother Edmund with great slaughter at Brunanburh in the year 937.

But what would Olaf and Constantine make of the claim of an English dominance from Bamburgh to the south coast? Clearly, Brunanburh, as far as the Scots were concerned had indeed taken place 'far into England', but this notion may not have been shared by Olaf and his successors. The subsequent history of the north Midlands showed very clearly that leaders at York had a very different idea of where their kingdom started and finished and it had much to do with the inheritance of the ideas of ancient Northumbrian independence from the south coupled with (at its most extreme extent) a desire to control again the territories defined as 'Danish' by the treaty of Wedmore.

One issue remains: why was Brunanburh forgotten? Why did a battle-field stained with blood and lauded in contemporary literature disappear from view? For as long as the line of Edward occupied the throne, Brunanburh would be remembered. We have to realise that the history of a medieval people is linked with the history of its monarchs. New dynasties could bring changes in historical perception which would be powerful enough to remove legends and replace them with stories more pertinent to the needs of their own justifications. To find the answer to the question, modern historians will need to look to the centuries after the Norman Conquest. A new rule of law, a new form of government, even a new form of language were now the controlling aspects of the governance of England. The work had been done. England was already more than an idea, it was a kingdom ready for the taking. It is a measure of the success of the later Anglo-Saxon kings of England that, despite their difficulties, the nation which had been born at Brunanburh managed to survive the Norman Conquest. Now England's fortunes would be tied in with feudal Europe and its Scandinavian struggles would be consigned to legend. The power of poetry and the oral tradition would no longer be the tools for justification of power. Power will now be administered with a mailed fist. Somewhere along the way, the place in space and time known as the field of Brunanburh, where the English legitimised their claim to Britain, was utterly lost and a new place became the celebrated turning point in English fortune – the field of Senlac Ridge.

# 8

# THE SHADOW RETURNS

*Here King Edmund, Lord of the English,*
*Guardian of kinsmen, beloved instigator of deeds,*
*Conquered Mercia, bounded by the Dore,*
*Whitwell Gap and Humber river,*
*broad ocean-stream; five boroughs:*
*Leicester and Lincoln,*
*and Nottingham, likewise Stamford also*
*and Derby. Earlier the Danes were*
*under Northmen, subjected by force*
*in heathen's captive fetters,*
*for a long time until they were ransomed again,*
*to the honour of Edward's son,*
*protector of warriors, King Edmund.*
The *Anglo-Saxon Chronicle*, Winchester Manuscript (A).
The same poem is in all versions except for the much later (E) and (F).

The kingdom of the English pre-dates the Norman Conquest by well over a century. It is an Anglo-Saxon institution. Tracing its evolution, however, is not a straightforward matter, since it is composed of many parts, each having their own story to tell. But despite the fact that there are many dynamics to the tale of the rise of England in the tenth century, it can be argued that there was a driving force in the unity of the English people and that it came from both Wessex and Mercia.[1] The increasing confidence of the West Saxon line is reflected in the way that it styled itself. The use of certain terms is revealing (see appendix). When, under Alfred, Wessex regained the balance of power over the Danes in the south and began to take the offensive after the capture and restoration of London in the 880s, a new cultural affinity amongst the English was promoted by their king. The 'kingdom of the Anglo-Saxons' thus became a politically and culturally distinct unit.

Throughout the reign of Edward the Elder, the kingdom of the Anglo-Saxons retained its title and swept away its enemies. The armies of Edward and his sister conducted a methodical re-conquest of the Danish areas. Under Athelstan, however, a great drama had unfolded. By 927 the kingdom had not just evolved into the 'kingdom of the English', but its ruler had decided that, as king of the English, he had been elevated by the right hand of God himself to total power in the island of Britain. Later in Athelstan's reign, as we have seen, this claim was justified at sword's edge somewhere on the plains of Lothlynn.

The remarkable claims of Athelstan to be emperor of Britain begin around 927 after the treaty at Eamont. He had begun his reign as king of the Anglo-Saxons and subsequent charters showed him to be king of the English and also ruler over the Danes in the region of York, but only after receiving the submission of northern rulers at Eamont did he style himself as the great basilius, or imperial ruler, a self-styled *monarchus totius Britanniæ*. The divine elevation was never forgotten by Athelstan, for it served as a method of justification. With his charters revealing the connection to God, he was recalling the day of his Carolingian-style anointing and coronation. But there was a secular side to it too. In an English translation of a charter for 934 is a wording of the king's title which recalls the power struggles of yesteryear, this being the competition between every Anglo-Saxon ruler in the island of Britain for the position of Bretwalda. The Bretwaldas of the centuries preceding Athelstan had been powerful rulers who literally 'wealded the widest amount of power' in Britain. Their inspiration may well have come from a desire to emulate the rulers of Late Roman Britain. The office, if that is what we can call it, swung from Sussex to Wessex, then Kent, East Anglia and then to Northumbria which held sway until the late seventh century. Two out of the last three Northumbrian Bretwaldas had died facing the threat of a rising Mercian power. And so, it is not beyond reason to compare the Bretwalda struggles to the wars of Danish Northumbria against a southern 'king of kings' in the age of Athelstan. A most ancient drama was being performed. By the end of Athelstan's reign, the governmental apparatus was strong enough to allow for his aspiration to become a reality. The charter's words are as follows:

> Ongol Saxna cyning [and] brytæn walda ealles ðyses Iglandæs þurh Godæs sælene.

The idea was simple. The king of the English was the wielder of the widest power in Britain. And, what is more, he was given that position by God and through him he would rule.

But Olaf may not have seen it like this. He returned again to England just three years after Brunanburh and this time, the shadow spread across the whole of the Danelaw, touching the lives of those Danes who had already thrown in their lot with the king of the English.

## THROUGH DANISH EYES

The story of how the English Midlands and the north of the country were transformed into an Anglo-Danish society during the late ninth and tenth centuries is as controversial as it is complex. The problems which historians have encountered exist in how we define the place which became known as the Danelaw and in when we begin our acknowledgement of it. A further problem exists in who exactly is being called a Dane in the first place. Are the individual burials which are dotted around northern England, with their Anglo-Saxon swords, strap-ends and hybrid spear types[2] really the remains of pagan Danish warriors? The truth is bound to be more complex.

Although the Great Army over-wintered in England in 865-866, its members cannot be described as having 'settled' as such. Then, the army of the sons of Ragnar were still very much in the throes of a long and drawn out military and political campaign. Their mere presence as an army would not yet be enough to have a long-term effect on the material culture of England. Even the Danish camp at Repton, for some time the political centre of Scandinavian activity in England in the 870s, could not claim permanence in the Anglo-Saxon landscape, despite its overt symbolism. Something more than mere campaigning activity would have to happen for Anglo-Saxon life to become Anglo-Danish life in the Midlands and the north.

When Halfdan's army (which had split from its cousin, the great summer army of 871) took to Northumbria and began to settle the land there, and when in 877 some of Guthrum's men found land in Mercia exclusive of that which the English Mercian Ceolwulf was allowed to keep, the origins of the Danelaw are usually observed. But there is a great risk in going this far back. The Danelaw was an institution which evolved sometime after the treaty of Wedmore and it constantly changed as its leaders switched their allegiances, farmed their estates and went to church. Even the laws of Athelstan and Edmund, of which there are many, make no reference to the legal autonomy of the Danelaw, yet by the time of Edgar there was clearly some recognition that practices there had been different for some time.

The boundaries outlined by Alfred and Guthrum's treaty at Wedmore divided the Danish area of the country from the English. For much of the length of the boundary the demarcation line was Watling Street and the River Lea. The wording of the delineation went as follows:

> … Up the Thames, and then up the Lea, and along the Lea to its source, then in a straight line to Bedford, then up the Ouse to Watling Street.

Although the general distribution of Scandinavian place names suggest that these boundaries were roughly those of the later Danelaw, we must take into account that a great many matters were negotiated by treaty and that the Treaty of Wedmore just happens to be a surviving one. There is no mention of the boundary running all the way along Watling Street to Chester, for example, so we are left wondering what sort of arrangement was being made in north-west Mercia.

The first time we come across the term 'Dane-law' is in a piece of writing by Archbishop Wulfstan set down in the reign of Æthelred II (979-1016). Æthelred's law code (VI) contains a description of the punishment due to anyone plotting against the king's person and it makes a distinction between the triple ordeal applicable in English areas and those measures which apply under Danish law. It seems that the earlier codes of Edward the Elder, which spoke of legal arrangements in Danish areas being made in accordance with 'treaties', were being replaced by more tacit admissions from the southern court that things were always going to be done differently in the north. Edgar had allowed the Danes a certain amount of autonomy to make their own laws, yet the codes of Æthelred suggest a legal recognition of those practices. The point is, however, that whatever the peculiarities or differences in the Danelaw, it was the king of the English who was trying to integrate the whole thing. Ironically, it would later be the great Danish king of England, Cnut, who would continue this line by making sure that the autonomy enjoyed in the Danelaw would not extend to the keeping of the peace there.[3]

Snorri Sturluson was the first historian, writing in the thirteenth century, to observe that the settlement names of eastern England were largely Scandinavian. They do indeed keep themselves to the east of the treaty line, with a small over-spill into Northamptonshire and Warwickshire. Separating the Danish from the Norwegian influence north of this line is not always easy, but it seems that the main areas of Danish influence according to place name studies were more or less where the history and politics of the period would suggest that they were. The areas of the Five Boroughs with their dependent territories (Nottingham, Leicester, Derby, Lincoln and Stamford) are rich with Scandinavian suffixes such as -thorpe and -by. In fact, Derby itself is a case in point. This place had previously been known to the English as Northworthige (pronounced 'Northworthy'). Its name was replaced by a Danish form that it has retained ever since. In Leicestershire the area of the valley of the Wreak (itself a Danish river name) was heavily settled by the Danes respecting, it seems, the areas of the densely populated English Soar valley.

The other area heavily influenced by the Danes was in the region of the territory dependent upon York. This had been a Danish area since the time of the split and settlement of the Great Army in the ninth century and the Danish names had enough time to effect the names in the landscape before the Norwegian dominance of York took place in the early tenth century. The extent to which Danish personal names lingered in the Danelaw is demonstrated by the tale of a boy born in the area of Whitby in about 1110 who was christened Tostig by his parents. The boy had fun poked at him wherever he went and his parents decided to rename him William, adopting the more respectable name of the Norman Conqueror. Only in the twelfth century do the Anglo-Scandinavian names of the Danelaw become Anglo-Norman. However, the transition is more or less complete by the thirteenth century: in a list of over 600 tenants of the bishop of Lincoln in 1225, under six per cent of the names are either Anglo-Scandinavian or Anglo-Saxon in origin, the remainder being shared by the popular post-conquest names of Robert, William and sundry others.[4]

Whatever the nature of the evolution of the Danelaw in the eleventh and twelfth centuries, the fact remains that, at the accession of King Edmund, the political future of the Midlands and Northumbria was far from certain. The jarls and holds of the Danish areas still held the balance of power in the great struggle between north and south.

## OLAF TAKES HIS CHANCE

These years after Brunanburh are the hardest for historians to pull together. There is so much political activity that the sources barely cover the basics. Everything that Athelstan had fought for in the north would have to be fought for again by his brothers.

Athelstan died on 27 October 939.[5] The *Annals of Ulster* state emphatically what their writer had thought of the English king: 'Athelstan, king of the Saxons, pillar of the dignity of the western world, died an untroubled death', they record. It had seemed, until that moment, that the road to the throne of York was firmly blocked against Olaf Guthfrithson. Throughout 938, Olaf licked his wounds back in Dublin.[6] But even here his life was not peaceful: he had to endure an Irish uprising and is also recorded raiding churches in Kildare in 939, perhaps as a way of accruing wealth in preparation for another campaign in northern England. But while Athelstan was still alive, the Northumbrian adventure would have to be postponed. When the news came that the architect of Brunanburh had died however, it must have been greeted with great relief by Olaf. Preparations were quickly made for another Norse-Irish invasion of Northumbria.

Although he had fought alongside Athelstan, the heir to the English throne was just eighteen years old at his accession. Olaf knew that he had his second chance and he would not waste it. By the end of the year his force had left Dublin and, upon its arrival in Northumbria, it quickly seems to have secured support from the Northumbrians, who let Olaf back into York without a fight. In the autumn of 940[7] Olaf had sufficient strength to campaign to the south, raiding extensively into the English Midlands with Archbishop Wulfstan at his side and meeting stiff resistance only as far south as Northampton. After the Northampton set-back, Olaf turned to Tamworth and, after a struggle, took the fortification. But he was deep inside English territory and, on hearing that the young Edmund had finally taken the field, he fell back to Leicester where the English army soon surrounded him. Despite being hemmed in at Leicester, Olaf, 'whose head was full of impossible ideas', had managed in 940 to do what he had apparently failed to do in 937, to penetrate England to the southern limits of the Danelaw.[8] At some time during the night, Olaf and his men burst through the besieging force, leaving behind them some very red faces in the English high command. His stealth at Leicester recalls that of the night before the great battle at Brunanburh. He clearly now felt that he was in a strong enough position for his claim to the Danish areas of England to be legitimised by negotiation and treaty. Odo, the archbishop of Canterbury, and Wulfstan, the archbishop of York, led the negotiations for both sides. The agreement must have been galling for Edmund. Everything which he and Athelstan had fought for at Brunanburh had been undone in one lightning campaign. Olaf, it seemed, had turned the tables on the brother of the Thunderbolt. This had been the very campaign which Brunanburh had prevented, but such punctuation marks in the prose of Anglo-Saxon history require an Athelstan as their author. Edmund, now humbled, would have to show the mettle of his royal lineage if these disasters were to be overcome.

Simeon of Durham leaves us in no doubt as to the extent of Olaf's conquest. He describes the boundary of Olaf's territory as being defined by Watling Street, to the south of which were Edmund's domains. Leicestershire, Lincolnshire, Nottinghamshire and Derbyshire were under Olaf's control, leaving only the areas of East Anglia, Northamptonshire, Huntingdonshire, Bedfordshire and Cambridgeshire of the original Danish areas in English hands. The Danes and the Englishmen of the Five

Boroughs, who had played such a pivotal role in Edward and Athelstan's northern designs, now found themselves under the Norse yoke, a government which some sources proclaim was favourable to neither of them.

For nearly a generation – that is to say beyond the living memory of some of the young warriors of the Midlands in 940 – their territories had been run by 'jarls' and other government officials on behalf of the English king. To them, the protection of the king was worth more than an alliance with the Norse at York. But not to all leaders in the Danelaw. Roger of Wendover's[9] account of the struggle sheds some tantalising light on the matter. Olaf had apparently married the daughter of one of the leading northern jarls, a man named Orm. His daughter, Aldgyth, had an English name, suggesting that her mother was an Anglo-Saxon, surely not an uncommon occurrence in the north during the tenth century. Orm, it seems, was of Danish descent, although this is disputed – some give him a Norwegian ancestry. But it seems that Orm and others like him were the 'Danes within England' who gave support to the coalition in 937. The implications of political co-operation between Orm and Olaf are difficult to play down. Edmund was humbled and Brunanburh, it seemed, had achieved nothing.

With the southern areas of his patrimony seemingly secure for the time being, Olaf turned his attention to the north of his domain in 941 and to the threat posed to him by the independent English state of Bamburgh. He campaigned widely beyond the Tees and attacked the ancient Bernician settlement at Tyningham on the Firth of Forth. He died, however, in this year and must have departed life a relatively happy man knowing that all the might of Wessex and Mercia had not stopped him from forming the northern power base that had been the dream of his relatives for years. Just as Athelstan's death had been the springboard for Olaf's second opportunity, so it was with Edmund at the passing of Olaf.

Olaf's successor was the man who had been at the centre of the brief war of 927 and who was well known in all the theatres of northern warfare – Olaf Sihtricson. He was the figure who had been exiled to Ireland after Athelstan's lightning strike on York in 927. Now he was older and wiser. He had been around the court at York for some time, probably having been recalled by Olaf Guthfrithson from Dublin for the 940 campaign, or even, as some argue, for the Brunanburh campaign of 937. Although it is generally considered that William of Malmesbury mistook Olaf Guthfrithson for Olaf Sihtricson in his story of the famous struggle, it is not unreasonable to assume that Sihtricson had been there, given that he later ruled again at York and was a key player in northern politics for a substantial period of his long career. The Northumbrians saw no reason not to support his claim to power. Northumbrian ambitions, whether expressed politically by fourth generation Dane, second generation Norwegian or long-established Englishman, were always the same: independence from the kings of the south. If anything, the new Scandinavian veneers in Northumbrian society strengthened their ancient claims to independence.

## THE RECAPTURE OF THE FIVE BOROUGHS

Before Edmund launched his successful campaign to reclaim the Five Boroughs, there appears to have been some serious campaigning in Wales. Anti-English feeling was still running high and Idwal ap Anarawd, king of Gwynedd, fought with the West Saxons and was killed. It is likely that this took place in the summer of 942 and that the subsequent campaign in northern Mercia occurred in the autumn of that year.

We know very little of Olaf Sihtricson's style of government at York, but what we do know is that subsequent events proved him to be no Guthfrithson. In 943, after receiving baptism from Edmund, he was driven from the kingdom and back to Dublin by the Northumbrians having had a disastrous year in 942 where all of Guthfrithson's territories south of the Humber were regained by Edmund, an episode captured in another of the *Anglo-Saxon Chronicle*'s glorious poems. The poem records some revealing details about the nature of the territory of the Five Boroughs. It reveals that the campaign was fought on the boundary between Mercia and Northumbria as bounded by the Dore, Whitwell Gate, the River Humber and the sea. It also names the boroughs as Nottingham, Leicester, Derby, Stamford and Lincoln. The inhabitants of this part of Mercia are described as Danes (despite the fact that we know the settlement here to be multicultural). But it is no surprise that the poet chose to describe them thus. To them, the coming of Edmund was something of a liberation.

They had endured Norse rule, which may well have been carried out with intimidating force. With perhaps one or two exceptions, the Danes of the Midlands, having had the governments of Athelstan and Olaf Guthfrithson to compare, seemed happier with the former.

The replacement for Olaf Sihtricson in York was a man called Rægnald, the brother of Olaf Guthfrithson. There seems to have been considerable tension between the two men, since Olaf Sihtricson was evidently still at large (as his visits to Edmund's court show). In fact, Rægnald visited Edmund as well, also receiving baptism at his court. In 944 Olaf attempted a coup to re-establish himself at York. It is not clear how successful he was in overthrowing Rægnald because before the year was over Edmund, in a strike reminiscent of his brother, marched on York with a huge force and drove out both men. The English king was clearly concerned at the long-term effects of a civil war in Northumbria between two of his subjects and must have been aware of the power of Northumbrian public opinion which could so easily bring a perfect stranger or an enemy of the king to the throne at York. York, once again, was in Edmund's hands, but the campaign had cost the life of Rægnald.

Archbishop Wulfstan of York had been a prime mover in the politics of these years and would continue to be so. He had supported Olaf Guthfrithson in his sacking of the ancient Mercian seat at Tamworth and yet was not so pliable that he would not readily expel troublesome Danes from York himself. His power was immense and it is worth examining his motives. He was a truly independent-minded northerner. He probably saw York as deservedly independent from Canterbury and he was happy to support any leader that could help promote this notion. He had brought about by negotiation the humiliating treaty which left Edmund with nothing north of Watling Street and yet he appears as a witness on Edmund's charters at least some of the time. He held the archbishopric between 931 and 956 and must have seen the most dramatic struggles for control of Northumbria. Between 935 and 941 he does not attest charters, but he does attest those of Edmund in 942, before Edmund's recovery of the Five Boroughs, and he is there again in 944. In 952 he was arrested by the king, a risk he had run throughout his entire career. He survived his incarceration to be finally buried at Oundle, but he had been kept from Northumbrian politics towards the end, having been given his dignity back at Dorchester, safe from contact with the north.

Meanwhile, there had been something of a sea-change in relations between the courts of the kings of the Scots and the English. In 937 Athelstan had faced an alliance instigated by the king of the Scots with the Britons of Strathclyde among the other long-established insular powers in support. Now, in Edmund's reign, there was an unlikely alliance between the English and the Scots. Edmund appears to have invaded Strathclyde in 944, laying it bare and then handing it over to Malcolm, the king of the Scots, so long as he gave Edmund future support by land and by sea. The implication is that there had been a tradition in Cumberland and Strathclyde of the harbouring of all sorts, particularly along the shores of the Solway Firth, and it was to these semi-independent Norse settlements, which had proved such fertile recruiting grounds in 937, that Olaf Sihtricson may have fled after he was driven from Northumbria in 943 and again after Edmund fell upon York in 944. In fact, Olaf does not appear to be back on the throne in Dublin until 945 so it is likely that Cumberland and its inhabitants did indeed harbour him for a while. The campaign was not without its unsavoury moments. Roger of Wendover's account, admittedly later, has it that the English king was supported by the king of Dyfed and that Edmund, during the course of events, had two of the king of Strathclyde's sons blinded. The whole campaign might have appeared at first to be a success, but Dunmail, the Strathclyde king, returned in due course to his seat.

Edmund's reign was cut short by a tragic incident. He was murdered by an outlaw who had returned from exile and had found the king at his court in Pucklechurch, Gloucestershire, and stabbed him there during a gathering. Although William of Malmesbury describes this moment of infamy, the impact of the deed has aroused the interest of people down the centuries, capturing the imagination of, among others, John Milton:

> Feasting with his Nobles... he spied Leof a noted thief, whom he had banish'd, sitting among his Guests: wherat transported with too much vehemence of spirit, though in a just cause, rising from the Table he run upon the Thief, and catching his Hair, pull'd him to the ground. The Thief who doubted from such handling no less than

his death intended, thought to die not ureveng'd; and with a short dagger struck the King, who still laid at him, and little expected such Assassination, mortally into the Breast. The matter was done in a moment, ere men sat at Table could turn them, or imagine at first what the stir meant, till perceiving the King deadly wounded, they flew upon the murderer and hew'd him to pieces; who like a wild beast at abay, seeing himself surrounded, desperately laid about him, wounding some in his fall.[10]

The murder must have sent ears pricking around the islands of Britain and Ireland. Although young at his death at just twenty-five years old, Edmund had begun to show something of the tenacity and imperialistic attitude of his brother, despite a hesitant start. The strike on York in 944 bore all the hallmarks of an Athelstan-style descent upon a recalcitrant city. Although he had lost them in the first place, Edmund's well-timed and decisive re-capture of the Five Boroughs won him deserved and wide acclaim.

## ERIC BLOODAXE AND
## THE END OF THE KINGDOM OF YORK

After the death of the king [Harold] there was great strife between his sons, for the men of Vik took Olaf for their king, but the Thronds Sigurd. But these two, his brothers, Eric slew at Tunsberg, one year after king Harold's death. All these things happened in one and the same summer, to wit, king Eric's going with his army eastwards to Vik to fight with his brothers, and (before that) the strife of Egil and Bergonund at the Gula-thing, with the other events that have just been related.

*Egil's Saga*, 59

The right of the king of the English to rule over Northumbria went unquestioned at the accession of Edred. He was the brother of Edmund and was crowned at Kingston upon Thames in 946. In fact, in 947 at Tanshelf, that important strategic location at the crossing point of the river Aire, a region where so much had been at stake ten years earlier and which as the boundary between the kingdoms of York and Mercia still had great significance, Edred secured promises and hostages from the Northumbrians at a meeting which included archbishop Wulfstan.

But the southern grip on Northumbria was about to be prized open by the arrival of an extraordinary character. A man whose name lives on in Viking legend came to England. He had been, for a short and tempestuous time, the king of Norway. His name was Eric and he became known as 'Bloodaxe'. His father, Harold Fairhair, had also been king of Norway. Eric had already murdered two of his brothers in the tangled accession crisis which followed his father's death. Athelstan had fostered his half-brother Hakon at the English court and it was Hakon who had gained the trust of the people of Norway against his brother. After some successful campaigning in what might be described as the old-fashioned style, he found the shores of Northumbria, arriving perhaps as an opportunist, or as some have said, at the invitation of the late King Athelstan.[11] At the time, it must have seemed like a blessing for the leading Vikings of the area, who were still under the yoke of the south. They accepted him as their king with a minimum of fuss. Eric's first rule in York began in 947. Even in this brief first reign which lasted only until the following year, Eric had coins minted by a local moneyer who readily locked away his King Edred dyes in favour of new Eric designs. Edred's response was unequivocal, but earned him some degree of disapproval from the historians of the age. He personally led an army which burned and ravaged its way through Northumbria as far as Ripon where it destroyed the Minster, which St Wilfrid had built. Prisoners were arrested and suspects interrogated. It was an unpleasant affair. What are we to make of such actions from a Christian king? It is probably best to interpret these actions as those of a man who had grown impatient of Northumbrian partisan politics. Ever since he was a boy, all he had known was trouble in the north. Any opportunity they had up there to elect a powerful opponent to challenge the might of his kinsmen they had taken, or so it had seemed to him. The northerners would have seen it quite differently indeed. The time had come, he thought, to teach the Northumbrians a lesson about the perils of fair-weather allegiances.

The legacy of Brunanburh might have been longer lasting if Athelstan himself had continued to live, but pitched battles were not the chief characteristic of military operations in Northumbria. Armies would instead concentrate on out-manoeuvring each other, razing the countryside, and destroying resistance in punitive campaigns. The experience at Ripon, however, would never be forgotten by the men of the north. Oda, the archbishop of Canterbury, had been there at Ripon's darkest hour and had even acquiesced in this dreadful affair by appropriating the suspected bones of St Wilfrid and taking them back to Kent.

Edred's army was in the process of returning south at the boundary of northern Mercia and Northumbria – Castleford, to be exact – when, as it was crossing the Aire, its rearguard was attacked and defeated by what must have been a shadowing force from York. There are hints that Eric had organised this ambush and it does not seem unreasonable.[12] Edred had been with his vanguard some distance from the incident and when he heard of it, he flew into a rage. He threatened a repeat campaign unless the Northumbrians abandoned their support for Eric. The Northumbrians saw that it made sense to accept these terms for the time being. Eric was duly exiled and huge compensation paid to Edred for the loss of noble life in his rearguard. For a few years Edred was king in Northumbria again. In 949 Olaf Sihtricson returned to York after a difficult spell in Dublin and began what seems to have been another reign at the Northumbrian capital. This time it must have been at Edred's discretion, with Olaf recognising Edred as overlord. Eric, it is thought, fell back upon the time-honoured occupation of Viking leaders and indulged himself in slave-trading, adding a further chapter to the colourful story of his extraordinary career.

In 952 Eric returned to York and swept back into power, forcing Sihtricson to flee. This was the same year in which Archbishop Wulfstan was arrested and he may have had much to do with soliciting Eric's return. Perhaps Sihtricson's rule was too acknowledging of Edred's overlordship. Eric's second reign was something of a more serious attempt at altering the political status quo of the north. It was unfortunate that he was just as antipathetic towards Dublin as he was to Winchester and he seems to have had enemies everywhere. The reign, which lasted from 952-954, began with what appears to have been a huge battle in the north, which for once did not involve Wessex or Mercia. A new Scottish king, Indulf, allied himself with the ruler of independent English Bamburgh and the tireless Cumbrians and took on a Norse force in a move reminiscent of the alliances of northern kingdoms back before the 920s when everyone, including Æthelflæd, had a vested interest in trying to check the Northumbrian ambitions of Rægnald. It may have been that Eric was becoming a threat to the interests of many around him. The Norse had the victory and it had been an emphatic one as far as we can tell from the sparse account. Eric ruled for another two years on his own and then in co-operation with his brother.

West Saxon sources tell us that in 954 Eric was expelled by the Northumbrians and that Edred succeeded to the kingdom of Northumbria. Simeon of Durham and Roger of Wendover shed further light on the events. The former states that after he was expelled, Eric was killed by Maccus, son of Olaf. Wendover elaborates a little with the comment that he was killed by Earl Maccus 'in a lonely place called Stainmore'.[13] The deed must have involved some form of treachery, it being unlikely that Eric would be unable to defend himself against anyone in a stand-up fight. The sources point to the complicity of the high-reeve of Bamburgh, an Englishman named Oswulf. The proud north Saxons had just been defeated by Eric and needed rid of him. Simeon suggests that Oswulf stood to gain from Eric's departure by being awarded parts of Northumbria to swell his own small northern empire. Whatever happened at Stainmore, Eric's memory passed into legend. There would be no more kings in Northumbria, only earls. Eric Bloodaxe, a true old-style warrior by tenth-century standards had been, for better or for worse, the last king of an ancient kingdom. Northern independence would continue to be fought for, and the politics of subsequent eras would demonstrate this deep desire, but the vision of a kingdom of the English promoted by Athelstan and his successors was now beginning to form. Wulfstan's vision of a glorious independent Northumbria, for the time being, would have to be viewed through the windows of a church at Dorchester. For him, the shadow had been cast from the south and not the north.

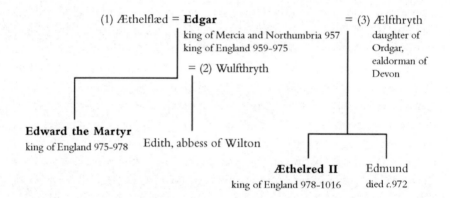

Descendants of Edgar, king of England. Names in bold indicate kings of England.

## 9

# THE EVENING
# OF A GOLDEN AGE

### THE BOY KING

> The lustful man suddenly jumped up and left the happy banquet
> and the fitting company of his nobles for the… caresses of loose
> women… repeatedly wallowing between the two of them as if in
> a vile sty.
>
> From an early *Life of St Dunstan*

Edred died on 23 November 955 without issue. Edwy and Edgar, the
sons of Edmund, were the obvious choices for the succession. Edwy
was a teenager and Edgar at the time was just twelve years old. Edwy
acceded to the throne and his short reign was one which lived in
infamy for the chroniclers of the age. In fact, it is testimony to the
strength of the institution that it managed to survive these extraordinary years without serious threat to its stability.

Edwy had the nickname 'all-fair' due to his shock of blond hair. He
could have had so many more nicknames. One of St Dunstan's earliest
biographers records a scene of debauchery at the night of the coronation of Edwy in Kingston upon Thames which shocked contemporaries and which passed into legend in subsequent centuries. The
traditional feast which follows a king's anointing and crowning was
vacated by Edwy, who went to seek the company of two ladies in an

177

adjoining room. As it turned out, the two women were mother and daughter and the prime mover in this great royal seduction was the mother. It was clear, however, that there was something between the younger girl Ælgifu and the young king because he ended up marrying her and she became a reasonably well-respected princess. The members of the clergy and senior noblemen present at the coronation feast were all somewhat offended by the absence of the monarch. Dunstan and the bishop of Lichfield were sent to fetch the boy. What greeted them was the sight of an extraordinary *ménage-à-trois* and, nearby on the floor, a discarded crown. Dunstan was apparently angered by his discovery and rebuked Edwy and the women. Edwy was equally angered at having been disturbed and it is probable that Ælgifu's mother subsequently encouraged him to strip the bishop of all his property and send him into exile overseas. Which is exactly what happened. Some histories (notably the *Anglo-Saxon Chronicle*, Worcester Manuscript D) say that it was archbishop Oda of Canterbury who discovered the scene at the coronation feast, although it is likely that many churchmen and statesmen were present at this embarrassing time. Most accounts are quick to provide moral judgement on the affair, but we must be more circumspect and perhaps more understanding of the young king. The subsequent rise to positions of prominence of those churchmen who witnessed the scene and who became leading lights in the reform movement may have much to do with the way in which the incident was remembered. We can permit ourselves, however, to observe that whichever way one looks at it, Edwy's actions and subsequent reactions were clearly bad politics.

What kind of a king Edwy was is perhaps deducible from the speed at which his grasp on power slipped away. By the end of 957 both Mercia and Northumbria refused to recognise him as king, a rift which might have had dangerous consequences. They did, however, choose to recognise Edgar as king, thus confirming their acceptance of the West Saxon line, although Edgar's personal background made him infinitely more acceptable in Danish areas. It seems that the private council, or immediate circle of friends which Edwy kept, were just as inexperienced and naive as he was and this was a cause for great concern up and down the kingdom. There were, however, some political appointments in Edwy's reign which stood the test of time and which show some degree of forethought. Ælfhere, ealdorman of Mercia, Byrhtnoth of Essex (who was to achieve immortality in a battle at Maldon against the returning Viking forces of 991) and Æthelwold of East Anglia, all rose to power during the reign of Edwy.

But the promotion of powerful Englishmen to the position of ealdorman in areas such as East Anglia, Mercia and Northumbria, was not new. In fact, it seems to have been part of Athelstan's policy of governance in these former Danish areas. During Athelstan's reign, a figure appears in East Anglia who was himself called Athelstan, but nicknamed 'Half-King'. The ealdorman Athelstan's region of rule was effectively the ancient kingdom of East Anglia, which he ran on behalf of the king. His family would remain powerful until the end of the century and his own household would accommodate a future king of England.

## KING EDGAR AND THE MONASTIC REVIVAL

If there had been something of a revolution in Edwy's reign then it was a very quiet one. With a relatively incompetent ruler and with some Mercian and Northumbrian dissent, Wessex stood its ground and the political geography of England, despite the appointments of these new and powerful ealdormen, remained much as it was. Edwy's death in 959 was followed by a quick acceptance of Edgar as king in Wessex. But, once again, there is a twist in the tale. Edwy, who had taken much from the monasteries during his reign, paid a very high price for it. 'Private profit has no priority over public loss' said William of Malmesbury on the matter of Edwy's ecclesiastical policy. According to William, the young man simply could not keep pace with the demands of kingship: '... stripped of the most part of his kingdom and under the shock of this, he died.'[1]

In some ways, Edgar and Athelstan share common ground. Both are remembered for what they did for the Church and both kings had a background in an upbringing somewhere other than Wessex. Athelstan had observed Mercian politics at close quarters in his youth and Edgar had seen East Anglian life from the house of Athelstan 'Half-King' of East Anglia. Nor do the similarities stop there. If we choose to trust the testimony, then we have another glimpse as to the appearance of an

Anglo-Saxon king from William of Malmesbury. Edgar, it seems, was a short man. So short, in fact, that he was often on the receiving end of barbed comments from others at court. One day, the Scottish king told him that he thought it ironic that the whole of Britain should be ruled by a dwarf. It was an unwise outburst, for Edgar had another character-istic: he was an impressive warrior. Edgar challenged his adversary to a duel and the Scottish king, rather than accept the challenge, fell to the floor pleading forgiveness. The story may sound dubious, but it does at least highlight an aspect of the king which we know to be true: he was extremely self-confident. His military machine was huge. He had an army drawn from the whole of Britain and a navy which regularly patrolled the whole island in search of troublesome fleets. His leadership was every bit as tenacious as Athelstan's but the lack of military crises in his reign gives us little historical material for us to judge his mettle. The 'Peace of Edgar' as it has become known, has obfuscated one important fact. Although the king owed his lofty position to the achievements of Athelstan and his brothers, he could not have maintained his peace without the threat of a mailed fist. Edgar did not need to campaign against those wishing to invade his kingdom. He was too strong for them to try. All he had to do, as the amusing story above shows, was to threaten action and his enemies melted away.

The reign of Edgar is characterised by the cultural and political activity which took place against this peaceful backdrop. This era was a triumph of art, literature and religion. The continental contacts which had been forged by Athelstan in Germany and France through marriage ties and embassies were bearing fruit now. The *Regularis Concordia*, an important monastic manual of Edgar's reign, was influenced by a synod amongst whom were clerics from Fluery and St Peter's in Ghent. Although Edgar claims to have funded the revival of monastic fortune in England, there is a trace of evidence that his conscience might have been held to ransom.

But first we must turn to Edgar's coronation. He comes in the mid-dle of a long line of kings who were crowned at Kingston upon Thames and it seems illogical that he should not have been crowned there too. In fact, his official coronation came much later than his accession, in 973, at Bath. The significance of this delay should not be misunder-stood. Edgar was crowned in his twenty-ninth year. This was the age when Jesus had begun his own public ministry according to St Luke.

Contemporaries who saw the coronation at Bath would have known of the amount of work Dunstan and his helpers had put into it. The loose form of the coronation ceremony had been tightened now into an evermore symbolic service, which, as one observer pointed out, further emphasised not so much the crowning, but the anointing of the monarch,[2] thereby giving the whole process a decidedly Carolingian ring to it. The replacement of David with Christ elevated the moral responsibilities of the king and made it that much easier for future critics to accuse the king of tyranny if he failed to live up to his promises. Dunstan and Edgar, it seems, were of a like mind in their view that the anointing of a king and the consecration of a bishop were both ceremonies demanding equal solemnity. The coronation had taken place on 11 May on the feast of the Pentecost. The significance of the choice of Bath as the coronation place may lie in the achievements of the empire of Athelstan. Now England was at peace and the borders of the kingdom of a lowland ruler had been pushed once again to the same northerly reaches as they had been in Roman times. There is something symbolic about the Romanitas which will still have been evident at Bath in 973. The sacredness of the site was undoubted. It had been an Iron Age and Roman shrine and now it would be the crowning place of a king who claimed power across the whole of Britannia. If *Rex Totius Britanniæ* had been an aspiration for Athelstan in his great struggle with the northern powers, then his success and that of his brothers had made it for Edgar a spectacular reality.

Soon after his grand coronation, Edgar took his fleet to Chester where we are told by the *Anglo-Saxon Chronicle* that six kings gave him their support by land and sea in the traditional manner of submission. This is supposed to have taken place on a single day and the story has become cloaked with legend, but it appears to be a reasonable enough assumption that other leaders of Britain, who Florence of Worcester names, did indeed row the English king along the Dee each with their own oar with Edgar at the rudder. It sounds somewhat dramatic, but it needed to be demonstrative for an attentive audience. They rowed from the palace to the monastery of John the Baptist. When Edgar entered the monastery for prayers he is supposed to have remarked upon how lucky his successors would be to be king of the English. Florence's expanded list of those kings who were present reads fairly truly, although there are one or two names which cause confusion or who are yet to be identified. They were Malcolm, king of the Cumbrians; Kenneth, king of the Scots; Maccus, king of 'Many Islands'; and the five princes Dunfal; Siferth; Jacob; Huwal and Juchil. Kenneth had come to power in 971 and Jacob is probably Iago of Gwynedd who reigned from 950-979. Huwal was Iago's nephew and enemy, and Maccus was the son of Harold, a well-known Viking seafarer. Dunfal must surely be Dunmail, king of Strathclyde, who had been at large since the 940s when Edmund had ravaged his country, and Malcolm was Dunmail's son.[3]

England and Scotland, it seems, were reaching an understanding. Edmund's grant of Strathclyde in return for support is but one example of a new relationship and there is evidence that Edgar granted land to the Scots king between the Tweed and the Forth in Lothian and later granted estates in England itself so that the Scottish king would have peaceful residence when he came to see Edgar. It all seems a remarkably long way from the mutual animosities of the Great War of 937.

One would expect Edgar to have been a model of Christian behaviour given what we know of the achievements in his reign, but legends were told about his lustful youth. Once again, we might choose to disbelieve the tales. A sexual liaison had taken place between Edgar and a nun for which Edgar was admonished by Dunstan and made to do seven years penance during which he could not wear his crown. Edgar is also supposed to have freed a slave girl after a similar encounter.[4] Such stories may be designed to reinforce the notion of an increasing influence of churchmen on kings. In the context of Edgar, where we have so little detail to go on, the stories remind us that there is often a deeper tale lurking behind recorded history.

But what of the state of church life in England at the beginnings of Edgar's reign? The depredations of the Vikings had led to some depopulation even in Wessex and land which had once been given by Edward the Elder to New Minster at Winchester in 903 was sold back to him by the Church for a lump sum. The Collingborne estate, which, after returning to the monarchy ended up in the hands of Wulfgar, is one such example.[5] Athelstan had gone a long way to bringing church life back to the very heart of the people at a local level and had promoted his own love of the Church. It was the direct intervention and ecclesiastical appointments, including imports, of Alfred the Great and the appointments of continental scholars and clerics in the reign of Athelstan that had achieved so much. Athelstan had been an energetic benefactor of religious houses, scarcely failing to adorn any one of them with gifts, books and relics, or so it was said. But the real need for reform in the reign of Edgar had come from the gradual encroachment into religious organisations of secular figures with powerful families, who in most cases expected to be able to nominate, from their own families, abbots to their appointments. The practice was rife. If a family did not have a candidate, it would still try to sell the promotion. Also, the Rule of St Benedict, by which these communities were supposed to be living, was not being fully observed in many cases. Edwy's reign had seen things get out of hand in this respect and it was only a matter of time before reform would be forthcoming. Four men were responsible for the change in the way that religious houses were run in England: Dunstan, Oswald, Æthelwold and Wulfstan.[6]

The second abbot of Cluny, Odo, had been the driving force behind the reform of the community at Fleury on the Loire. He had also managed to persuade St Peters in Ghent to see his ways. When, in Athelstan's reign, Bishop Oda of Ramsbury had escorted Louis d'Outremer back to France, he had visited Fleury and had himself tonsured there. Later, as archbishop of Canterbury, he sent his nephew Oswald (who had received his abbacy at Winchester by courtesy of his uncle's purse) to Fleury to be a monk for a few years. On his return, Oswald's career took off. He became bishop of Worcester and then archbishop of York, these two centres having a very close relationship throughout the second half of the tenth century. In fact, Fleury acted as something of a training school from which monks would graduate to become in some cases abbots of important houses in their own right. And so Oswald, as archbishop of York, and Æthelwold, as bishop of Winchester, sent their followers there.

So what were the unreformed clerics like? Why did they attract so much consternation from the new order? Inevitably there is a great deal here that is down to propaganda, but it does seem that those who were not following *The Rule* to its full were at the very least giving the impression of living an indulgent and relaxed way of life. They were often married with children, were individual landowners instead of being landowners in common and accusations of drunkenness, gambling and adultery abounded. The kindred group was the dynamic by which these

houses were driven and the tenth century reform movement was designed
to smash it. What the reformers desired were properly trained clergy in
high places, and throughout the reigns of Edgar and his successor, Edward,
a great drama unfolded across England.

Although he was no supporter of the reform movement, it was
Edmund who had appointed Dunstan as abbot of Glastonbury. Edmund
had also provided refuge at Bath for the unreformed clerics ousted from
St Peters at Ghent. Edred was more sympathetic, however, and gave
Æthelwold at an early stage in his career the estates of the deserted
monastery at Abingdon which had passed into royal hands. Here he
built a reforming community. Although King Edwy had exiled Dunstan,
Æthelwold remained loyal and became Edgar's tutor.

In Edgar's reign, Beorthelm, the recently appointed archbishop of
Canterbury, was sent packing to Wells whence he had been promoted,
and Dunstan, who had briefly held Worcester and London, took his
place. It was an extraordinary move by Edgar, whose powers were not
supposed to extend to the demotion of clergymen. Soon Æthelwold
would receive Winchester and Oswald, Worcester. These two places
would be the spearheads of the reform movement, while at Canterbury
Dunstan was still working on the community there. Æthelwold's
establishment at Abingdon continued to recruit and train abbots and
bishops while Winchester and Worcester promoted an observance
of *The Rule* at the expense of those who would not accept it, who
had their property confiscated. The ingredients for a long period of
profound secular disaffection among families promoted to great power
in the age of Athelstan were being stirred.


## THE GOVERNMENT OF ENGLAND

Edgar's approach to government was clearly an intelligent one.
The country under his rule had changed remarkably, even in his own
lifetime. Now there were in the north and Midlands second and third
generation Danes and Norwegians in permanent residence with a
part to play in the running of the kingdom. But how firm was Edgar's
control of these groups? As strong as any other medieval monarch, it
seems. But Edgar was, like Alfred before him, a realist. He knew that it
would make political sense to recognise the clear differences between

Danish and English areas and saw also that there would be some matters upon which his subject's cultural affinities would have no bearing at all. We must remember where Edgar had come from. Despite being the son of Edmund and the brother of Edwy, his background was in the Danelaw. This is where he was first recognised and promoted as the favoured candidate for the whole kingdom of England in preference to the unpopular Edwy. Edgar's subsequent style of government clearly reflected the debt that he felt he owed to the leading political figures of Anglo-Scandinavian England. In 957, Edgar gained power in Mercia and Northumbria. Two more years passed before he would accede to the whole kingdom. The *Anglo-Saxon Chronicle* is rather reticent about the early years of the reign of the king who came to be regarded as the leading light of the Anglo-Saxon Golden Age and the reason for this is the same as it was in the days of Edward's suppression of Mercian independent sentiment: the West Saxon chroniclers were reluctant to accept that the political impetus for the choice of a king of all England had come from anywhere other than Wessex.

Although the sub-division of shires into hundreds, or wapentakes, has an ancestry going back to Alfredian times, in Edgar's period a new dimension can be observed and its inspirer was probably the German king Otto the Great, who had created a liberty for Cologne. The hundreds had provided warriors for the imperial army. Now there would be shipsokes, groups of three hundreds which must provide a ship for the royal fleet and a crew of sixty men. With his fleet constantly patrolling the island, Edgar's kingdom was virtually unassailable. But the giving of shipsokes to bishops had a damaging effect on some of those secular nobles who had come to expect to wield a great deal of power. Groups of three hundreds whose men were under the control of a bishop sat uncomfortably in the middle of a territory controlled by a secular authority. Such was the case at Oswaldslow in Worcester, and Ælfhere of Mercia, like many others, would not like it a bit.

The charge brought against Edgar that he encouraged and loved foreigners to the detriment of the country is somewhat unfair, but has its foundation in the fact that Edgar was famous, like Athelstan had been before him, across the whole of Europe. Old Saxons, Flemings and Danes had flocked to England to be closer to the king and brought with them, it is said, some vices that the English are not supposed to have been familiar with according to William of Malmesbury.[7] The

Saxons had brought with them great ferocity, the Flemings a spineless effeminacy and the Danes a penchant for drinking. All of these traits could quite conceivably be levelled at the English themselves before this time, particularly by their enemies. Nevertheless, Edgar's death prompted some more laudatory words from the quill of the Anglo-Saxon Chronicler:

> 8 July. Here departed Edgar, ruler of the English, friend of the West Saxons, and protector of the Mercians. That was widely known throughout many nations over the gannet's bath, that kings greatly honoured Edmund's offspring, widely submitted to the king, as was natural to him. There was no fleet so proud, nor raiding-army so strong, that fetched itself carrion among the English race, while the noble king governed the royal seat.
>
> *Anglo-Saxon Chronicle*, Manuscript D Worcester
> Entry for 975 recording the death of King Edgar

The death of Edgar also gave rise to the return of the feuding clerics, those who had been ousted from their communities during the great reforms and whose families had a score to settle. The constant push and shove between competing factions would eventually weaken England. Its consequences are most clearly seen in the reign of Edward the Martyr.

### THE GATHERING STORM

> The barking of those whelps while their mother was asleep signifies that after your death, while those who are now alive and powerful are asleep, a set of rascals not yet born will bark like dogs against the church of God. As for the fact that a second apple followed the first... this indicates that from you, who overshadow all England like a tree, there shall come two sons. The supporters of the second shall do away with the first... If the larger pot could not fill the smaller, this means that the northern peoples, who are more numerous than the English, will attack England after your death.
>
> William of Malmesbury, *Gesta Regum Anglorum*, 156.1

The interpretation of a dream of King Edgar as spoken to him by his mother and recounted by William of Malmesbury conjured up powerful images of trouble ahead for the English. The strength of Anglo-Saxon unity would be challenged as soon as Edgar unexpectedly died in 975. The crisis which followed his death threw the kingdom into temporary turmoil and events must have been closely observed by dark forces overseas. Edgar's son Edward, by his first wife, was a teenager when his father died. The surviving boy from the third marriage was Æthelred and he was very young at this time of the crisis. Edward, despite the claims of romantic fiction which have grown up around the young man's troubled life, was an unsavoury character with a sharp tongue and short temper. This notwithstanding, Edward had his supporters including the two archbishops and the heirs of Athelstan 'Half-King' of East Anglia. Æthelred, for his part, had his mother and the energetic Ælfhere of Mercia. The country was certainly split, but it was the young Edward who was elected and crowned before the year was out. For now, the reformers had won, but in its record for the year 975, the *Anglo-Saxon Chronicle* is quick to change its tone from one of adulation for Edgar to one of dark foreboding. No sooner have the glories and achievements of Edgar's peaceful reign been recorded than famine, strange comets and 'manifold disturbances' visit themselves upon the English people.

The confusion of Edward's accession gave some leading ealdormen, such as Ælfhere of Mercia, an opportunity to redress the balance of land ownership which had seen monastic communities in his, as in many other areas, develop into the principal landowners. This 'enemy of the monks' overthrew all the Mercian monasteries which had been built by Æthelwold during Edgar's reign. Such attacks on the Church did not go unrecorded by the chroniclers. The reformers could be forgiven for thinking that providence was on their side. At the Synod of Winchester, a vision of the Lord appeared routing the clerics and their supporters. As if that was not enough, during a meeting at Calne, where Dunstan was heavily under fire from various magnates for his reforming policies, the first-storey floor upon which they were all seated collapsed, taking with it some senior figures. Dunstan, of course, was left standing on a supporting beam, unharmed.

Except for his unusual temperament, there is very little recorded about the reign of Edward the Martyr. It is clear that he was unpopular with some of the nobility of England and clearer still that he was murdered in cold blood on the evening of 18 March 978. Although it is reasonable to presume that there was a climate of mistrust of the young king during his reign, the incident which brought both his reign and his life to an end did much to permanently sow the seeds of suspicion between the monarchy and the leading political figures of the day:

> Here King Edward was killed in the evening-time on 18 March at Corfe 'passage'; and they buried him at Wareham without any royal honours.
>
> No worse deed for the English race was done than this was, since they first sought-out the land of Britain. Men murdered him, but God exalted him. In life he was an earthly king; after death he is now a heavenly saint. His earthly relatives would not avenge him, but his Heavenly Father has much avenged him. Those Earthly slayers wanted to destroy his memory upon earth, but the sublime avenger has spread abroad his memory in the heavens and on the earth. Those who earlier would not bow to his living body, those now humbly bow the knees to his dead bones. Now we can perceive that the wisdom and deliberations of men, and their counsels, are worthless against God's purpose...
>
> *Anglo-Saxon Chronicle* entry for 979 [978]
> Peterborough Manuscript (E)

Once again, the passing of a king inspired a chronicler to use dramatic language. But who had committed such a foul deed? The strength of the rivalry between the Æthelred and Edward camps does not seem to be disputed. The boys' father had married three times. With Æthelflæd, King Edgar's first wife, he had Edward. With Wulfthryth, his second wife, he had Edith, who became an abbess at Wilton. His greatest issue was with his third wife Ælfthryth, daughter of a Devonshire ealdorman. Their two children were Edmund, who died in about 972 and who might have been king himself, and Æthelred, the young man who would have one of the longest and most eventful reigns in English history. But there were other tensions. Æfhere of Mercia and the descendants of Athelstan 'Half-King' of East Anglia were set against each other in a fight for supremacy and each supported a different candidate. The reason for the expression of horror in the *Chronicle* probably rises from the fact that the deed was carried out with such calculated brutality. Kings often died violently – and have done so throughout the medieval period across the world – but this event had something positively Byzantine about it. Edward was apparently visiting his half-brother and stepmother informally when he was murdered. Later and more colourful versions of the event implicate Ælfthryth as the prime mover in the assassination implying that she had intrigued on behalf of her son. The earliest account, however, firmly suggests that the motive lay with the personal retainers of the young Æthelred. Of Ælfthryth's character we know but a little. She had once accepted as her partner a nobleman called Æthelwold who had been sent to judge her beauty by Edgar. When Edgar finally came for his prize, she readily dropped Æthelwold in favour of the king. We do not know who was really behind it, but we know that Edward was greeted with great warmth and, in a moment when he was least expecting it, both his arms were grabbed and an assailant stabbed him.[8] There was a struggle as Edward stayed on his horse and wheeled it around to flee, but got his foot caught in the stirrup and a little distance later he fell and was dragged along the ground. When his murderers reached him, they simply tossed him down a well. Locals retrieved his body and took it to a church. The body rested for some time at Wareham, perhaps for even a year, lying apparently in a bog where sometimes columns of fire could be seen to mark its position.

The remains were subsequently removed to St Mary's at Wareham. Among the many legends and miracles surrounding the remains of the young king were that a lame man walked and a dumb man spoke in the presence of the relics. Ælfthryth herself started on a journey to see what all the talk was about but her usually swift horse was rooted to the spot as was its replacement. She chose, it is said, a life of hair-shirted penance at Wherwell.[9] In 980, Ælfhere of Mercia arranged for Edward's body to be brought to Shaftesbury where it was placed at the north side of the principal altar. This single act might even implicate Æfhere in the murder. It is while the king's bones laid here that the most famous stories of miracles occurred. In 1001 the bones were properly translated and then there follows a somewhat confused history. The fact that within just a few years, Edward's cult had grown into full legitimacy with the saint and martyr being named as such in law, charter, prayer, calendar and litany, should not surprise us. Even the

Witan – the great council – passed a law in 1008 honouring Edward's day. But the point is this: the late tenth and early eleventh centuries was a period when the cult of saints was once again becoming fashionable. In Edward's story, the hagiographer has everything he needs. Here we have a 'boy victim', always a popular subject, whose tale reads like a lamb slaughtered by a Judas. Other saint's lives have aspects of Edward's story, but few have as much detail. The killing of innocent people who are actively engaged in something mundane or benevolent is an oft-repeated feature of cults in this period, such as those of St Kenhelm or St Æthelbert. With Edward, we have the victim innocently out hunting and visiting his brother in a good-will gesture, being handed a chalice before he is brutally murdered. There is the penance of Æthelred and the complicity of his mother and the unhealthy disrespect for the victim's body, too. As cults of the era go, that of Edward, king and martyr, has it all. This may explain the extraordinary history of his relics, which are still actively revered as objects of devotion today.

The story of Edward's bones is remarkable. It shows just how powerful such matters can be over a very long period of time. Soon after the translation – at what time or times is uncertain – the bones were split up and dispersed to Leominster (a possession of Shaftesbury before it became a dependency of Reading in 1125), Salisbury, Bradford upon Avon and Abingdon. Tradition asserts that much of the body still remained at Shaftesbury (sometimes known in medieval chronicles as Edwardstowe), probably including the heart and viscera. William of Malmesbury claims to have seen one of the king's lungs there 'still panting and completely fresh'. There is a school of thought which states that only the viscera had been left with the nuns of Shaftesbury and that all of the bones were dispersed before the twelfth century.[10] The thirteenth-century Abingdon chronicle says that Abingdon acquired most of the parts in 1034 with Leominster, Salisbury and others subsequently acquiring pieces. So, by the time William saw the lung in 1125 at Shaftesbury, there were no bones to be seen there, since they had long departed.

There is no doubt that throughout the medieval period Shaftesbury was an important pilgrimage destination and the abbey was proud of its relics. The dissolution of the monasteries in the mid-sixteenth century brought to Shaftesbury much the same wanton destruction that it brought to other great monastic institutions and the abbey fell into ruin. A tomb was unearthed in 1861 and was discovered to be empty. It is not until the 1930s that the story can be picked up again. The owner of the private gardens in which the abbey remains were located was a certain Mrs Claridge. She did not allow excavations, but by chance in 1931 her gardener was digging in the north-east section of the north transept where he discovered a lead casket (2ft by 9in) in which were some bones and part of a skull. Bert Richard's famous discovery was lauded in *The Times* for the 26 January 1931 as the recovery of the bones of St Edward the Martyr: '[A discovery] of great importance... of unique interest... setting at rest the speculation of centuries'. The nuns of Shaftesbury, or so it is thought, had clearly reburied these remains in a contemporary lead casket to avoid detection at the time of the dissolution of the monasteries. A stone shrine was built for the bones in the grounds of the abbey and during the war years they spent the first of several spells behind the door of a bank vault.

The bones were examined in 1968 by a Dr Stowell who reported to the Roman Catholic Church that these were the bones of an Anglo-Saxon male in his late teens.[11] Doubt was soon cast on the integrity of these observations, but still the saga continued. John Wilson Claridge (1905-1993), one of Mrs Claridge's two sons, then removed the bones, claiming them to be his property. He offered them to the Roman Catholic church of St Edward in Shaftesbury, but negotiations broke down after Claridge demanded that he should retain some of the bones for himself. There was still the nagging doubt over the authenticity of the bones. There followed a series of earnest attempts to deposit the bones somewhere appropriate. The Roman Catholic bishop of Plymouth, the abbot of Buckfast, St Edward's church in Oxford and the Anglian bishops of Winchester and Exeter were all approached but none of them could meet the demands of Claridge who said that he wanted the bones properly enshrined.

In what was described by John Wilson Claridge as an act of divine providence, in 1980 he met a Mr Pobjoy who was also known as Father Alexis of a Russian Orthodox Church sect in exile. Father Alexis was, and still is at the time of writing, the Archimandrite of the St Edward Brotherhood which formally set itself up at the Brookwood cemetery in Woking, Surrey, in 1982. Father Alexis gladly agreed to take the bones and put them in a specially tooled wooden box, with a view to placing them on a shrine in a converted chapel at the Brookwood cemetery. Then came Geoffrey, John's brother, into the fray. He claimed that he had equal right to decide the destiny of the bones and he had fallen in with the Shaftesbury lobby who wanted them back in their ancestral home. But plans were already made at Woking. The enshrinement of the bones would be a huge affair: the bishop of the Russian Orthodox Church outside of Russia and thirty other clerics were already on an aeroplane from their base in New York fully intent on attending the great ceremony. But all of them were nearly confounded. Although a formal ceremony took place between 15-16 September 1984, the Shaftesbury lobby via Geoffrey Claridge had sought an injunction claiming that the bones were his and objecting to the Russian donation (the archbishop of Canterbury and several leading Catholics had declined their invitations anyway). The injunction was not successful in its original aim, but the judge ordered, for the purposes of security, that the bones be removed to a bank vault in Woking pending a full hearing. An interim hearing came in 1988 when the sect was allowed to take the bones back to Brookwood, but another hearing was pending. Shaftesbury continued its pressure and was annoyed at the suggestion that it should foot the bill for the accommodation of the bones in Surrey. Even Nicholas Baker, the Member of Parliament for North Dorset, was aroused by the controversy. But in December 1992 on the feast of St Æthelgifu, Athelstan's aunt, the first abbess of Shaftesbury, the brotherhood brought back their relics to the church having obtained some months before a ruling from the High Court regarding the security arrangements at the church.

Today the bones are still at Brookwood in the care of the community which had campaigned hard to keep them. The year 2001 marked the 1,000th anniversary of the original glorification of the bones and a special service was held in the St Edward Brotherhood's church on 31 March 2001 to celebrate the event. The Hierarchical Liturgy was led by Archbishop Mark who is in charge of the parishes of the Russian Orthodox Church in Britain. The community continues to flourish at Brookwood although it is likely that the controversy of the Martyr's bones will never entirely disappear.

The problems of the luckless but extraordinarily long reign of Edward's brother Æthelred are well documented and their details are not within the scope of this book. There would be a dawning of a new age under the unfortunate king, an age that saw the second coming of the Vikings and the resurgence – if, indeed, it had ever gone away – of an independent Anglo-Danish cultural identity in the Danelaw. It was a complex period of English history in which many of the achievements of the previous decades seemed on the face of it to have been undone by internal disputes and rifts. The accusations of treachery and incompetence that seem too often to be assigned to Æthelred's history are the result of unfair judgements handed down by posterity. But it remains a fact that the king was not universally popular. Indeed, the medieval reputation of Æthelred could hardly have been in more stark contrast to that of Athelstan. It is to the notion of the image of kings that the rest of this volume is addressed.

Æthelred ruled from 979-1016 amid a tumult of confusion and shifting allegiances of powerful magnates. His son would be the last truly English king of England, a nation which, as we have seen, had only recently come into being. Eventually, England would pass into the hands of the Danish King Cnut, whose dynastic ambitions would be disputed by the heirs of Æthelred. The second coming of the Danes in England was just as bad as the first. In fact, it was worse, since it seemed that by the 990s, English morale at a local level had completely collapsed. But Æthelred had his supporters, despite the huge payments of Danegeld and the disastrous St Brice's Day Massacre where he ordered the killing of Danes in England. Leading political figures even asked for him to come back from exile, if he could show that he would rule differently from how he had before. It is in this continuing belief in the institution of the Old English monarchy at a time when it was allegedly at its weakest, that we can find an ideal. The ideal was an Alfredian creation in England, borrowing heavily from the Carolingian model. Edward the Elder kept the ideal alive at sword's edge and Athelstan had personally promoted it in almost every way imaginable. Athelstan's brothers had fulfilled their roles reasonably well despite some pressing military problems, but it was with Edgar under the influence of the reformers that the Carolingian light shone brightest.

And yet it is the nature of Anglo-Saxon kingship that despite the quality of the tools of government, the royal secretariat and the revival of the Church, so much still depended upon the character of the incumbent. Æthelred's problems were no greater than Athelstan's. But the two men were decidedly different in the way in which they approached them.

William of Malmesbury's assertion that Æthelred merely occupied the throne rather than ruled is too broad a statement for a very complicated reign and contrasts with what he had to say about Athelstan. But there are some endearing links between the two men and they are dynastic in nature. Æthelred clearly knew his lineage. It is reflected in the names which he gave his children. His first son was called Athelstan and there was an Edmund (Ironside), Edred and Edwy from his first marriage to Ælfgifu, daughter of Thored earl of Northumbria, and a further Edward (the Confessor) and Alfred from his second marriage to Emma of Normandy. There is a confidence in the choice of names here. But it would not be enough to save his reputation.

The memory of good kings and bad kings is traceable through the medieval and later histories and creative works such as plays, songs and stories. The remainder of this volume is dedicated to the notion that it was Athelstan, above all others, whose style of kingship was held as a model for hundreds of years, a reputation that does not place him merely somewhere between Alfred and Edgar, but which elevates him to a position of great historical importance. The ultimate degeneration of his reputation, a fact which is undisputed, can be explained. Athelstan, for all his magnificence, had his failings too.

# IO

# THE LEGEND
# OF KING ATHELSTAN

*Come hither, Athelstan. Stay where thou art.*
*My son, the dearest of all to me,*
*Proven in battle, faithful to God and men,*
*The end draws near for me and I must go*
*To join my mother, Ecgwinne the fair,*
*Love of my youth, as thou art of my age.*
*I pray thee Athelstan, forget not thou*
*To hold that standard high before thine eyes*
*Set thee by Alfred, Alfred the Great now hight.*
*O govern thou this realm*
*In holier ways than I have done. Thou ever*
*Art pious, wise and virtuous. Perchance*
*Thy better prayers will ease my tortured soul*
*In purgatory.*
From *Athelstan, A Pageant Play*, by M.L. Kerry and P.N. Maby,
1924. As performed by pupils of the County Secondary School,
Malmesbury, for the Athelstan Millenary Celebrations.

The words of Edward the Elder, as written by Kerry and Maby in
1924 may seem a little mawkish today. But, sentimentalism aside, they
capture something of the spirit of the time. Notwithstanding some
erroneous names in this excerpt, the play goes on to portray the

jealousies of the thegn Alfred regarding Athelstan's accession and the doubts which were expressed by the characters regarding the legitimacy of his birth. Athelstan's background – the son of a king and his beautiful concubine – clearly had much to do with the challenges which he faced in the opening years of his reign. The way in which Athelstan dealt with the threats has been viewed by later historians as an example of an immensely strong king exercising his power to its fullest extent and showing himself to be humble and remorseful in the eyes of God.

As in Malmesbury, the people of Kingston upon Thames did not miss the opportunity to dramatise his life, choosing to do so in 1925. The work of W.E. St Lawrence Finny, who had attended the Malmesbury celebrations as a civic guest, owes much to an active imagination and yet it too draws upon a legend that had grown in the centuries immediately after the king's death. No matter what the nature of the artistic licence, or how far from the historical Athelstan these portrayals might be, the tradition which they represent is an ancient one and it deserves to be understood.

There can be little doubt, if the medieval texts are to be believed and interpreted correctly, that the memory of the tenth century was profound in the minds of Englishmen, perhaps more so than that of the disastrous eleventh century. There had been a Golden Age during the reign of Edgar and it had been made possible by Athelstan. Furthermore, it seemed that everyone knew it. Embodied within this Golden Age were certain virtues in kingship which Edgar inherited from Athelstan and prosecuted with great zeal. The notion that a king rules through God and that his laws are just and Christian laws is one which is promoted by the poets of later medieval England as one of Athelstan's great legacies. Of course, this idea was hardly Athelstan's invention, there being many Anglo-Saxon law-making monarchs who had ruled in this way, such as his predecessors Ine and Alfred, but it was Athelstan to whom this reputation became most firmly attached. With this comes the necessity in the face of an enemy intent on breaking down the social fabric, to defend the realm with force of arms, another of Athelstan's lasting achievements.

There is a tendency to see Athelstan as a notable warrior king some-where along the road of Anglo-Saxon state development between Alfred and Edgar. Indeed, Ælfric, the great churchman of the later tenth century, included him in his praise of kings who 'were often victorious through God' and had Athelstan as 'the king who fought against Anlaf and slaughtered his army and put him to flight and afterwards with his people he dwelt in peace'.[1] Ælfric, however, heaps the greatest praise on Edgar whom, he says, by spreading the praise of God everywhere among his people, safeguarded the country from attack. Yet it is clear that the achievements of Athelstan were not just military. There were cultural and governmental improvements too.

Little wonder then that William of Malmesbury had discovered the laudatory Latin discourse on Athelstan and borrowed from it in his own work on the king in his *Gesta Regum*. The poem which William includes in his work has been the subject of some controversy. It has sometimes been identified as the 'ancient volume' (which was almost certainly a tenth-century manuscript written in a very formalised and bombastic style praising the king) which William had said that he had recently found, a work which told of Athelstan's education among other things. The work was written in a style which William detested, although he excused the author his literary excesses, putting this down to the practice of his time, a time when the great king was still living. But it seems that he chose not to quote from it as it stood, even though a number of historians have claimed that he did. Instead, he inserted a twelfth-century Latin poem which may very well have been roughly contemporary with his own time and which was written in a style that he evidently preferred. In fact, he may even have had it specially written for his own volume. But the inspiration for the twelfth-century work was clearly the original tenth-century material and without it our knowledge of the extraordinary king would be much poorer than it is.

Before introducing the subject of the 'ancient volume', William tells of the popular conception of the king's impact on his subjects. The extent of Athelstan's compassion, law-making and martial prowess prompted a meaningful sentiment from the twelfth-century historian:

> Concerning this king, there is a vigorous tradition in England that he was the most law-abiding and best-educated ruler they have ever had.

Notwithstanding the controversy surrounding the Latin poem in William's work, a remarkable piece of scholarship has demonstrated that there were indeed contemporary works in Latin written about Athelstan and their study makes interesting reading.[2] One of the earliest known poems to mention Athelstan was written when he was just a boy. It is written as an acrostic. This means that the letters which start and end each line will make up two separate words when read vertically. It was quite a skilful art to write a Latin acrostic whilst keeping hold of both structure and meaning in the work and sometimes poets tortured their words to make the important letters fit the acrostic puzzle. However, this particular poem[3] which bears the two legends ADALSTAN/ IOHANNES is a fairly accomplished work which only mutilates the first word of the second line in order to satisfy the art. It was almost certainly written by John the Old Saxon, Alfred's mass-priest, who was one of the earliest continental ecclesiastical imports in the reign of Alfred, brought over to help restart the campaign of letters and learning which was to characterise Athelstan's England. Here, he casts himself as the biblical Samuel foretelling a great future for a young prince. Athelstan was only a boy when it was written and it may well have been penned to commemorate the 'Investiture' of Alfred's favoured grandson in a ceremony which echoed that which Alfred had undergone in Rome at the hands of Pope Leo IV when he himself was a boy. At this ceremony, Alfred had been decorated 'with the dignity of the belt and the vestments of the consulate, as is customary with Roman consuls.'[4] William of Malmesbury tells us that a similar ceremony occurred when Athelstan was a boy and that Alfred bestowed upon him a scarlet (sometimes taken to be imperial purple) cloak, a gem-studded belt, and a 'Saxon' sword with golden scabbard. With this investiture came the symbolism which signalled that Edward's line, in the form of his eldest son Athelstan, would be the line of power in the kingdom of the Anglo-Saxons. But soon young Ælfweard would arrive as a more legitimate claimant from a recognised second marriage. The notion that Athelstan came to throne by accident at the death of Ælfweard, who died in the same year as Edward the Elder, must be tempered by a consideration of this acrostic poem. Whatever the struggle for legitimacy in 924, this event in Athelstan's childhood remains a conspicuous feature. Rome is resoundingly echoed in these ceremonies. The pope was aware of the struggle on the northern frontier of Christendom and the English kings needed a form of legitimacy to fight against the Pagan and to impress the counter-claimants. Here, John the Old Saxon provides in poetic form the literature of justification:

*'Archalis' clamare, triumuir, nomine 'saxI'.*
*Diue tuo fors prognossim feliciter aeuO:*
*'Augusta' Samu-cernentis 'rupis' eris —elH,*
*Laruales forti beliales robure contrA.*
*Saepe seges messem fecunda prenotat altam; iN*
*Tutis solandum petrinum solibus agmeN.*
*Amplius amplificare sacra sophismatis arcE.*
*Nomina orto- petas donet, precor, inclita —doxuS*

*You, Prince, are called by the name of 'sovereign stone'.*
*Look happily upon this prophecy for your age:*
*You shall be the 'noble rock' of Samuel the Seer,*
*[Standing] with mighty strength against devilish demons.*
*Often an abundant cornfield foretells a great harvest; in*
*Peaceful days your stony mass is to be softened.*
*You are more abundantly endowed with the holy eminence of learning.*
*I pray that you may seek, and the Glorious One may grant, the [fulfilment implied*
*in your] noble names.*[5]

Later in his reign, in 927, when Athelstan was at his imperial height, having secured the submission of northern kings at Eamont, another contemporary poem appears to have been written. This poem survives in two different versions, one of which only includes (in prose) what one scholar thinks would have been stanzas 1, 2 and 4 written down as a footnote on the page of a sumptuous eighth-century gospel book probably written at Lindisfarne whilst the other full poem accompanies several other works in a composite manuscript probably from a centre on the extreme western fringes of Wessex. So, in both surviving examples we can see the successful emperor at the head of a great army establishing himself now as ruler of all Britain, a country now made whole – the aspiration of every powerful monarch since the time of the Roman governors. The poem must be closely dated to the events at Eamont since it records the loyalty of Constantine and mentions his support which was apparently withdrawn in 934 and which prompted the great English expedition into Scotland of that year. It is thought that the author of the work was Peter, another foreign import into the New Minster *familia* at Winchester, since he mentions himself as the announcer of the king's news in the poem:

| | |
|---|---|
| Carta dirige gressus | *Letter, direct your steps* |
| per maria nauigans | *sailing across the seas* |
| tellurisque spacium | *and an expanse of land* |
| ad regis palacium | *to the king's burh.* |
| | |
| Rege primum salutem | *Direct first of all your best wishes* |
| ad reginam, clitonem | *to the queen, the prince,* |
| claros quoque comites | *the distinguished ealdormen as well,* |
| armigeros milites | *the arm-bearing thegns.* |
| | |
| Quos iam regit cum ista | *Whom he now rules with this* |
| perfecta Saxonia: | *England [now] made whole:* |
| uiuit rex Æ?elstanus | *King Athelstan lives* |
| per facta gloriosus! | *Glorious through his deeds!* |
| | |
| Ille, Sictric defuncto | *He, with Sitric having died,* |
| armat tum in prelio | *in such circumstances arms for battle* |
| Saxonum exercitum | *the army of the English* |
| per totum Bryttanium | *throughout all Britain.* |
| | |
| Constantinus rex Scottorum | *Constantine, king of the Scots,* |
| aduolat Bryttanium: | *hastens to Britain:* |
| Saxonum regum saluando, | *by supporting the king of the English* |
| fidelis seruitio. | *[he is] loyal in his service.* |
| | |
| Dixit rex Æ?elstanus | *King Athelstan said [these things]* |
| per Petri preconia: | *through the announcements of Peter:* |
| sint sani, sint longeui | *may they be well, live long,* |
| saluatoris gratia! | *Through the saviour's grace!* |

Most things in this poem might appear to be self-evident. It was intended to be read and heard by the court household, probably at Winchester. Among them are the queen (probably Eadgifu, the mother of Edmund and Edred) and the prince, perhaps Edwin, who would soon be drowned at sea on the king's orders. But what is clear is the achievement of Athelstan even before the great showdown at Brunanburh.

One more contemporary poem, which can be dated to the years between Brunanburh in 937 and the death of Athelstan in 939, deserves attention. The poem *Rex pius Æþelstan* was written into a beautiful gospel book which had come into Athelstan's possession probably from the Ottonian court. The poem's sumptuous accommodation is matched by its Latin eloquence. Once again written by a foreign hand, it praises the king at the end of his illustrious career. It begins with the lines:

> *Holy King Athelstan, renowned through the wide world,*
> *Whose esteem flourishes and whose honour endures everywhere...*

The tone remains like this, praising the king's military achievements thus:

> *... so that this king himself, mighty in war, might be able*
> *to conquer other fierce kings, treading down their proud necks.*

Clearly, the poet had Brunanburh on his mind here. Although he gives Athelstan the sort of praise one might expect in a poem incorporated in one of the king's own precious books, he is not alone in his admiration. An unknown scribe added a note into the margin of the chronicle of Florence of Worcester which described the king as *Strenuus et Glorius rex Athelstanus solus per totam Angliam regnum Anglorum regnavit*, a description which instantly captures the imperialistic achievements of the reign.

So, Athelstan's good reputation clearly survives him. But why do we come across a different kind of Athelstan by the later medieval and Tudor periods? His achievements would seem to us to be enough to guarantee him the same sort of lasting fame that his grandfather had. Perhaps the seeds of doubt were sown by William of Malmesbury himself, who with a full and frank account of the king's life will have given people with an axe to grind some room for manoeuvre by reminding his reader of the popular songs from which he was taking some of his material. Athelstan does not always come out of it smelling of roses. It is in this difficult to define grey area of popular feeling about Athelstan that the essence of the legend can be found. Truth may well be a hostage to the legend, but the important point is that the legend became its own beast and we can identify its embryo in the tales recalled by William.

The first story concerns the legitimacy or otherwise of the king's birth. One night, whilst lying in bed at her home in a small village, a beautiful shepherd's daughter had a dream. Her belly shone as bright as the moon and it lit up the whole kingdom. She told her friends of the curious vision the next day and word soon spread to the wet-nurse of king Alfred's sons. The wet-nurse took the girl into her own home, showing her the delights of a more polite lifestyle and dressed her accordingly. One day, the young Prince Edward rode through the village and came to the house of his former wet-nurse to briefly pay his respects to her and her family. On seeing the girl, he was instantly smitten and asked if he may spend some time with her. That night, Athelstan was conceived and the girl's earlier vision of a bright light enveloping the whole kingdom would become true. And so, when Edward died and his son Ælfweard, who was born of a legitimate marriage between Edward and Ælfflæd, followed him soon after, the hopes of all were set upon Athelstan. All that is, except the seditious thegn Alfred.

The other popular tale surrounds the role of Edwin in all the plotting at the beginning of the reign and tells of his death at the hands of Athelstan, an event which the *Anglo-Saxon Chronicle* (version E) records, without assigning the blame. Both Simeon of Durham and Henry of Huntingdon implicate Athelstan in the drowning of Edwin, but William of Malmesbury gives the fullest account of it in its popular form. Edwin had been accused of plotting against Athelstan and protested his innocence to the king, yet was still exiled despite swearing on oath. Edwin, 'who even strangers could not choose but pity' was cast adrift in a small oarless boat with his servant. In time, Edwin threw himself overboard rather than suffer anymore, but his servant manfully continued to paddle the vessel with his feet, collecting the body and bringing it to the shore 'in the narrow sea that flows between Dover and Wissant'. The king was apparently overwhelmed with remorse at what he had done and, submitting to a seven-year penance, turned upon the cup-bearer who had informed against Edwin. The cup-bearer gave himself away one evening when he slipped while pouring wine at a feast, losing his balance with one foot and regaining it with another. He uttered the words 'Thus does one brother aid another'. Athelstan heard the remark and had the man's head cut off. The king later reflected on the help

Edwin might have given him if things had been different. There is another, more curious tradition surrounding this whole affair. It does not come from the pen of a medieval historian, but from the firmly held traditions of the origins of the Freemasons in England. Their tale places the whole incident in the bay of Weymouth, stating that Edwin had returned from a trip to the Orient whence he had brought back the secrets of Freemasonry. Edwin, it is said, created the first English Lodge at Ely which soon aroused the interest of the king who summoned him to his court at Weymouth to explain himself. Edwin refused to reveal the secrets of the Lodge or even account for what was said at their meetings. He did, however, offer to make an oath of allegiance to the king, provided he was not made to break his vow of secrecy. The anger of the king rose, and he set his brother adrift in the boat. The rest of the story told in the Freemasons' mythology is much as it is in William of Malmesbury.

And so, armed with the popular tales about Athelstan, the later works of medieval literature would portray a very human character indeed. The Anglo-Norman poet Geffrai Gaimar tells of the military prowess of the king in his *L'Estoire des Engleis* of *c.*1135-40, which appears to be largely, if not entirely, based on the famous poem in the *Anglo-Saxon Chronicle*. Later, the facts become mingled with fabrications and distorted out of all proportion to the truth, but still retain some useful aspects of Athelstan's life. Layamon's *Brut* which is derived from Wace's *Roman de Brut* demonstrates the link between Athelstan and the ancient Saxon king of Wessex, King Ine, another notable law-maker, but he only separates them by an inaccurate sixty-five years. Importantly, despite highlighting the piety of the king (being responsible here for the restoration of Peter's Pence and the founding of churches), the ghost returns once again to haunt the memory: Athelstan holds his office as an illegitimate claimant. He had come to London, we are told, to be appointed king, rather than to walk in as the rightful heir. Much of the topographical and political references (such as the attributing to Athelstan of the establishment of Parliament and the creation of royal forests) have as much to do with the prevailing conditions of the thirteenth century when he was writing, but it is revealing nevertheless. Athelstan, despite his human failings, is clearly being held up to the medieval audience as an exemplar of kingship:

'How he set shire and set hundred; and the names of the towns in Saxon Runes'.[6]

The English translations of the Anglo-Norman *Gui de Warewic* of *c.*1230 have Athelstan summoning his council to deliberate on the impending invasion of King Anlaf of Denmark. Athelstan is loved for his good deeds and loves just a chosen few himself, so much so that jealousies abound at the court. The chosen one is Gui, who meets the Danish challenge in a fight of champions and wins against the Danish candidate, but prefers to have his identity kept secret. So here there is indecision in the face of the Danish threat, something which William of Malmesbury's Latin panegyrist mentions and even condemns, putting Athelstan's slow military build up down to some sort of negligence whilst the allies ravaged the northern limits of his empire. Here too, is the reliance on a hero figure to sort the problem out for Athelstan. In this case it was Gui, but in another work, the Scandinavian saga of Egil Skallagrimson, the English king has a different champion of the battlefield.

The fact that Athelstan's character deteriorates in the thirteenth and fourteenth centuries may have something to do with the interpretation of works such as William of Malmesbury, but it may also have as much to do with the way in which poets chose to represent their own prevailing monarch by dressing him up as a positive and well-known figure from history whose failings are brought out to show those of the current king in a subtle way. This line of interpretation of the Athelstan legend is taken by the author of the medieval work *Athelston* and it deserves closer scrutiny, for here we can get to the very bottom of the legend.[7]

*Athelston* was a romance written in Middle English at the end of the fourteenth century and it survives in a copy datable to the early fifteenth century. It represents the pinnacle of all of the later works on the king. Athelston is first introduced to us as a messenger, who becomes king since he is the dead king's cousin and closest heir. At his accession, he promises to look after his three sworn 'brothers'. Alryke gets the archbishopric of Canterbury, Egeland receives the earldom of Stane and marries Athelston's sister Edith (who is an historical figure) and Wymound gets the earldom of Dover. Wymound, because he is jealous of the king's love for Egeland, plots against him and fabricates a charge of treason against him. The king sends for Egeland and his family (who by association, must be guilty also) and plans to have Egeland executed. Athelston's pregnant queen tries to intervene, but is kicked in the stomach by the king who unwittingly kills his unborn heir. Alryke arrives to try to plead on behalf of Egeland but is rebuffed and dispossessed into the bargain. The picture of a tyrant emerges. But Alryke's reaction is to excommunicate Athelston and to gather against him a great council of barons. This act is shot through with huge symbolism to its medieval audience given the struggles of the barons and English kings in the thirteenth century. In the face of this religious and secular disapproval, Athelston repents and allows the archbishop to pass judgement on Egeland by arranging a trial by ordeal of fire for Egeland and his family in an act which recalls the spirit of the Anglo-Saxon age of law making. Egeland, his wife and children come through their ordeal absolved and Edith gives birth to a son, Edmund, whom Athelston names as his heir. Alryke presses the king to break his vow of silence against the true conspirator, Wymound, who is subsequently put through the same ordeal and found to be guilty of treason. His punishment is execution by drawing and quartering. Our poet is determined to point out to us that treason, or wrongly accusing someone of it, is a very serious offence and that anyone found guilty of it should go the same way as the hapless plotter Wymound.

This imaginary Anglo-Saxon world would have been recognisable to its medieval audience. At its heart was the king, who must rule justly and wisely in the eyes of God. Athelston abuses his position and it is only the intervention of the archbishop which gets him to change his ways and rule once again with piety and respect for God. The ancient rite of trial by ordeal is brought in to give the tale an authentic flavour, as are the oath-swearing and bonds of allegiance scenes (the real Athelstan was famed for his laws regarding the sanctity of the oath and pledge and for the creation of Peace Guilds). But the point is this: in order to make sure that his medieval audience fully understood the consequences of tyranny and treason, the power and righteousness of the Church and its relationship with the king and the validity of the law, the *Athelston* poet chose a figure from history whose reputation was well established. Athelstan was someone who was the very model of medieval kingship and yet he had a greater than usual grip on power. All the poet had to do was characterise him for a contemporary audience. People knew about Athelstan and knew that he was a just and wise ruler, a great warrior and a true patron of the Church in a time when it faced its greatest external threats. They will have known perhaps that Athelstan was capable of dark things too, such as the killing of his brother – we are all fallible, of course. By rooting the story in the age of Athelstan, the poet constructs the authentic and legiti- mate framework within which to work his allegories. There is an obvious connection in the tale between Athelston's tyranny and that of Richard II, about whom the poet is probably writing. Furthermore, both Athelstan and Richard II had no direct heir. The tale could be a re-telling of so many struggles between Church, monarch and noblemen in medieval England – the struggle between Henry II and Thomas of Canterbury; the tyranny of King John and his battle with the barons of England; the protracted debate between Henry III and the English nobility are all possible inspirations for the story. But the choice of Athelstan is important, and the message is clear for all: Athelston can only rule properly when he does so in co-operation with the Church.

But then there seems to have been something of a shake-up in the way that the English viewed their history. Some scholars put this down to the arrival of the Tudor dynasty and claim that there was an attempt to re-tell history in a different way. The fact that the Tudor line traced itself from the very dynasty which Athelstan had all but crushed may have something to do with it. And yet, Athelstan just about survives as a legend after this era.

Thomas Dekker, a contemporary of Shakespeare, wrote a comedy entitled *Old Fortunatus* in 1600.[8] Dekker's style is certainly different from that of the writers we have already examined, but his Athelstan, even at the beginning of the seventeenth century, still seems to embody some of the characteristics that were displayed by the later medieval literary Athelstans, a strong grip on power being one of them. But there is a notable degeneration. Athelstane, as he is called in *Old Fortunatus*, is proud and greedy. The play is set in Cyprus, Babylon and England and has as its central theme the failings of people who are hostage to either Vice, Fortune or Virtue. Athelstane has a daughter Agripyne who he clearly cares for, but when she pinches the purse of Andelocia, he has this to say:

*More than a second kingdom hast thou won.*
*Leave him, that when he awakes he may suspect*
*Some else has robbed him; come dear Agripyne,*
*If this strange purse his sacred virtues hold,*
*We'll circle England with a wall of gold.*

Agripyne is subsequently abducted by Andelocia and rescued by another character. There is much amusing soul-searching before the king and his daughter finally come through their ordeal at the end of the play. It is here that the most powerful message comes across. Dekker's play was performed in front of Queen Elizabeth I and the words of Virtue towards the end of the play seem to be loaded with meaning and intended for her ears. Here again, we have a monarch being told of the dangers of immorality and once more it is Athelstan who is the conduit for the message:

*Fortune triumphs at this, yet to appear*
*All like myself, that which from those I took,*
*King Athelstane, I will bestowe on thee,*
*And in it the old virtue infuse:*
*But, king, take heed how thou my gifts dost use.*
*England shall ne'er be poor if England strive*
*Rather by virtue than wealth to thrive.*

And so the circle is complete. Athelstan has gone from being a hero of the battlefield and an ideal of kingship to being a greedy and immoral man in the space of 700 years. But one thing remains obvious: he is always depicted as being extraordinarily powerful. Creative writers over the centuries had portrayed the darker side of the king because they knew that he had one. He was not perfect, but because of his famous grip on power, he was the ideal king upon which to base tales of tyranny, of repentance and justice. His legend was simply bound to degenerate over time.

The real Athelstan had modelled his court on that of the Carolingians. In it had been scribes, poets, scholars and warriors from all over Christendom. The court had benefited from the presence of Breton, Frankish and German clerics and scholars and even an Italian Jew. Most of them often travelled with the king on his journeys to the outlying parts of his empire and some of them were responsible for prosecuting the great campaign of learning which had been initiated by Alfred in the face of the Pagan menace. Alfred had imported John the Old Saxon and Grimbald of St Bertin's to help him. By Athelstan's time, the numbers had swollen. Most of the contemporary poems outlined above were penned by foreign scribes, which is not to say that the English ones were incapable of such expression as the poems of the *Anglo-Saxon Chronicle* indicate. It has been shown that the scribes of Athelstan's era played a key role in the decades after his death in the revival of Roman fortune in England.[9]

Athelstan's short reign had been remarkably eventful. The military campaigning and itinerant style of government with an extensive entourage showed him to be an energetic king like no other of his age. A huge programme of legislation – financial, criminal, military and economic – had been set in place between 924-939 upon which later kings would build. His military activities even stretched to foreign shores with the Breton campaigns of the 930s. Such expeditions would not be seen on the Continent again for generations, when things would be so very different for England. The Church was brought closer to the people of England in the reign of Athelstan and the monastic reform movement of the tenth century was promoted by men who rose to prominence in the age of Athelstan. But if we are to remember one thing about Athelstan then it must be this: he was the founder of a country. A nation called England was already arguably in the making during the reigns of Alfred and Edward, but it would take a self-styled basilius, an imperial majesty, to see that it happened in reality. Somewhere on a blood-stained battlefield in 937 Athelstan had justified himself as the first king of England. History would soon show that this kingdom was an enviable possession indeed.

# APPENDIX

The list below contains the descriptions in Anglo-Saxon charters of how English kings styled themselves from the time of King Alfred to the end of Athelstan's reign. Occasionally, through letters written to the kings, we also get a glimpse of how they were addressed by others. Alfred's Kingdom of the Anglo-Saxons was superseded by the Kingdom of the English which was given an extraordinary makeover in the charters of King Athelstan. The charter numbers on the left indicate the charter or document numbers in Birch's *Cartularium Saxonicum* (1885) Volume 2. The dates on the right are the dates of the charters where known.

| BIRCH NO. | DESCRIPTION OF KING | DATE | BIRCH NO. | DESCRIPTION OF KING | DATE |
|---|---|---|---|---|---|
| | *Reign of Alfred* | | | *Reign of Edward* | |
| 550 | Saxonum Rex | 882 | 584 | Edwardo Angolsaxonum | |
| 553 | Westseaxena cinge | 880x885 | | gloriosissimo (In a grant by | |
| 555 | Regi Anglorum (in a letter | | | Malmesbury Abbey | |
| | from the archbishop of Rheims | | | to Earl Ordlaf) | — |
| | addressing Alfred thus) | c.885 | 588 | Angul Saxonum rex | 901 |
| 561 | Ælfred rex Anglorum et | | 592 | Angul Saxonum rex/ | |
| | Saxonum... | 889 | | Anglorum Saxonum rex | 901 |
| 563 | Rex Anglorum | — | 596 | Rex Anglorum | — |
| 564 | Anglorum Saxonum Rex | 891 | 598 | Anglorum Saxonum rex | 901 |
| 565 | Angulsaxonum Rex | — | 601 | Angul Saxonum rex | 903 |
| 567 | Angol Saxonum rex | 892 | 604 | Rex Anglorum | 904 |
| 568 | Angol Saxonum rex | — | 612 | Angul Saxonum rex | 904 |
| 571 | Rex Saxonum | — | 613 | ...occidentalium Saxonum rex | 904 |
| 576 | Saxonum rex | 898 | | | |

| BIRCH NO. | DESCRIPTION OF KING | DATE |
|---|---|---|
| 620 | Angulsaxonum rex | 909 |
| 623 | Angul Saxonum rex | 909 |
| 624 | Angul Saxonum rex | 909 |
| 625 | Angul Saxonum rex | 909 |
| 627 | Angul Saxonum rex | 909 |
| 628 | Angul Saxonum rex | 909 |
| 635 | rex Anglorum | 921 |

*Reign of Athelstan*

| BIRCH NO. | DESCRIPTION OF KING | DATE |
|---|---|---|
| 641 | rex Saxonum et Anglorum | 925 |
| 642 | rex Anglorum | 925 |
| 646 | ADelstanus rex Dei gratia regni Angliæ omnibus hominibus suis Eboraci… (in a grant of liberties and privileges to the church at Ripon) | 925 |
| 648 | Æðelstani Angelsaxonum Denmorumque gloriosissimi… (in a grant for three lives by monastery of St Saviour, Winchester of land at Chisledon with the consent of the king) 925x941 | |
| 658 | Rex Angulsaxonum | 926 |
| 659 | Angul saxonum rex | — |
| 660 | … monarchus totius Brittanniæ | 927 |
| 663 | Rex Anglorum | 928 |
| 666 | rex Anglorum | 929 |
| 667 | Æðelstanum regum Albionis | 930 |
| 671 | Quapropter ego ÆDelstanus desiderio regni cœlestis exordens favente superno numine basyleos… and as witness… Ego – Atheustan rex tocius Britannie præfatam donacionem Sigillo sancte crucis confirmavi | 931 |
| 674 | ego ÆDelstanus rex Anglorum. per omnipatra'n'tis dexteram totius Bryttaniæ regni solio sublimatis | 931 |

| BIRCH NO. | DESCRIPTION OF KING | DATE |
|---|---|---|
| 675 | ego ÆDelstanus rex Anglorum. per omnipatra'n'tis dexteram totius Bryttaniæ regni solio sublimatis | 931 |
| 676 | ego ÆDelstanus rex Anglorum. per omnipatra'n'tis dexteram totius Bryttaniæ regni solio sublimatis | 931 |
| 677 | ego Æelstanus rex Anglorum. per omnipatra'n'tis dexteram totius Bryttaniæ regni solio sublimatis and as witness… Ego Æðelstanus florentis Brytaniæ monarchia praeditus rex | 931 |
| 680 | Rex et Primicerius tocius Albionis regni | 931 |
| 681 | Rex et Primicerius tocius Albionis regni | — |
| 682 | Rex Anglorum et eque totius Albionis and as witness… Ego Æðelstanus rex tocius Brittannia | 931 |
| 683 | … tocius Brittanie basileus… | 931 |
| 689 | … per omnitenentis dexteram tocius Britanniæ regni… | 932 |
| 690 | … rex Anglorum | c.932 |
| 692 | … rex Anglorum, per omnipatrantis dexteram totius Britanniæ regni | 932 |
| 694 | … per omnipatrantis dexteram apice totius Albionis… and as witness… totius Brittannie rex… | 933 |
| 695 | rex Anlorum per omnitonantis dexteram totius Bryttaniæ regni… and as witness… totius florentis Bryttanniæ rex | 933 |
| 697 | Rex [and] rector tocius hujus Britannie insule largiente domino and as witness… rex totius Britannie | 933 |

| BIRCH NO. | DESCRIPTION OF KING | DATE | BIRCH NO. | DESCRIPTION OF KING | DATE |
|---|---|---|---|---|---|
| 701 | … divinæ dispensationis providentia tam super Brittanicæ gentis quam super aliarum nationum huic subditarum imperium elevatus rex | — | 711 | Dedication by king Athelstan of four gospels to Christchurch, Canterbury: …Anglorum basyleos. et curagulus totius Bryttanniæ | after 936 |
| 702 | … rex Anglorum per omnipatrantis dexteram totius Britanniæ regni… | 934 | 712 | … rex Anglorum et eque totius Albionis… | 937 |
| 703 | … rex Anglorum, per omnipotentis dextram, quae Christus est. totius Britanniæ | 934(?) | 713 | … totius loculentæ Brittannie rex… | 937 |
| 704 | …rex Anglorum per omnipotentis dexteram totius Britanniae regni… | 934 | 720 | … Rex Anglorum… | 937(?) |
| 705 | …rex et rector totius hujus Brittanniae insule largiente domino et omnimbus ejus sanctis…and in the English version of the same charter… Ongol Saxna cyning [and] brytæn walda ealles ðyses Iglandæs purh Godæs sælene | 934 | 721 | … rex monarchus totius Bryttanniæ insule…and as witness… rex totius Bryttanniæ | 937 |
| | | | 723 | …rex Anglorum… | 670 (938) |
| | | | 724 | …rex Anglorum… | 670 (938) |
| | | | 725 | …rex totius Bryttanniæ insulæ.. and as witness… rex Anglorum | 670 (938) |
| 707 | … Dei gratia basileus Anglorum et equæ totius Bryttanniæ orbis… and as witness… … tocius gentis Anglorum rex | 935 | 726 | …rex Anglorum… | 670 (938) |
| | | | 727 | …rex Anglorum… | 938 |
| 708 | … nodante Dei gratia basileos Anglorum [and] eque tocius Britannie orbis…and as witness… Dei Rex Anglorum | 935 | 728 | basileos industrius Anglorum and as witness… Rex totius Britannie | 938 |
| 709 | … nodante Dei gratia basileos Anglorum et eque tocius Britannie orbis…and as witness… rex totius Britannie… | 936 | 729 | rex Anglorum et æquæ totius Brittanniæ orbis curagulus pre electus and as witness… rex tocius Brittanniæ | 938 |
| | | | 730 | … basileus industrius Anglorum… and as witness… rex tocius Brittanniæ | 938 |

# FURTHER READING

The works below represent a good mixture of both basic and detailed reading on the subject of the life and times of King Athelstan. There are general works on the period as a whole as well as some more detailed investigations into tenth-century history.

Campbell (ed.), 1982 *The Anglo-Saxons*. Harmondsworth. Good general account of the entire period with many references to Athelstan's laws and influence.

Dumville, D.N., 1992 'Between Alfred the Great and Edgar the Peacemaker: Athelstan, First King of England' in *Wessex and England from Alfred to Edgar. Six Essays on Political, Cultural, and Ecclesiastical Revival*. Detailed examination of the reign of Athelstan and his achievements in comparison to Alfred and Edgar.

Fisher, D.J.V., 1973 'The Anglo-Saxon Age *c*.400-1042'. Good general coverage of the whole period.

Hill, D., 1981 *An Atlas of Anglo-Saxon England*. Oxford. Very good for maps of Athelstan's campaigns.

Loyn, H.R., 1977 *The Vikings in Britain*. Oxford. Good account of the Scandinavian background to the age of Viking invasions.

Reynolds, A., 1999 *Later Anglo-Saxon England - Life and Landscape*. Stroud. Very good background reading setting the period in a landscape context.

Sawyer, P. (ed.), 1997 *The Oxford Illustrated History of the Vikings*. Oxford. Good for general background on the Viking Phenomenon across the whole of Europe including Britain and Ireland.

Stafford, P.A., 1989 *Unification and Conquest: a Political and Social History of England in the Tenth and Eleventh Centuries*. London. Places Athelstan's reign in a wider context.

Stenton, Sir F., 1971 *Anglo-Saxon England*. Oxford. Classic account of the whole period includes a detailed section on Athelstan.

Swanton, M., 1996 *The Anglo-Saxon Chronicle*. London. Particularly for the years 924-939.

Whitelock, D., 1952 *The Beginnings of English Society*. Harmondsworth. Still a good introduction to the whole period.

Wood, M., 1981 *In Search of the Dark Ages*. BBC Books: London. Very good consideration of Athelstan's importance in English history.

# NOTES

## 1 RECOVERING ATHELSTAN

1. A homilist is a sermon-giver.
2. See Swanton, M., *The Anglo-Saxon Chronicle* (J.M. Dent: London, 1996), p.xv.
3. A full and detailed account of the chronological difficulties of the *Anglo-Saxon Chronicle* is expertly summed up in Swanton, *The Anglo-Saxon Chronicle*, pp.xi–xxxv. See also Wainwright, F.T., *The Chronology of the Mercian Register* (EHR, 1945) LX p.386.
4. Swanton, *The Anglo-Saxon Chronicle*.
5. *Archaeological Journal* (1851), pp.425–6.
6. See Hadley, D.M., 'In Search of the Vikings' in Graham-Campbell, J., Hall, R., Jesch, J. and Parsons, N. (eds) *Vikings and the Danelaw: Selected Papers from the Thirteenth Viking Congress,* (Oxbow: Oxford, 2001), p.16.
7. *Ibid.* p.19.
8. See Butters, S., *The Book of Kingston* (Baron Birch for Quotes Ltd, 1995), p.33.
9. *Ibid.* p.33.
10. See Wood, M., *In Search of the Dark Ages* (BBC Books: London, 1981), p.132.
11. I am very grateful to Shaan Butters, author of *The Book of Kingston*, for conversations past and present on the matter of the Kingston coronations. The research she has undertaken on this subject, which was published in her book, is the only modern summary of the authenticity of Kingston's claim to be the place of the coronations and its findings are simply outlined here.
12. The oldest charter which supports this claim is one granted by Edward III in 1371, which makes a reference to a charter granted by Athelstan.
13. This passage of text is taken from an extract by R. Sadler, quoted in Luce, Major-General Sir R.H., *The History of the Abbey and Town of Malmesbury* (The Friends of Malmesbury Abbey, 1979), p.191.
14. The way in which military service was organised on a personal and lordship basis was covered emphatically by Professor Richard Abels in 1988. He deduced that English warriors throughout the entire Anglo-Saxon period turned up for battle for much the same reasons: that they owed this service to their lord. Harold's men at Hastings were little different in their obligations than the men of Dark Age warlords. The work unravels that of other authorities, and its general emphasis on lordship bonds is taken here to be of great significance. See Abels, R., *Lordship and Military Obligation in Anglo-Saxon England* (British Museum Press: London, 1988).

15. The division of the Anglo-Saxon fyrd into 'Select' and 'Great' groupings was the work of C. Warren Hollister. For years it was a seminal work, though by the author's own admission it was an institutional rather than a military history. See Hollister, C. Warren, *Anglo-Saxon Military Institutions on the Eve of the Norman Conquest* (The Clarendon Press: Oxford, 1962).

16. The *Duguð* of the early Saxon period was an important social figure. He was a proven warrior and if he had been given land by his lord, he was likely to set up his own estate and attract to it young warriors who themselves were in search of honour, glory and reward. These young men were known as *Geoguð*, or 'youth'. A successful *Duguð* would expand his estate and preside over what was known as his *Scir*. Here in its earliest form was the origin of the later Saxon shire which is still with us today.

17. The word used in the *Chronicle* is *Folcgefeoht*, probably best translated as 'general engagement involving the entire king's host'.


## 2  IN THE SHADOW OF THE VIKING

1. In Old Danish *uge soes*, in Old Swedish *veckosjoe*. The distance is thought to be anything from 3-15km.

2. Fought in Essex at the Blackwater Estuary in 991 between the famous Byrhtnoth, ealdorman of Essex and a Danish force, at the head of which might have been the renowned Olaf Tryggvason.

3. See Loyn, H., *The Vikings in Britain* (Blackwell: Oxford, 1994), p.3.

4. For a succinct breakdown of the effects and course of the Viking raids in Ireland right up to the end of the Viking period, see Ó Corráin, D., 'Ireland, Wales, Man and the Hebrides' in Sawyer, P. (ed.), *The Oxford Illustrated History of the Vikings* (OUP: Oxford, 1997), pp.83-109.

5. The *Annals of Ulster* state in an entry for 841, with a dry mixture of resignation and disbelief, that there were 'Pagans still on Lough Neagh'.

6. The longphort was attacked by a joint Irish force from Ossory and Laois at the end of the long hot summer of 862. The natural water defences had dried up by September and the Irish were able to attack over the flats.

7. See Hill, D., 'Offa versus the Welsh' in *British Archaeology*, No.56 (2000), pp.18-23.

8. The Abingdon Manuscript of the *Anglo-Saxon Chronicle*. Version C. Entry for 916.

9. See Kirby, D.P., 'Hywel Dda: Anglophil?' in *The Welsh History Review 8* No.1 (1976-7), pp.1-13 for a more modern examination of the reign, and Lloyd, Sir J.E., *A History of Wales from the Earliest Times to the Edwardian Conquest* (London: Longmans and Co., 1911) for a more traditional view.

10. See Ritchie, A., 'Viking Farmers at Jarlshof' in *British Archaeology* No.69 (2003), pp.22-23.


## 3  THE CALLING OF ALFRED

1. Æthelwulf was, in fact, a Mercian. Berkshire had passed into West Saxon control in the 850s and the ealdorman's body was taken away after his death at Reading to Mercia, to a place which Æthelweard refers to as 'Northworthig', but 'Derby' in the Danish tongue.

2. The time of Ivar's death is somewhat problematic. Æthelweard says that he died in the same year in which the murder of St Edmund took place (869), but the *Annals of Ulster* have his death recorded in 872 (really 873). His absence from the Great Army

in 871 is probably explained by the fact that, according to the *Annals of Ulster*, he is supposed to have sacked Dumbarton that year and then sailed back to Dublin with captives and booty. Biddle and Biddle put together a seductive argument that the rich Viking burial place in the converted Anglo-Saxon mausoleum at Repton was in fact for Ivar himself and that he had returned to be with the Great Army before he died. See Biddle, M. and Kjølbye-Biddle, B. 2001 'Repton and the "great heathen army"'. In *Vikings and the Danelaw. Select papers from the proceedings of the Thirteenth Viking Congress.* Eds Graham-Campbell, J., Hall, R., Jesch, J. and Parsons, N. (Oxford: Oxbow) p.82.

3. There is every reason to believe that this 'foolish king's thegn' was a very carefully chosen appointment. The Vikings were hardly entering a political vacuum in the Midlands and would have been well aware of the recent dynastic politics in Mercia where there seem to have been at least three competing families. Ceolwulf, it is suggested, had a reasonable enough degree of acceptance in Mercia because he was probably from the house of Cenwulf, which was one of these families. His degree of acceptance amongst the Mercians would have meant that the Danes could do business with him that much easier. Puppet leaders are rarely chosen at random.

4. Excavations are being carried out at Ingelby by Julian D. Richards in order to establish the nature of the relationship between the two sites.

5. David Sturdy points out that among those who fled abroad was ealdorman Wulfhere of Hampshire, one of Alfred's greatest noblemen. Sturdy. D., *Alfred the Great* (Constable: London, 1995), p.147.

6. The brother was very probably Ubba, the same man who had killed St Edmund in 869. Ubba was buried after the battle and, according to Gaimar (3141-7), was placed in a barrow named Ubelaue, or 'Ubba's Barrow'.

7. See Sturdy, *Alfred the Great*, p.149.


4 A VISION OF ENGLAND

1. William of Malmesbury, *Gesta Regum Anglorum: The History of the English Kings*, edited by Mynors, R.A.B., Thomson, R.M. and Winterbottom, M. (Clarendon Press: Oxford, 1998), paragraph 125.

2. Mainly in Simeon of Durham, *Historia Regum*.

3. Stenton, Sir F., *Anglo-Saxon England* (Oxford: Oxford University Press, 1971), p.322.

4. Stenton, *Anglo-Saxon England*, p.322. Stenton points out that the Æthelstan charters of 926 contain the statement that the lands which were being confirmed as belonging to Englishmen were 'bought from the heathen at the command of King Edward and the ealdorman Æthelred'.

5. However see the discussion of the location of the Battle of Brunanburh on page 151.

6. This site remains unidentified. Swanton has it probably as Wigmore in Herefordshire on a Roman road at the Welsh border (see Swanton, *The Anglo-Saxon Chronicle*, p.101). Stenton suggests that it lay deep within Danish territory, which would make military sense when compared to the positions of the other fortifications (see Stenton, *Anglo-Saxon England*, p.327), but see Cockburn, J.H., *The Battle of Brunanburh and its Period Elucidated by Placenames* (London and Sheffield: Sir W.C. Leng and Co., 1931) for an identification for Wigingamere as Wincobank near Sheffield. If Cockburn's identifications of Wincobank and nearby Bremesburh are correct, then the East Anglian

and Northumbrian Danish attack on Wigingamere which dominated the route to Northumbria via Ricknild Street would have been an attempt to relieve the stranglehold which Æthelflæd had created by blocking access from one Danish polity to another. Brunanburh hunters should not let this notion pass them by.

7. The validity of this source is questioned because of its unknown background. According to O'Donovan, who published it in 1860, the text he used was taken from a copy of a manuscript which Dubháltach Mac FirBhisigh (Duald Mac Firbis) himself copied in 1643 from 'a vellum Manuscript, the property of Nehemias Mac Egan'. Both Duald's copy and the original manuscript are lost and we are left with O'Donovan's copy of Duald's copy (O'Donovan, *The Annals of Ireland, Three Fragments* Irish Archaeological and Celtic Society: Dublin, 1860). The other main objection to the validity of the source rests upon its dramatic and legendary style, but as has been skilfully observed, the tale of Ingimund and his attempted settlement in the Wirral at least is sound enough to be reconciled with more reliable English and Welsh sources of the period (Wainwright, F.T., 'Ingimund's Invasion' in Finberg (ed.), *Scandinavian England* (Phillimore: Chichester, 1975), pp.131-161.

8. Both the Welsh sources *Annales Cambriae* and *Brut Y Tywysogilon* mention this event, stating that Ingimund landed at the same place (*Osmeliaun* and *Ros Meilon* respectively).

9. The Norse kings of Man played a pivotal role in the politics of the north. Recent excavations at Govan have shown clear similarities between Strathclyde and Man. Five hog-back tombstones and twenty-one recumbent slabs with interlace crosses are thought to indicate the burials of members of the Strathclyde royal house, or some very notable Scandinavians. Alongside the evidence for the working of jet at the Govan monastic site, was the striking discovery of an arrangement of church, road and court centre which had its closest parallels at Tynwald on the Isle of Man. The assumption is that the Strathclyde and Manx dynasties were closer than has been previously thought and that Scandinavian influence was profound. This does not, however, suggest that the kings of Strathclyde were not still fiercely independent in the face of political threat. Their expansionist tendencies at this time tell a different story. The excavations were summarised in *British Archaeology*, No.27, September 1997.

10. The sources are comprehensively surveyed for these battles in an essay which sheds much light on northern politics in this period, written by Wainwright, F.T., 'The Battles at Corbridge' in Finberg (ed.), *Scandinavian England*, pp.163-179.

11. According to the Irish document 'The War of the Gaedhil with the Gaill'.

12. The problems raised by this line of argument are mainly based on the fact that the Mercian register is used by many to tie in dates from other less reliable documents. If we suggest scribal copying errors for 918-919, then reliability becomes the victim. The notion that Edward acted in the same year as the death of his sister makes perfect sense, however and is summed up in a short essay by Wainwright, F.T., 'Ælfwyn's Deposition' in Finberg (ed.), *Scandinavian England*, pp.127-129.

## 5 THE THUNDERBOLT

1. Malmesbury's 'Flash of Lightning' as translated by Mynors, R.A.B., Thomson, R.M. and Winterbottom, M. in William of Malmesbury, *Gesta Regum Anglorum: The History of the English Kings*. The term is often interpreted as a 'Thunderbolt'.

2. William of Malmesbury, *Gesta Regum Anglorum*, 134.5. William claims to have seen the king in his tomb and confirmed that his hair was indeed 'beautifully intertwined with golden threads'.

3. The *Anglo-Saxon Chronicle* is not the only source to mention this incident. William of Malmesbury, Henry of Huntingdon and Simeon of Durham mention it too. So does the account written at the Abbey of St Bertin where Edwin's body was taken after it had been washed ashore. 'Drowned whilst escaping from England in a time of commotion' is how they describe the incident, mindful of Athelstan's gratitude for the burial they had given him. In fact, it was Edwin's own cousin Adelulf (Æthelwulf) who oversaw the proceedings. For a detailed account of the story, including the legend of the Freemasons, see pages 202-203 of this volume.

4. This suggestion is put forward by Dumville, D.N., 'Between Alfred the Great and Edgar the Peacemaker: Athelstan, First King of England' in *Wessex and England from Alfred to Edgar. Six Essays on Political, Cultural, and Ecclesiastical Revival* (Woodbridge: Boydell & Brewer, 1992), p.151.

5. I am grateful to John Bowen for this observation.

6. Stubbs, W. (ed.), *Memorials of St Dunstan* (London: Public Record Office, 1874), p.360. The text tells of the continued strength of the relationship between the kings of England and the counts of Flanders some three generations later.

7. See Stenton, *Anglo-Saxon England*, p.346.

8. There is some evidence to suggest that Bretons were not the only immigrants into Britain in the early tenth century. Between 901-903 the people of Ponthieu in Picardy were mauled by the Vikings and fled to England, giving their names to Pointou (Cobham) and Pontefract (meaning 'the height of the Ponthieu men'). This argument is put forward in Cockburn, J.H., *The Battle of Brunanburh and its Period Elucidated by Placenames*, p.170.

9. For a full discussion of the significance of the Breton connection see Brett, C. 'A Breton Pilgrim in England in the Reign of King Æthelstan' in Jondorf, G. and Dumville, D.N. (eds), *France and the British Isles in the Middle Ages and Renaissance. Essays in Memory of Ruth Morgan* (Woodbridge: Boydell & Brewer, 1991).

10. Dumville, D.N., 'Between Alfred the Great and Edgar the Peacemaker: Athelstan, First King of England' in *Wessex and England from Alfred to Edgar*, p.157.

11. BL., MS. Cotton. Tiberius A. XV.

12. Michael Wood has outlined the significance of the grant made to Wulfgar of Inkpen at Lifton which was made on 12 November 931 and which effectively elevated Wulfgar and his wife Aeffe into the nobility. As a clear example of Athelstan's land-awarding policy in action, it is made all the more significant that the original document with its attendant witness list and an attached will of Wulfgar both survive in good condition. See Wood, M., *Domesday. A Search for the Roots of England* (BBC Books: London, 1986), pp.108-9.

13. See Richardson, H.G. and Sayles, G.O., *Law and Legislation From Æthelbert to Magna Carta* (1966), p.19. This view demonstrates a complete misunderstanding of the way in which Athelstan was trying to rule the country.

14. See Davis, R.H.C., 'The Warhorses of the Normans' in *Anglo-Norman Studies X* (1987), pp.67-82. This is the most succinct account of the dangers faced by medieval horse

breeders and is especially useful for the background for horse management in early medieval Francia. Davis's careful translation of the Capitulare de Villis, based on Loyn and Percival's translation, is used here.

15. *Ibid.* p.73.
16. Pope John VIII in 876 requested such horses from the Christian king of Galicia describing them as 'excellent'.
17. English translation taken from William of Malmesbury, *Gesta Regum Anglorum: The History of the English Kings.* The reference to the statement of Virgil relates to *Aen.* vii. 279.
18. Davis, R.H.C., 'The Warhorses of the Normans' in *Anglo-Norman Studies X*, p.74.
19. The Old English word used is Eorodcistum/Eoredcystum, meaning 'mounted troop', but which has its root in 'eoh', meaning 'warhorse'. In this particular translation (Swanton, *The Anglo-Saxon Chronicle*, p.108), the translation 'elite cavalry' is used.

## 6 BRUNANBURH – THE GREAT WAR

1. William of Malmesbury, *Gesta Regum Anglorum,* 134.
2. Florence of Worcester. *Chronicon Ex Chronicis I*, 132. Florence states that as well as giving Olaf Sihtricson his daughter's hand in marriage, Constantine was the instigator of the Northumbrian campaign in 937.
3. The identification of the site at Brougham Castle has been persuasively argued by Lapidge in Lapidge, M., 'Some Latin Poems as evidence for the Reign of Athelstan' in *Anglo-Saxon England 9* (Cambridge: Cambridge University Press, 1981), pp.92-93.
4. William of Malmesbury, *Gesta Regum Anglorum.* 156.2.
5. Smyth, A.P., *Scandinavian York and Dublin II* (1975), p.43.
6. *Ibid.* p.43

## 7 OF MYSTERY AND MEANING

1. See Campbell, A., *The Battle of Brunanburh* (1938) for a comprehensive discussion of the evidence.
2. The arrangement for the battle may seem odd in the light of our knowledge of English and Danish armies chasing each other over England on giant strategic campaigns, bringing each other to battle only when conditions clearly favoured one side more than the other. This should be set against the notion that in generations gone by, when competing Anglo-Saxon kings wished for a military showdown, that similar arrangements were indeed made between forces and that there seems to have been something of an ancient code of conduct for pitched battles of this kind. For an in-depth account of the anthropological aspects of Anglo-Saxon warfare in the period before Brunanburh, see Halsall, G., 'Anthropology and the Study of Pre-Conquest Warfare and Society' in Hawkes, S.C. (ed.), *Weapons and Warfare in Anglo-Saxon England* (Oxford Committee for Archaeology: Oxford, 1989), pp.155-179.
3. These variations are largely based upon the exhaustive etymological study of Brunanburh undertaken by John Henry Cockburn in 1931, which led him to deduce with good reason that the site of the battle was at Brinsworth, near Rotherham. See Cockburn, H., *The Battle of Brunanburh and its Period, Elucidated by Place Names.*
4. In 1907 Francis Tudsbury wrote an almost unfathomable leaflet based on etymological meanderings which still represents a difficult read for the most hardened of

researchers. See Tudsbury, F.W.T., *Brunanburh* (Henry Frowde and Chester: Philipson and Golder, London, 1907).

5. See Dodgson, J. McN., 'The Background of Brunanburh' (1957), reprinted in *The Place Names of Cheshire V*, Pt 2, EPNS 74 (1997). pp.249-61.

6. Cited in Thomas Booth's writings and correspondence held by Burnley Central Library under classification K18.

7. Wilkinson, T.T., quoted in the *Burnley Express* in the collection of Louis Lang's papers on the subject, 1856.

8. See Neilson, *Scottish Historical Review VII* 1910, pp.37-55.

9. Florence of Worcester, *Chronicon Ex Chronicis I*, 132.

10. Wilkinson, T.T., *Transactions of the Historical Society of Lancashire and Cheshire IV* 1857, pp.21-43.

11. Hardwick, C., *Ancient Battlefields in Lancashire*, 1882.

12. Hardwick, C., *The Borough of Preston and its Environs*, c.1882.

13. Smyth, A.P., *Scandinavian York and Dublin I*, 1975, pp.63, 95-6, 107-108.

14. See Holderness, T., *The Battle of Brunanburh – An Attempt to Identify the Site* (Driffield, 1888).

15. Wood, M., 'Brunanburh Revisited' in Townsend, J.A.B., *Saga-Book of the Viking Society* (1980) and Smyth, A.P., *Scandinavian York and Dublin II* (1975), pp.43-89.

16. Wood, M., 'Brunanburh Revisited', pp.200-17.

17. Cockburn, J.H., *The Battle of Brunanburh and its Period, Elucidated by Placenames*.

18. Wood, M., 'Brunanburh Revisited', p.216.

19. *Ibid*. p.216.

20. This translation overstates the case here. Anglo-Saxon armies did not use cavalry in the same way that we have come to picture it being used in the era of the Normans or Crusaders. See also note 19 for chapter 5.

21. Henry of Huntingdon, *Historia Anglorum*, edited by T. Arnold (Rolls Series: London, 1879), pp.159-60.

22. See Thormann, J. (1991) 'The Battle of Brunanburh and the Matter of History' in *Mediaevalia* 17, pp.5-13, for a succinct analysis of the meaning of Brunanburh.

23. Niles, J.D., 'Skaldic Technique in Brunanburh' (1989) in Niles, J.D. and Amodio, M. (eds), *Anglo-Scandinavian England. Norse-Irish Relations in the Period before the Conquest*, Old English Colloquium Series No.4 (University Press of America: Lanham), pp.69-78.

24. *Ibid*. p.76.

25. It should also be noted that the o+ nasal consonants and u- for standard o- in the inflexional endings of this poem have led some to deduce that despite its skaldic influence, the poem is in fact a Mercian production, possibly from Worcester. See Walker, S., 'A Context for Brunanburh?' in Reuter, T. (ed.), *Warriors and Churchmen in the High Middle Ages. Essays presented to Karl Leyser* (Hambledon: London, 1992), pp.21-40.

## 8 THE SHADOW RETURNS

1. For an analysis of how this phenomenon grew out of Alfred's vision, see Keynes, S. 'King Alfred and the Mercians' in Blackburn M.A.S. and D.N. Dumville (eds), *Kings, Currency and Alliances: History and Coinage in Southern England in the Ninth Century*, (Boydell & Brewer: Woodbridge, 1998), pp.1-45.

2. Many of the spearheads discovered in such graves display a mixture of Viking and Anglo-Saxon forms and methods of manufacture. For a general analysis of this phenomenon see Hill, P.R. 'The Nature and Function of Spearheads in England c.700-1100' in *Journal of the Arms and Armour Society*, Vol. XVI, No.5. (2000), pp.257-280. Also, for a specific example, see Evison, V.I., 'A Spearhead from Bletchley, Milton Keynes', Records of Buckinghamshire, Vol. XX, Pt 3 (1977), p.342.

3. See Holman, K., 'Defining the Danelaw' in *Vikings and the Danelaw: Select papers from the proceedings of the Thirteenth Viking Congress*, pp.1-12.

4. Both these points are observed by Robert Bartlett in a passage which looks at the changes in personal names and saintly cults in the era after the conquest. See Bartlett, R., *The Making of Europe* (Penguin: London, 1993), p.271.

5. Beavan points out that the entry for Athelstan's death in the *Anglo-Saxon Chronicle* under the year 940 is one year post-dated. See Beavan, M.L.R., 'King Edmund I and the Danes of York', *EHR*, Vol.CXXIX (1918), pp.1-9.

6. The *Annals of Ulster* (I, 457) recorded Olaf's return 'with a few' in the new year of 938. The suggestion has been made that he had cooled his heels with either the king of the Scots or the Strathclyde king for some time before he sailed from Dumbarton to Dublin.

7. The difficulties of conflicting chronicles are discussed and analysed in detail by Beavan in a paper which has become required reading for students of the history of this period. See Beavan, 'King Edmund I and the Danes of York'.

8. This view depends upon whether we accept Smyth's assertion that Olaf had been down here before on his Brunanburh campaign. See page 150 of this volume.

9. Roger of Wendover, *Flores Historiarum*, (ed.) H.O. Coxe, I, pp.395-6.

10. From John Milton's *The History of Britain, That Part especially, now call'd England; From the First Traditional Beginning, continu'd to the NORMAN CONQUEST*.

11. There is a curious tradition which may have some basis in truth, that Athelstan had granted Northumbria to Eric, this being mentioned in *Egil's Saga* (59).

12. Written down in the much later source – the notebook of John of Wallingford.

13. Roger of Wendover, *Flores Historiarum*, I, H.O. Coxe, pp.402-3.

# 9 THE EVENING OF A GOLDEN AGE

1. William of Malmesbury, *Gesta Regum Anglorum*. 147.4.

2. Vita Sancti Oswaldi, *Historians of the Church of York* (Rolls Series: I, 1879-94), pp.436-8.

3. This list of those present at the ceremony on the river Dee is based squarely on Sir Frank Stenton's account. See Stenton, *Anglo-Saxon England*, p.369.

4. William of Malmesbury, *Gesta Regum Anglorum*, 158-160.

5. See Wood, M., *Domesday. A Search for the Roots of England* (BBC Books: London, 1999), p.109.

6. This Wulfstan is not the Wulfstan whose political career we have already observed earlier in this volume. Wulfstan would become one of the most famous figures of the later tenth and early eleventh centuries, and a vital churchman during the reign of Æthelred.

7. William of Malmesbury, *Gesta Regum Anglorum*. 148.3.

8. The descriptions of the murder are not as fanciful as they might seem. In the early Middle Ages, Theoderic had killed Odovacer in much the same way, by getting his retainers to pull him both ways by his arms, so that Theoderic could slice him in two with his sword.

9. William of Malmesbury, *Gesta Regum Anglorum*. 163.4.

10. This line is taken by William Smith in his response to an earlier President's piece on the bones of the Martyr in the Council for British Archaeology's *British Archaeological News* Vol. 4 (July 1989), p.50.

11. Dr Stowell's short report appeared in *The Criminologist* in 1970. He tried to assign various signs of pathological injuries to the types of injuries the king might have received at his death. A subsequent and fuller report was produced in 1973 by Don Brothwell who had reason to challenge almost every contention in the Stowell paper.

## 10 THE LEGEND OF KING ATHELSTAN

1. From Ælric's epilogue to a translation of the Old Testament Book of Judges (*c*.1002-5).

2. See Lapidge, M., 'Some Latin poems as evidence for the reign of Athelstan' in *Anglo-Saxon England 9*, pp.61-98. This paper addresses the issue of the controversy over Malmesbury's 'ancient volume' and brings to light the poems which I have included here.

3. Oxford. Bodleian Library, Rawlinson, C. 697 (S.C. 12541).

4. Quoted from a letter which the pope wrote to King Æthelwulf of Wessex who had sent Alfred to Rome.

5. This is Lapidge's tentative translation as published in Lapidge, M., 'Some Latin poems as evidence for the reign of Athelstan' in *Anglo-Saxon England 9*, (Cambridge: Cambridge University Press, 1981), p.73.

6. *The Brut of Layamon*, line 31, p.990.

7. The poem *Athelston* has been examined with relation to the events in the reign of the real tenth-century figure in Treharne, Elaine M., 'Romanticizing the Past in the Middle English Athelston' in *Review of English Studies* 50 (1999), pp.1-26. I am grateful to Professor Treharne for her advice and I follow her line of reasoning here.

8. Rhys, E. (ed.), Thomas Dekker 'Old Fortunatus' in *The Best Plays of the Old Dramatists* (London 1887), The Mermaid Series edited by Havelock Ellis.

9. Wood, M., 'The Making of King Athelstan's Empire: An English Charlemagne?' in Wormald, P. (ed.), *Ideal and Reality in Frankish and Anglo-Saxon England* (Oxford: Blackwell, 1983), pp.250-272.

# LIST OF MAPS AND
# GENEOLOGICAL TABLES

MAPS

GENEOLOGICAL TABLES

# INDEX

Page numbers in *italics* refer to illustration numbers